W9-BXL-296

A Dictionary of Fishes

ELEVENTH EDITION

GREAT OUTDOORS PUBLISHING CO.
4747 TWENTY-EIGHTH STREET NORTH
ST. PETERSBURG, FLORIDA 33714

Foreword

O ANSWER THE ETERNAL QUES-
TION, "What kind of fish is this?"
there has been set down between
these covers a collection of 4,000 answers.
This is really a small number compared to
the possible 400,000, which are on file in a
good library of scientific books. Only a person dedicated to a lifetime of study on this
subject would ever need or seek that many
answers, yet a great many every day fishermen do need to know the answer to the first
4,000. Not only for curiosity, but for his very
life. Some fish are deadly poisonous.

It is for that reason this book has been
compiled with unvarying foremat, to answer
the most important questions about essential
fish. As a text book, the fundamentals are set
down, to build a foundation for higher learn-
ing. As a research volume, there are many
answers published between these covers,
which have never been put into type before.

Always keeping to an eight-point foremat, the 700-odd fish described on the
following pages are explained as to common
name, Latin name, size, edibility, color,
characteristics, habitat and food. Sometimes
it is easy to get these eight answers, sometimes it is very difficult. So difficult, in fact,
that one researcher alone could never accu-
mulate these answers in a lifetime.

Thus it is that the signed author of this
book gives credit to the persons who have
made ths information possible. The 1,000
(and more as time passes) of the Great Outdoors Association, scattered throughout the
civilized world, have contributed the information published herein.

There is probably no other group of
animals on this earth in which so much
change takes place, as the fishes, thus it is
impossible to publish a book of information
on this subject and have it remain authentic
throughout the ages. Two years is the very
maximum life of a text on this subject, which
often gets out of date while on the press.

If you are a layman and you discover a
rare fish, seek out a member to report your
find. If you have a great interest in this
subject, then become a member yourself.
Some of the most important members are
captains of charterboats and fishing camp
operators.

About Sharks

In the summer sharks are more plentiful, in the inshore waters. They appear to thrive in warmer water—and find more carrion on which to feed. At this time of year they drop their young. All sharks are born alive with the exception of one remote deep water species.

It is fairly simple to identify a shark because of the following characteristics:

They have a torpedo-like shape.

Skeleton composed wholly of cartilage.

Jaws, teeth and paired fins.

Skin covered with minute tooth-like scales, sandpapery texture.

Differ from whales and porpoises in that they do have gills and scales and the mammals do not.

Differ from bony fishes in that bony fishes have only one pair of gill openings.

To determine what kind of a shark it is, poses a different problem. The large sharks, such as Hammerhead, Tiger, White, Mako, Basking and others are fairly easy to identify, but the inshore sharks, such as the Sandbar, Bull, Dusky, Sand, Blue and Lemon Shark are more difficult to differentiate. The sketch on this page supplied by the U. S. Fish and Wildlife Service, will be of considerable help in this matter.

There is a large population of sharks in northern Atlantic coastal waters—and many species. Among these are several species reputed to be maneaters, but they rarely attack swimmers in the area of Atlantic coast population centers.

The Shark Research Panel of the American Institute of Biological Sciences has found records of only 22 unprovoked attacks, with nine fatalities, north of Cape Hatteras, N. C., between 1865 and 1966. The White Shark has been definitely identified in reported attacks; it was evidently this species that caused five of the nine fatalities—and one White Shark was credited with four fatal attacks in New Jersey in 1916, and another with one death in Massachusetts in 1936.

The White Shark is not the only one to treat with caution, however. Sharks with very bad reputations in other parts of the world include the Tiger Shark, Hammerheads; Lemon Sharks and occasionally the Sandbar Sharks have injured bathers in tropical waters. The Gray Shark is also considered quite dangerous. Although attacks by the Mako, Porbeagle, Blue and Whitetip sharks remain unproven, these large, heavily toothed and unpredictable animals should be regarded as dangerous.

As a sport fish, sharks are increasing in importance. It is estimated that sport fishermen caught 1,715,000 sharks in U. S. coastal waters in one year; about 45 per cent of these were taken between Maine and North Carolina.

The Mako, Blue, Porbeagie, White, Thresher, Tiger and Sawfish rank as big-game fish, and are formally recognized among the 50 species of game fish on which the International Game Fish Association keeps worldwide records. Anglers in the Northeast who are interested in trying for record sharks are in an excellent area. Of the current world records for different tackle sizes, 21 were taken in New Jersey, New York, Rhode Island and Massachusetts.

Anglers agree that few game fish can equal the spectacular leaps and swift runs of the Mako.

Other species seldom leap—and opinions on their fighting abilities may be varied, but one thing is certain; any large shark, caught on suitable tackle, will test the fisherman's patience and endurance. The excitement of landing a voracious shark has an appealing element of danger that other fishing seldom affords.

All sharks found off the northeastern coast of the United States are edible. The Mako, Porbeagle, Thresher and Dogfish are considered the most desirable; young fish are preferred to old ones. The meat can be boiled, fried or chowdered, but it should be cooked or cured as soon a possible. Cured, the meat is excellent whether smoked, salted or kippered.

PARTS OF A SHARK

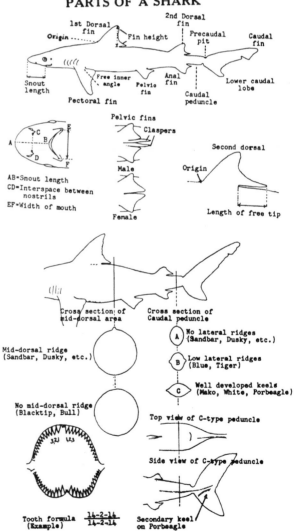

AB=Snout length
CD=Interspace between nostrils
EF=Width of mouth

4

Sharks

FROM EVERY CORNER OF THE WORLD come the sharks. Vicious scavengers of the deep. With them come conflicting stories of their preying on man and the upsetting of boats to kill and eat occupants. Of course 95% of these stories are not true. Sharks are undoubtedly characters disliked by all men and fish, but on the whole they are only Jackals and take the old, the weak and the crippled from the water.

The White Shark is considered one of the most dangerous. This brute spends most of his life off shore and feeds on porpoises and sea lions when he can get them. If a human were to come in grasp, you can bet he'll grasp the unfortunate.

The largest of all sharks, and largest of all fishes, the Whale Shark, is harmless to mankind. Feeds entirely on small microscopic fishes and would not even kill a larger fish. When harpooned does not defend itself, but swims away from its enemies.

Other sharks are not like this. It is the general custom of most all sharks to turn and attack a boat when hooked. Many a rowboat has scars of shark teeth embedded in the chine when a shark, unable to break away, returns and attacks the boat.

Any Shark, except the Whale Shark, will attack if wounded. Quite often when suffering from a back injury, possibly inflicted by a porpoise, a common Shark will cruise the shallow waters and attack anything which is in range, including the legs of a fisherman or bather. This would be a rare occasion, however.

It is not that sharks do not eat meat, they do. Might be called swimming garbage disposal units. They'll actually eat anything and that includes tin cans. The list of articles which have been taken from a shark's belly is like the inventory of Fibber McGee's closet. According to information gathered by the Office of Naval Research, in underwater accoustics tests, Sharks are stimulated by sound waves in locating their prey. Therefore, when Sharks are in the vicinity, a swimmer would be safer making smooth, steady strokes rather than splashing about without any rhythm.

The Sharks are of the Dogfish family and closely related to the Rays. These fish are all viviparous, which means they bear their young alive. For the most part they will give birth to a dozen or two dozen young each year. The young must be nimble, quick and hardy when they are born, for the parent shark does not hesitate to make a meal of them if they can be caught.

In the Sharks and Rays, the skeleton is still cartilaginous but they have mouths and lower jaws movable. Gill openings are slits and number from five to seven. While they are restless and rove the

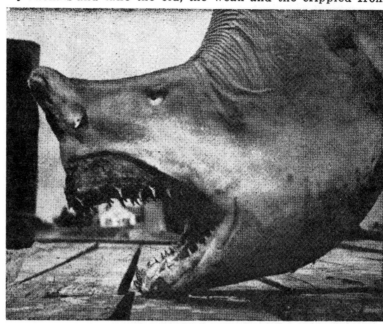

Mouth of a Ground Shark open showing teeth.   Photo by author

seas, it is very difficult to keep them in captivity, even though as a rule they do not swim at great speed.

● SMOOTH HAMMERHEAD SHARK
Sphyrna zygaena

Average length 6 feet; largest on record, 13 feet, weighing 725 pounds, caught by Frank Cavendish, Anna Maria, Fla., June 27, 1967. He was fishing off Rod and Reel Pier, with a cut bait. There have been reports of 2,000 pound specimens some 15 feet in length, but none of these claims have been verified.

Grayish above, becoming paler on belly. Easily identified by typical cross-bar on head. Eyes on extreme ends.

A nervous, roving beast of prey in all warm seas. Feeds on other fish, preferring Dogfish or Rays and other Sharks. Will attack anything in the water that looks edible. They're dangerous to man.

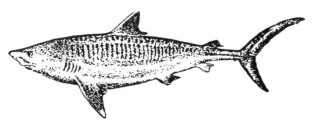

● **TIGER SHARK** *Galeocerdo cuvieri*

Also called Fox Shark, Leopard Shark.

Average length 8 feet; largest on record, 1,780 pounds, caught by Walter Maxwell, Charlotte, N. C., at Cherry Grove Beach, S. C., June 1966. Not edible.

Bluish-gray to slaty-gray, shading to white beneath. Fins all dark near edges.

A true rover of the seas. Will attack and eat anything in the water, including other Sharks. A veritable cannibal of the seas. A scavenger; will eat anything, including tin cans and rubbish.

● **GREENLAND SHARK** *Somniosus microcephalus*

Average size about 200 pounds; largest not determined. May reach 24 feet.

Brown to gray to black below and above; sometimes with indistinct dark bands or whitish spots. Mostly in North Atlantic. Feeds on fishes. One of the few Sharks that is oviparous.

● **LEMON SHARK** *Negaprion brevirostris*

Size: mature at 7 feet. Largest on record 272 pounds, caught May 18, 1966, fishing in the Gulfstream, near Miami by Guide Ralph Knowles. He was using a specially built salt water flyrod and claims the world record for the catch as a fly-rod record.

The Lemon Shark is very numerous in the Gulf of Mexico and the Caribbean. It is found from Cape Hatteras to Brazil. It is not unusual to find specimens in the South Pacific and the Indian Ocean.

The coloration is yellowish-brown, fading to a distinct yellow on the belly. It has a rather small dorsal for a Requiem Shark and a rather large second dorsal.

This Shark is dangerous to skin divers as he is found close to shore with a disposition that is unpredictable. It is mainly a fish eater, but has been known to attack man when harpooned. A very common Shark in the Caribbean and Gulf of Mexico.

● **GREAT WHITE SHARK** *Carcharodon carcharias*

Also called Man-Eater, Pointer.

Average length 8 feet, 250 pounds; largest on record, 17 feet 2 inches, weighing 4,500 pounds caught near Montauk Point, N. Y. by harpoon in July, 1965. The catch was made by Harvey Fersten and group of anglers under his direction working from charterboat Crickett II. Female with a 13-foot girth. Not edible.

Found in all warm seas and strays into temperate seas. A truly dangerous Shark, the most formidable creature in the water. Will attack on sight and take a human.

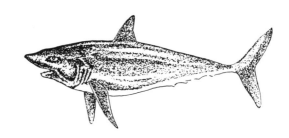

Atlantic: *Isurus oxyrinchus*
● **MAKO SHARK** Pacific: *Isurus glaucus*

Sometimes called Mackerel Shark.

Average 8 feet; largest on record 12 feet. Official largest ever taken on rod and reel 1,000 pounds by B. D. H. Ross in New Zealand waters, March 14, 1943. Unofficial record of a 1,200 catch by Al Hack off Florida Coast near Egmont Key. Food value poor.

This Shark is famous as a gamefish. Will strike most any bait. Prefers Jackfish. Not considered a dangerous Shark, although has been charged with attacking humans, especially when wounded. Found in all warm seas.

Large Sharks, Mostly Harmless

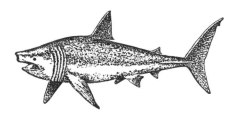

● **BASKING SHARK**   *Cetorhinus maximus*

Average size 15 feet; largest on record 32 feet weighing 1500 pounds; caught by Harold W. Simmons Jr., & Robert Damrell, Boothbay Harbor, Maine, Capture made with a harpoon, August 15, 1966, two miles west of Monhegan Island. Not edible.

Bluish-grey and greyish-brown. Sometimes nearly black on back.

This enormous Shark is found in temperate waters. Exceeded in size only by the Whale Shark. A sluggish and inoffensive creature and not considered dangerous to man.

Feeds on plankton along the surface of the water, thus the name Basking comes from the sight of the fish lazily moving along with fins out of water, sweeping up quantities of minute creatures.

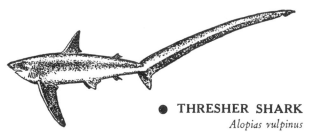

● **THRESHER SHARK**
Alopias vulpinus

Also called Fox Shark, Whip-Tail Shark, Swingletail. Average length 8 feet; largest on record weighed 922 pounds, caught in the Bay of Islands, New Zealand, March 21, 1937 by W. W. Dowling.

Dark greyish-brown to nearly black on upper area, changing abruptly to white on belly. Easily identified by long tail. Abundant in Atlantic and Mediterranean and found in all warm seas. Although quite formidable looking is considered harmless to man. Feeds on fish. Usually circles a school of small fish and using the tail to thresh water, feeds by throwing food into mouth with tail.

● **WHALE SHARK**   *Rhincodon typus*

Average size 20 feet; largest sighted in the water, 60 feet, off Johns Pass, Florida, in 1957. Largest authentic weight, 26,594 pounds, caught

near Knight's Key, Florida in 1912. This one measured 38 feet in length.

Brownish or greyish. Head and body covered with round white or yellow spots. Has a marble or mottled appearance. The largest fish in the sea.

This immense creature is easily distinguished from all other fish by the striking color pattern. A surface swimmer and feeder. Cruises on the surface feeding on small creatures. Entirely harmless to man.

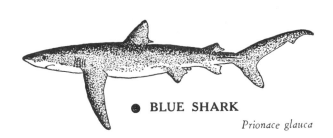

● **BLUE SHARK**

Prionace glauca

Also known as Blue Pointer.

Average size 9 feet; no authentic record of the largest, but thought to be close to 12 feet. Easily recognizable by its blue color; long pointed snout and long sickle-shaped pectoral fin. Blue on upper surface, shading to pure white below.

Reputedly the most numerous of the large oceanic Sharks; it is the one which is most often found around whaling operations. They will eat anything, often following a ship and consuming the garbage tossed over the side.

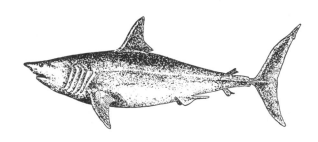

● **PORBEAGLE SHARK**   *Lamna nasus*

Also called Mackerel Shark, Salmon Shark, Blue Shark. Average length 5 feet; largest on record 8 feet, 10 inches long, weighing 390 pounds and 8 ounces with 53 inch girth, caught near Fire Island, New York on May 20, 1962 by Joseph Monty.

Food value is slight. The pointed snout identifies a Porbeagle. World traveler; strong swimmer able to catch fast-swimming fish.

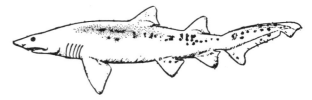

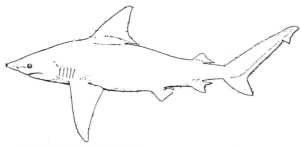

● **SANDBAR SHARK**   *Carcharhinus milberti*

Also called Brown Shark.

Average size 75 pounds; largest not known. Records solicited. U. S. Fish and Wildlife says they grow to seven feet in length.

Gray to brown above. Paler below. Fin margins slightly darker. Commonly found in inshore waters along the Atlantic coast, Cape Cod to Florida. Probably the most commonly reported Shark around bathing beaches. Only the females come inshore to bear their young. Males stay offshore. Much the same diet as the Dusky Shark, feeding on bottom fishes.

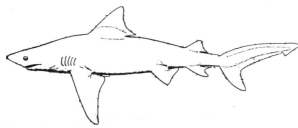

● **BULL SHARK**   *Carcharhinus leucas*

Also called Cub Shark.

Average size 20 pounds; largest not known. May grow to 12 feet in length.

Gray above and white below; lower tips of pectorals sometimes dusky. A common shark of tropical waters. A sluggish, heavy-bodied Shark which often enters estuaries and travels up rivers. Feeds on anything that can be digested, and has a keen taste for garbage.

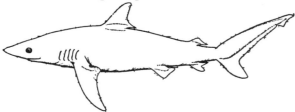

● **DUSKY SHARK**   *Carcharhinus obscurus*

Average size 20 pounds; largest not known. Records solicited. U. S. Fish and Wildlife says they grow to 11 feet.

Lead gray, bluish, or copper above, white below. A common Shark of inshore waters along the Atlantic, Cape Cod to Florida. Feeds primarily on Searobins, Skates, Headfish and Flounders. Can be a menace to bathers on the beaches. Not dangerous unless wounded or hungry.

● **SAND SHARK**   *Carcharias taurus*

Also called Slender Tooth.

Average size 60 pounds; largest on record not determined. U. S. Fish and Wildlife says they grow to over 10 feet.

Gray-brown above becoming grayish white below. Found in all warm seas. A very dangerous Shark penetrating far up estuaries into shallow water. Grows to 10 ft. and is responsible for most shallow water attacks in South Africa. Considered a serious menace in East Indian and Australian waters. Not many Sand Shark attacks reported in the U.S. though it is often seen in summer months.

Reported to be a cunning and quick scavenger, it creeps along the bottom toward shore, hardly visible against the sand. If an unwary bather approaches within reach, the Shark attacks in a savage rush.

● **BLACKTIP SHARK**   *Carcharhinus limbatus*
● **SPINNER**   *Carcharhinus maculipinnis*

Two Sharks or one? The *C. limbatus* is given the name Blacktip Shark or Small Blacktip and is said to reach 7 ft. The *C. maculipinnis* is named Spinner (a name also bestowed on *C. limbatus* by some authorities!) or Large Blacktip and is known to reach 8 ft. or more. Similar enough to be very difficult to distinguish. Experts point out some differences in eye size, swimming speed, slimness of body.

Occasionally seen on both coasts, but more often Atlantic, particularly in Gulf of Mexico.

Grey-black above, tips of all fins are black.

Largest Spinner—weight 305 lbs. caught by Mrs. Katheryn Herwitt of Monroeville, Pa., off Abaco, Bahamas, Nov. 26, '68. A record Small Blacktip, 132 lbs. was caught by Norman Jansik fishing out of Miami on May 15, '68.

Honored as a gamefish. Will leap from the water when hooked, oftentimes executing a spinning maneuver. Sometimes mistaken for Tarpon. Not considered dangerous unless of maximum size.

Deep Water Sharks

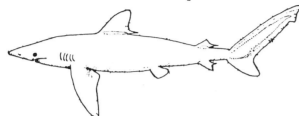

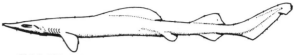

● FALSE CAT SHARK   *Pseudotriakis microdon*

Average size 10 pounds; largest on record not determined. Records solicited. U. S. Fish and wildlife says they could attain a length of nine feet, eight inches.

Uniformly dark brown shading to gray; darkest on the front margins of fins. Ranges all the Atlantic, mostly northern limits. A deep water Shark. Little is known about habits, food, etc.

● BIGNOSE SHARK   *Carcharhinus altima*

Average size about 80 pounds; largest on record not known. Information solicited. U. S. Fish and Wildlife says they grow to 9 feet.

Grayish-brown above, sides a lighter tint; belly dirty white. Warm water fish, found mostly around the coast of Florida and tropical waters. Seldom found in shallow waters. Little is known of feeding habits.

◉ CHAIN DOGFISH   *Scyliorhinus retifer*

Average size, one pound; largest on record not known. Information solicited. U. S. Fish and Wildlife says they could be three feet long.

Dark reddish-brown above, yellowish below, with a very characteristic pattern of sooty black stripes. Mostly found on the bottom close to the outer part on the Continental Shelf, seldom strays into shoal water. Little is known of its habits or food.

◉ WHITETIP SHARK
Carcharhinus longimanus

Average size, 20 pounds; largest not known. Records solicited. U. S. Fish and Wildlife says this shark can grow to 13 feet.

Grayish-brown above and yellowish below. Dorsal and pectoral fins are white tip, but sometimes there are exceptions. Range warm waters of South Atlantic. Usually found near the surface in offshore waters. Diet includes squid, Dolphin, Mackerel and other schooling fishes. Has a liking for garbage from ships at sea.

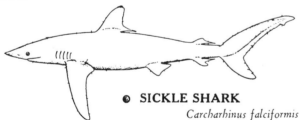

◉ SICKLE SHARK

Carcharhinus falciformis

Average size 100 pounds; largest not known. Records solicited. U. S. Fish and Wildlife says they grow to 10 feet in length.

Black to gray above, white below. Range the tropical belt of the Atlantic, north limit Cape Cod. Mostly found offshore and in warm water they are plentiful. Feed on squid and small fishes.

● PORTUGESE SHARK   *Centroscymnus coelolepis*

Average size, 3 pounds; largest not known, records solicited. U. S. Fish and Wildlife says they attain a length of three feet and eight inches.

Dark brown above and below. Somewhat similar to Greenland Shark, except much smaller. Ranges the Atlantic, mostly in temperate waters. A deep water species, never taken in less than 180 fathoms.

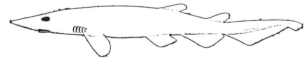

● DEEP WATER CAT   *Aspristurus profundorum*

Average size, unknown; largest unknown, information solicited.

Grayish-brown above and below. Found only on the Continental Shelf, off Delaware Bay. This is a rare species. Coloration suggests a deep water habitat.

● ATLANTIC SHARPNOSE
Scoliodon terraenovae

Average size 3 pounds; largest not known. Records solicited. U. S. Fish and Wildlife says maximum is three feet.

Brownish to olive gray above; white below. Range both sides of tropical and subtropical Atlantic. A small shallow water Shark, feeding on shrimp and small fishes.

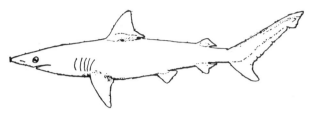

● FINETOOTH SHARK   *Aprionodon isodon*

Average size four pounds; largest not known. Records solicited. The U. S. Fish and Wildlife Service says that the maximum length of this Shark could be four feet or more.

Bluish-gray above, shading to gray on sides; white below. A tropical Shark, found mostly around Florida coast and Gulf of Mexico.

Distinguished by its smooth-edged straight teeth which are similar in both jaws; also by the presence of well-developed labial furrows around corners of the mouth. Differs from the Sharpnose Shark by the origin of the second dorsal fin which is located over the origin of the anal fin.

Apparently an inshore fish which feeds on a variety of small fishes.

● SIXGILL SHARK   *Hexanchus griseum*

Also called Griset Shark, Cow Shark.

Average size 10 feet; largest on record 26 feet, 5 inches; no food value. Flesh has a strong purgative effect.

Dark brownish-grey or black above, shading to paler below. Usually a pale streak along middle of each side. Said to be fierce and voracious. Feeds upon fishes. Found in Atlantic and Mediterranean.

● BRAMBLE SHARK   *Echinorhinus brucus*

Also called Spinous Shark. Average size 4 feet; largest to 10 feet; poor food.

Dark brown above and paler to whitish beneath. Skin is armed with button-like denticles, some surmounted by tuft of small prickle hairs.

Lives mostly in deep water; all oceans. Feeds on fish and crustaceans of the ocean bottom. Will take baited lines and sometimes caught from deep-sea fishing boats.

● SEVENGILL SHARK   *Notorynchus maculatus*

Also called Perlon Shark, Cow Shark.

Average size 7 feet; largest to 10 feet; food value slight. Brown or grey above, shading to paler below.

This Shark is regarded as dangerous in some waters, especially around Australia. Found in all oceans. Oil yield is considerable.

● GOBLIN SHARK   *Scapanorhynchus sp.*

Also called Elfin Shark. Average size 8 feet; largest known 14 feet; no food value.

Long snout and mouth which can be protruded, marks this Shark for easy identification.

Is a bottom feeder and probably lives off shellfish buried in the bottom mud, or in grass. Not too much is known of the habits for they are not plentiful. Mostly in the Pacific Ocean.

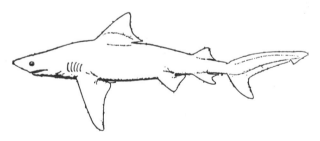

● NICARAGUAN SHARK   *Carcharhinus nicaraguensis*

Found only in Lake Nicaragua, this is the only Shark known to have adapted completely to a fresh water environment. Gray, heavy-bodied with broad stubby nose; long pectorals. A bottom dweller—takes any bait.

Largest reported to Great Outdoors caught by Frank L. McGinn of Lighthouse Pt., Fla., fishing at Tarpon Camp, Rio San Juan; weight 50 lbs. (length not reported). A very dangerous Shark—known to be a man-killer.

Unusual Sharks

○ SILVER SHARK
Chimaera monstrosa

Black striped on back and silvery belly.

A Shark of the deep water and only rarely taken in fishing waters of ocean and gulf. They move mostly by use of their large pectoral fins, indicating the connecting link to the Rays.

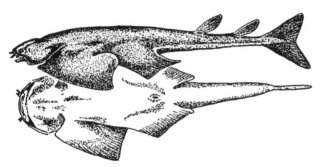

● ATLANTIC ANGEL SHARK   *Squatina dumerili*

Also called Monk Fish, Fiddlefish, Shark Ray, Mongrel Skate. Average size 4 feet; largest possibly 8 feet. Coarse-grained flesh. Sometimes eaten.

The upper surface is generally grey or brown, but varies from yellowish to nearly black and is usually blotched. Lower surface is plain white.

This creature is just halfway between a Shark and a Ray. It is a true Shark, however. Diet mostly shellfish.

Found throughout Atlantic, although not plentiful anywhere.

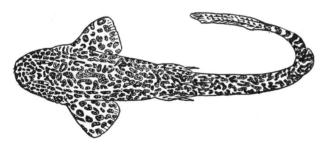

● IZAK SHARK   *Holohalaelurus regani*

Also called Lazyshark, Leopardshark, Tigershark. Average size 36 inches; largest 48 inches; food value nil.

Head is broad and depressed. Markings variable but distinct. Found in the Atlantic and Pacific. Not too uncommon.

● SMALLTOOTH SAWFISH   *Pristis pectinatus*

Average size 10 feet; largest on record 31 feet long, weighed 5,700; taken by F. A. Mitchell, Hedges, Panama Bay, 1923; food value poor.

Grayish over all. Darker on back and lighter on belly. Resembles the coloring of a Shark.

The Sawfish is fairly common on the Florida Gulf Coast and because of peculiar habits is more dangerous than the Spearfishes.

Of the Dogfish family, as are Rays and Sharks, the Sawfish does not have anything in common with the Swordfish or Sailfish, except a nose which is used as a weapon. Like the Sharks, Sawfish bear their young alive instead of laying eggs.

◑ ZEBRA SHARK   *Stegostoma fasciatum*

Also called Monkey-mouth. Average size 6 to 7 feet; largest 11 feet; food value nil. Easily recognized by the cross bars and spots.

Found throughout the warm seas of Indo-Pacific. A sluggish creature and harmless to man. Feeds on shellfish.

● CARPET SHARK   *Orectolobus barbatus*

Also called Wobbegong. Average length 6 feet; largest possibly 10 feet; no food value.

Yellowish, greyish or brownish. Color is quite variable. Sometimes spotted, barred or striped.

There are five species of this genus and they occur mostly in Asiatic waters. Easily identified by the blunt head and mottled coloration. They are quite different from other Sharks.

Spend most of their time on the bottom lying motionless in the weeds or half buried in mud. When a lobster, crab or bit of sea life comes within reach, the Shark takes off at great speed.

● **MOTTLED CATSHARK**   *Chiloscyllium plagiosum*

Average length 20 inches; largest on record 28 inches; no food value.

Can be identified by peculiar mottled coloring and a ridge along middle of back. Color variable. Spots sometimes blue. A rare Shark found in the waters of Indo-Pacific.

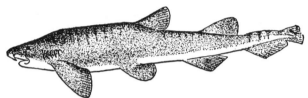

● **SKAAMOOG SHARK**   *Haploblepharus edwardsi*

Also called Puffadder Shark, Dogfish. Average size 30 inches; largest 40 inches; food value fair.

Head rather wide and bluntly pointed snout. Reddish-brown.

A shallow water Shark, feeding on shellfish. Found mostly on African Coast.

● **SMOOTH DOGFISH**   *Mustelus canis*

Average size 3 pounds; largest not known, records solicited. U. S. Fish and Wildlife says they grow to five feet in length.

Gray to brown above and grayish white below. Range throughout the Atlantic from Cape Cod to South America. A most abundant shark. Feeds on crabs, lobsters and small fishes.

A fairly abundant Shark on the Atlantic Coast, but rare on the Gulf Coast. Like other Sharks, it is viviparous and gives birth to a dozen young at a time. Will pick up any kind of bait, preferably dead.

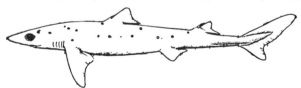

● **SPINY DOGFISH**   *Squalus acanthias*

Average size, 5 pounds; largest not known, records solicited. U. S. Fish and Wildlife says they attain a length of four feet.

Slate gray above, pale gray to white below. Young specimens have white spots. World wide in range. A common shark, found inshore and to depths of 10 fathoms. Feeds on fish, squid, shrimp and jellyfish. The spines are poisonous.

● **MILKSHARK**   *Carcharhinus walbeehmi*

Average length 3 feet; largest 4 feet: food value good. Grey to brownish above.

A harmless Shark fairly common in all warm seas. Has a rather sharply pointed snout and depressed head.

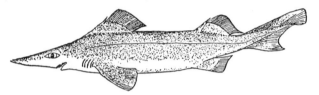

● **SHARK EGLANTINA**   *Deania eglantina*

Average size 30 inches; largest 4 feet; food value unknown. Easily identified by elongated snout, and big eye.

Found mostly in water up to 150 fathoms. Seen off the coast of Japan and the Philippines.

● **SWELL SHARK**   *Cephaloscyllium uter*

Also called Balloon Shark. Average size 24 inches; largest 36 inches; no food value.

Snout rather pointed, head broad. Able to inflate so as to become almost spherical. Found mostly on African Coast and Red Sea. A rare specimen.

● **SCHOOL SHARK**   *Galeorhinus galeus*

Also called Liver-oil Shark, Tope. Average size 4 feet; largest 6 feet; food value fair.

Brownish above; lighter below; eyes rounded.

Harmless to man, but likes to hang around fishing boats. Often takes the fish from the lines. Will bite well on bait. Sought after for the valuable liver oil which is rich in Vitamin A.

 # Medium Sized Sharks

● **ZEBRA SHARK**   *Stegostoma tigrinum*

Average length 4 feet; largest known 6 feet; no food value.

Yellowish-brown, with many vertical series of rounded dark spots. In the young these are cross-bars. Body long. Hind part flattened.

Widely distributed in tropical seas from California to Australia. A harmless Shark feeding on crustaceans. Usually inhabits waters close to shore.

● **HOUND SHARK**   *Mustelus punctulatus*

Also called Spotted Gully Shark, Gummy Shark, Speareye Shark, Sweet William.

Average size about 48 inches; largest about 6 feet; food value fair. Uniformly grey with black spots. Pupil of eye rounded.

Found in coastal regions of Atlantic and Indian oceans. Fairly common. Not considered dangerous.

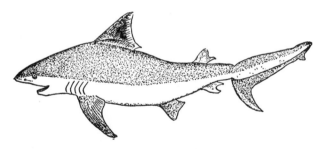

● **RIVER SHARK**   *Carcharhinus gangeticus*

Average size 5 feet; largest 7 feet; food value nil. Grey to bluish above, lighter below. Head rather wide. Body fairly slender.

A ferocious and savage Shark. Enters rivers freely and is as much at home in fresh water as the seas. Will attack bathers or anything in the water. Can inflict a terrible wound. Human no match for this Shark in the water. Found in all warm seas. Not abundant in temperate zones.

○ **PORT JACKSON SHARK**   *Heterodontus japonicus*

Also called Bullhead. Average size about 3 feet; largest 5 feet; food fair.

Brown or rusty-red with cloudy markings. Usually a dark bar on head running through eye.

A harmless Shark, living on shellfish. Found mostly on the coasts of Australia.

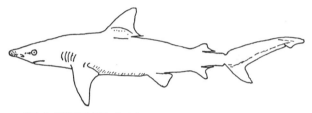

● **BLACKNOSE SHARK**   *Carcharhinus acronotus*

This shark is easily recognized by its long dusky snout. The snout is darker in young specimens, becoming more diffuse and obscure on adults. The body color is cream or yellowish-gray above and a paler shade below. Other specimens exhibit a uniform brown above and below.

Ranges from North Carolina to Rio de Janeiro. Southwest Florida is only area that it is seen in numbers. Size averages from 3 to 4 feet in adults. Seldom exceeds 5 to 6 feet.

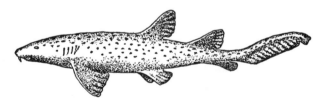

● **NURSE SHARK**   *Ginglymostoma cirratum*

Also called Gata. Average size 6 feet; largest possibly 12 feet; no authentic record available. Not gourmet, but could be eaten. Uniformly brownish. Smaller and younger specimens have small spots. Small mouth with barbels of sucker type.

Inhabit warm seas and most common in the waters about the Florida Keys. A shallow water Shark, feeding on crustaceans.

There is evidence that this Shark, once considered harmless, will fight back if provoked. Though teeth are weak, it will tenaciously hold on, and could drown its victim.

The Ray Family

THE AMERICAN RAYS are mostly enormous fish, ranging from over 500 pounds for the Stingray to thousands of pounds for the Manta. They are related to the Sharks, of the Dogfish family, yet they have none of the jackal traits of the Sharks.

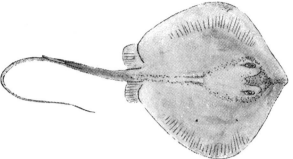

● **ATLANTIC STINGRAY**   *Dasyatis sabina*
Also called Stingaree.

Average size 5 pounds; largest Stingray on record caught in a commercial fisherman's net off Bradenton Beach, summer of '69; width 6½ ft. weight over 600 lbs. Tentatively identified as a Southern Stringray, *Dasyatis americana*, a deep water specimen seldom seen.

Olive-brown on back; lower surface whitish.

● **ATLANTIC MANTA RAY**   *Manta birostris*

Also called Devilfish.

Average size 500 pounds; largest on record believed to be 5,500 pounds. No food value.

Black on top with white underside. Has two large flippers on each side of mouth to sweep in plankton from the surface.

While not dangerous, these fish often leap from the water to terrorize fishermen in small boats— an awesome sight to see a 10 ft. 600 lb. Manta leap and turn a summersault within a few feet of your craft.

● **SPOTTED EAGLE RAY**   *Aetobatus narinari*
Also called Leopard Ray, Mussel Ray, Whip Ray.

Average size 10 pounds; largest on record 262 pounds, established by Grant H. Hansley of Sugar Grove, Ohio, Feb. 27, 1958, fishing from Spanish Harbor bridge, Marathon, Fla. Food value poor.

Grayish to black with pale spots. Females said to leap from water giving birth to young.

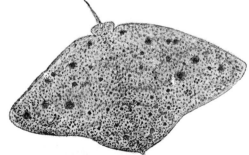

● **SHOVELNOSE GUITARFISH** *Rhinobatus productus*

Also called Sand Shark.

Average size 3 feet, 24 pounds; largest on record weighed 48 pounds, caught by Jody and Jeff Schiefler, Fort Myers, Fla., June 19, 1967, in Big Marco Pass.

Some of the experts state that this specimen attains a length of 10 feet and 500 pounds in weight, in the Pacific. Not edible.

● **SPOTTED BUTTERFLY RAY** *Pteroplatea micrura*
Average size 22 inches across wings.

Named because their swimming motions resemble a butterfly in flight; have a tendency to jump clear of the water more often than other Rays. Often seen over grassy flats in bays and inland waters.

American Skates

AMERICAN SKATES, quite common on the Atlantic Coast, are the same as the European Skates in appearance. Americans however, do not consider them good seafood, as do the Europeans.

Most Rays, like their relatives the Sharks, bear their young alive, whereas the Skates lay eggs which are frequently picked up along the shore and called "Mermaid Purses". A Skate will take most any cut bait.

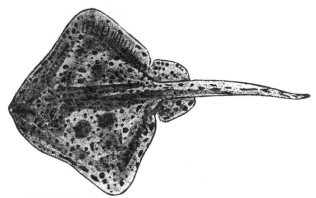

● **WINTER SKATE**   *Raja ocellata*

Also called Big Skate. Average size 2 pounds; largest on record 25 pounds; food value poor.

Lighter colored background, with finer mottled black spots as compared to the Clearnose Skate. This example has been found as far north as Labrador.

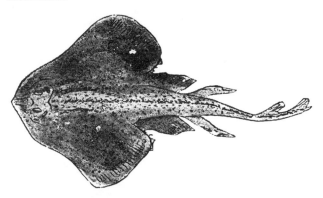

● **LITTLE SKATE**   *Raja erinacea*

Also called Tobacco Box. Average size 16 to 20 inches; the smallest and most common of the Skates found along the Atlantic shore. Light brown in color with small round spots of dark brown; food value poor.

Prefers shallow sandy bottom where it is easy to stir up a cloud of sand with a flap of the wings. The Skates soon settle in the sand and are secure from observation above.

In this position they feed by snapping up the next crab passing that way. Their diet is almost exclusively crustaceans.

Native to the shores of United States from the South Carolina border to Halifax. Most common about New England.

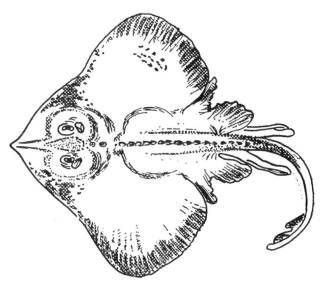

● **SMOOTH SKATE**   *Raja senta*

Average size 12 inches; largest on record 29 in. in length, caught by Mrs. Raymond L. Zuppinger, Punta Gorda, Fla. fishing off her seawall Aug. 3, 1969. Rusty-brown above; white below; not spotted.

Can be recognized by its sharp snout and rounded outer margins of the wings. There is a row of thorns running down the back to the tail.

A rare Skate, seldom seen in the Gulf of Mexico. Found sometimes on the offshore banks and occasionally inshore on the beaches.

● **CLEARNOSE SKATE**   *Raja eglanteria*

Also called Brier Skate. Average size 1 pound; largest on record 12 pounds; food value poor.

Prettily marked with alternating splotches of black, brown and silver.

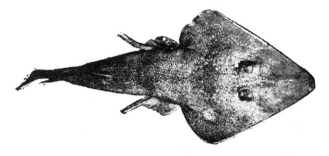

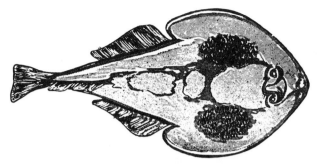

● **ATLANTIC GUITAR FISH** *Rhinobatus lentiginosus*

Also called Fiddle Fish. Average size 2 feet.

Elongated, with narrow wings and somewhat pointed nose. Grayish-brown on top, densely peppered with yellow spots. Although a member of the Rays, it appears to be a missing link between a Skate, a Ray, and a Shark.

Found from the Carolinas southward, fairly common on the Florida coast. They are occasionally caught on grassy bottom in the bays by trout fishermen. They feed on bits of fish and small shellfish. Will pick up a cut bait or dead minnow. Edible, according to some authorities.

● **LESSER ELECTRIC RAY** *Narcine brasiliensis*

Also called Numbfish. Average size 14 inches; largest on record 28 inches; food value, none.

A rounded head with dark spots on each wing top, has a thicker tail than the Skates and does not have the whip-like tail of the Rays.

This large Skate, which is a rarity in all waters, mostly found in Florida, carries its own storage batteries. A charge in the head of this fish is sufficient to knock a man down.

On one occasion, a fisherman jabbed a knife into an Electric Ray, and the shock knocked him unconscious. On another occasion, a shock was administered through wire leader to the fisherman's hand, who unfortunately suffered from a heart attack and died from the shock.

They pick up baits which are allowed to lie on the bottom of the fishing grounds and are usually caught accidentally. The grassy flats of bay water is the hangout for this shocking member of the flat-fish tribe.

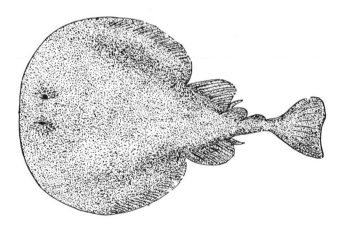

● **ATLANTIC TORPEDO** *Torpedo nobiliana*

Also called Crampfish, Numbfish.

Average size 30 pounds; largest 200 pounds; no food value.

A Ray which inhabits the coastal waters from Maine to Cuba and Key West to Vera Cruz. Not found in large numbers anywhere. This Ray ·can administer an electric shock so severe as to cause unconsciousness or death to a person. They feed on fish and are taken on hook and line. The leader wire attached to a hook and embedded in the Ray's mouth is sufficient conductor to administer a fatal shock to a fisherman.

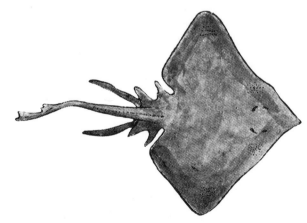

● **BARNDOOR SKATE** *Raja laevis*

Average size 3 feet; largest on record 6 feet; food value fair. Many fisherman claim the wings of this Skate are excellent eating.

Ground color with blotches on wing tips.

The largest of the Altantic Skates. Maine to Florida; from near shore to depths of 100 fathoms, depending on the season.

 # Eels, Salt & Fresh Water

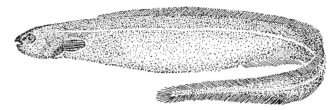

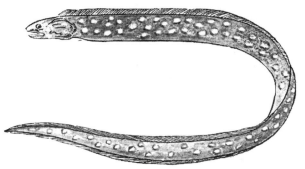

● **SLIME EEL**   *Simenchelys parasiticus*

Average size 24 inches; largest on record 43 inches, caught by David Brassell, Murrell's Inlet, S.C. Nov. 27, 1961. Food value nil. Dark brown, belly paler, sometimes more or less silvery.

Distinguished by snub nose and long dorsal fin; stouter and sway-bellied, head is shorter than a Conger; mouth small.

Preys on Halibut; very slimy. Found in shallow water mostly.

● **SHARP-TAILED EEL**   *Myrichthys acuminatus*

Average size 18 inches; largest not known; food value, nil. Brownish color. Has many round spots in two rows forming a somewhat regular pattern.

Found mostly on the Grouper banks off Tampa Bay, in Florida. One of the Snake Eels.

● **GREAT SIREN**   *Siren lacertina*

Also called Mud Eel. Average size 17 inches; largest on record 36 inches.

Black in color with yellow markings. Has a mouth nearly as large as a Mudfish. Equipped with 2 feet (just behind the gills) with 4 toes each. Gills have 3 slits. Not a fish but an amphibian sometimes found in river mouths or up to 100 yards from the water. Seldom seen in normal weather conditions. Believed to spend most of existence buried in water and mud.

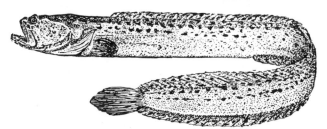

● **WRYMOUTH**   *Cryptacanthodes maculatus*

Light brownish; small dark spots arranged in more or less regular rows from head to base of caudal. An albino Wrymouth (entirely white) is called the Ghostfish.

Eel-shaped with a large head and the mouth sharply oblique like that of a Stargazer. A native of the Atlantic coast of North America. Lives in burrows of mud. Only rarely caught on a hook.

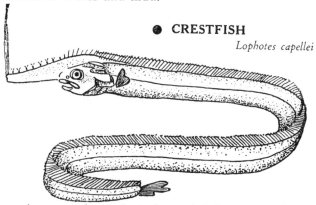

● **CRESTFISH**

Lophotes capellei

Average size 4 feet; largest 6 feet, 10 inches; captured by Jean Thomas, Ft. Lauderdale, Fla., May, 1956. Not edible.

Silvery with iridescent orange spots, which appear to light up in the water like neon illumination. A rare fish indeed. Not more than half a dozen have ever been recorded. The record, from Florida tops others of lesser size found in Japanese and African waters. Undoubtedly a deep water fish.

The fish was taken when a Shark chased it ashore at the feet of Jean Thomas, a boatbuilder of Ft. Lauderdale, who was surfcasting. He took it to the Reese taxidermy for mounting.

● **SEA LAMPREY**

Petromyzon marinus

Also called Lamper Eel.

Eel-like fishes with round sucker mouths, equipped with sharp cutting teeth arranged in circular formation. Have round holes on side instead of gills.

Average size 10 inches; largest on record 30 inches; food value poor.

This species lives in the ocean, but ascends streams in the spring to spawn. They build dams in fresh water brooks, using stones.

Many of these eels become landlocked in lakes and streams and are very destructive to other fishes. They feed by attaching themselves to the bodies of their victims and gnaw their way in.

Morays and Other Eels

THERE ARE AT LEAST TEN well known species of Moray Eels, all the same shape but with different coloring. The largest of the family is the Green Moray, which attains a length of 6 feet and presents an awesome spectacle when out of the water.

The open mouth discloses a bristling cavity of needle-sharp, curved teeth, which can tear flesh from the bones on short order. The Morays have thick leathery skin, brightly colored. Are found in tropical seas, where they live coiled around rocks or sulking in the reefs.

The flesh of Morays is seldom eaten and not considered wholesome as that of the true Eels.

Following are the names of Morays found in American Tropical waters:

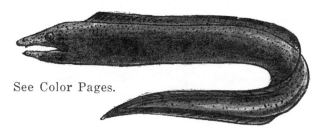

See Color Pages.

● **GREEN MORAY** *Gymnothorax funebris*
The greenish color is produced by a yellowish mucous layer which overlies the darker skin.

● **CALIFORNIA MORAY** *Gymnothorax mordax*
Used as a food fish in the Pacific. It is darker in color, resembling the Common Eels to greater extent.

● **SPOTTED MORAY** *Gymnothorax moringa*
A smaller size of Moray, marked with yellow and black; largest on record 19½ inches, caught by Bill Cope, off Murrell's Inlet, S. C.

● **PURPLEMOUTH MORAY** *Gymnothorax vicinus*
Uniform brown to yellow mottled. Roof of mouth lavender; floor dark purplish. Attains about 4 feet.

● **CHAIN MORAY** *Echidna catenata*
Has wine-colored body crossed by numerous white rings. Not as vicious as its relatives.

● **GOLDENTAIL MORAY** *Muraena miliaris*
Dark brown with numerous yellow dots; tail usually yellow. Max. length 20 inches. Found in Caribbean.

● **PYGMY MORAY** *Anarchia yoshiae*
Grows to 8½ inches. Generally brownish with marbling. This species never has been found alive. Native to Florida and Bahamian waters.

● **VIPER MORAY** *Enchelycore nigricans*
Adult has long slit-like posterior nostrils; coloring uniformly chestnut-brown; grows to 2½ feet—young are mottled in color. Native to So. Atlantic waters.

● **CONGER EEL**

Conger oceanicus
Also called Snake Eel. Average weight 2 lb. 8 oz. Largest on record caught by G. L. Caudell of La Marque, Texas. He caught the Eel while fishing 35 mi. off the coast in July 1969. Official weight 21 lbs. 15 ozs.

Brownish with yellow spots interspersed by black. An Eel which lives in the rocks and crevices of the Florida reefs usually in the same locality as the Morays. While not as vicious as the Morays, nevertheless a bad customer.

● **ELECTRIC EEL** *Electrophorus electricus*
Also called Horse Killer. Average size 12 inches; largest on record 36 inches; food value poor.

Dusky on top, shading to silvery belly. Round body, fins very small. There is only one species of this Eel and the natural habitat is South America, rivers of Brazil. Specimens have been imported to America and are on rare occasions found in creeks.

It is the most powerful of all electric fishes and stories are told of horses being killed by the shock of this creature.

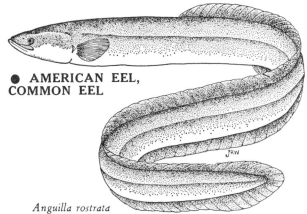

● **AMERICAN EEL, COMMON EEL**

Anguilla rostrata
Average size 18 inches; largest on record 48 inches; girth 13½ inches; weigh 10 lbs., 15 ozs. Caught by Mrs. Junie Becton, Richmond, Va., off Norfolk, Va., July 31, '63.

Food value good; color, dusky black.

The American Eel reverses the procedure of life of all other fishes. Instead of spawning in fresh water, it goes to the depths of the ocean to spawn, then dies. The young live in the ocean for a year or more then migrate to fresh water streams and brackish bays. Found mostly on muddy bottoms.

Snake-like Fish

● **ATLANTIC CUTLASS FISH** *Trichiurus lepturus*

Also called Scabbard Fish, Silverfish, Sable, Savola, Ribbon Fish, Hairtail.

Average size 20 inches; largest on record 52 inches long, weighing 4 pounds and 3 ounces, caught by Gordon W. Hasenfus of St. Petersburg, Fla. while fishing at Port Canaveral, Fla. near Jack's Fish Camp. Recorded June 8, 1959. Not recommended as food.

Silver in color, olive-toned dorsal fin with rays ivory-white. About 125 rays to the tail, brownish in the lateral area from pectoral fin back, just above median line.

Rarely caught in the bay fishing grounds; sometimes seen in Mackerel nets. Have been reported in large schools in some areas of Florida keys and the Florida East Coast. As a rule a rather rare fish.

● **AMERICAN SAND LAUNCE**

Ammodytes americanus

Also called Sand Eel, Lant. Average size 6 inches; largest on record 14 inches; food value, excellent. Colored to correspond with surroundings, usually the sand of the beach.

This little fish is abundant along the entire length of American shores at various times. They appear and disappear with great mystery. When a school comes in at some point, they bury themselves in the sand and often remain there after the tide has receded. At some points the natives take advantage of this and dig them out.

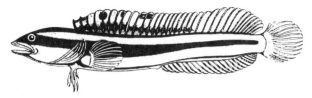

● **WRASSE BLENNY** *Hemiemblemaria simulus*

Average size 4 inches; largest not known; food value, nil.

Silvery with dark stripe running from nose to tail on the lateral line. A deep water fish of the coral bottoms, very rare.

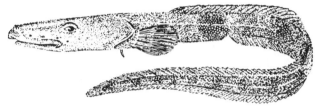

● **WOLF EELPOUT** *Lycenchelys verillii*

Average size 7 inches; largest 12 inches; no food value. Light grayish-brown above lateral line, pearly-white below; livid blue belly; sides marked with irregular patches of brown.

This is a fairly rare fish. Not too many specimens have been examined. Those found have come from deep water. Believed to live in mud or sand.

● **RIBBONFISH** *Letharchus velifer*

Only one specimen of this fish has ever been examined. This was approximately 5 feet long and was mounted by Al Pfleuger of Miama, Fla. Found on the beach near there.

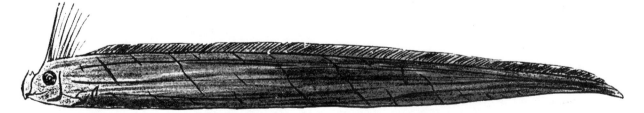

● **OARFISH** *Regalecus glesne*

Also called Sea Serpent. Average size 10 feet; largest on record 30 feet; food value, none.

Strikingly colored. Bluish-silver. High crest of bright scarlet fin rays behind head.

This is the Sea Serpent of the high seas. It is a deep water fish and is rarely seen. When observed upon the water or cast on the shore, the sea serpent stories begin to roll. It is the only such fish in the ocean which attains a length of 30 or more feet.

Largest speciman ever measured and authenticated, was reported as 11 feet and two inches, caught in the waters of the Gulf of Mexico, as a derelict, being washed on the beach. This incident occurred April 6, 1967, at St. Petersburgh Beach, witnessed by Rear Admiral Edward Ellsberg, St. Petersburg, Fla.

Snake-like Fish

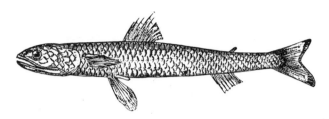

● **SHORTJAW LIZARDFISH**   *Saurida normani*

Also called Longley Lizardfish.

Average size 9 inches; largest on record 20½ inches, taken by Robert L. Levine, M. D. TESN, in Little Sound Bermuda, March 26, 1955, weighed 2 pounds and 3 ounces.

Gray on back with pale blue spots above the lateral line. Sides and belly silvery.

One of the Lizardfish group found in southern waters from Bermuda around the coastal waters of the Gulf of Mexico. Considered quite rare.

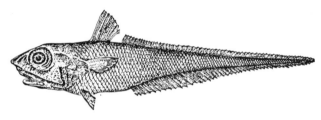

● **MARLIN-SPIKE**   *Nezumio bairdii*

Also called Common Grenadier; Rat-Tail.

Average size 12 inches; largest on record 18 inches; food value nil. Light brownish-gray above, silvery below; surface of snout, pink; throat deep violet; eyes dark blue.

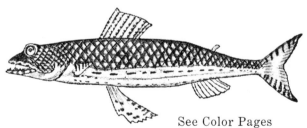

See Color Pages

● **INSHORE LIZARDFISH**   *Synodus foetens*

Also called Pike and Sand Pike.

Average size 8 inches, largest on record, 17 inches, caught by Capt. Black aboard the boat Pinellas out of St. Petersburg, 1955. Not a food fish, considered poisonous.

Body and sides grayish, finely mottled with brownish-green. Belly, white; caudal, dusky; head, brownish. Eye placed high. A mouth of formidable teeth.

Feeds on small fish, crabs, shrimp or worms, most anything. A voracious feeder. Cape Cod to Mexican coast and Indies.

20

● **ALLIGATORFISH**   *Aspidophoroides monopteryguis*

Also called Seapoacher. Average size 6 inches; largest not known.

A deep water fish, usually found in northern waters and considered out of environment when taken in southern fishing grounds.

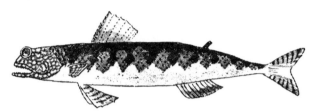

● **SNAKEFISH**   *Trachinocephalus myops*

Average size 7 inches; largest on record 19½ inches, caught in Boca Ciega Bay, Fla., by Jay Cook of Blind Pass, Fla. Weight 2 pounds. Not edible.

Greenish on top with white blotches on the side, usually about 10. Head is brownish; nose rounded.

This is the smallest of the Lizardfishes and most commonly taken by hook and line fishermen. Ranges over all southern waters and throughout the Caribbean.

● **TRUMPET FISH**   *Aulostomus maculatus*

Average size 10 inches; largest 14 inches. A bony fish, with snout somewhat resembling Pipe-fish. Feeds on tiny fishes.

Occasional specimens found in all waters of the Gulf of Mexico.

● **CORNET FISH**   *Fistularia tabacaria*

Average size 14 inches; largest on record, 5 feet even, weighing 6 pounds and 8 ounces, reported by Joe Walker, Arco Taxidermy Co., Tarpon Springs. Caught west of Tarpon Springs in the Gulf of Mexico, Aug. 26, 1965.

Color dark olive on back, pink on belly with bright blue dots, slightly smaller than a dime — all over body. Length of head 17 inches. This fish has been said to attain greater length, but no authentic catch reported larger than the one listed above. A rare fish, but has been found as far north as Nova Scotia. Is a tropical inhabitant.

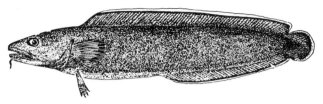

● **CUSK**   *Brosme brosme*

Average size 7 pounds; largest on record 30 pounds; food value good. Dark slaty to dull reddish-brown on back; pale yellowish on sides and dirty white on belly. The dorsal, caudal and ventral fins all have black at margin and are narrowly edged in white.

Found usually on rocky bottom and considered an offshore fish. In New England states it figures as an important food fish. They are taken chiefly on hook and line.

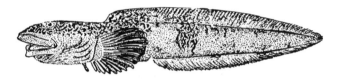

◉ **ARCTIC EELPOUT**   *Lycodes reticulatus*

Average size 18 inches, largest on record 22 inches, food value nil. Brownish with network of black lines on head; dorsal fin is dark edged.

A ground fish, living in moderately deep water.

● **FAWN CUSK-EEL**   *Lepophidium cervinum*

Average size 18 inches; largest on record 25 inches, reported by Roy Martin, Panama City, taken in Gulf of Mexico in 1957. Food value nil. Brownish-yellow marked on back with roundish white spots; narrow black margins on dorsal fins.

Differs from true Eels by the ventral fins. Usually found in deep waters of Florida.

● **PUGJAW WORMFISH**   *Microdesmus floridanus*

Also called Coral Eel.

Average size 3 inches; largest 6 inches. No food value.

A pale color, straw color or darker. Small specks on back. Burrow in the coral rock among the tiny holes or vents. Usually in deep water.

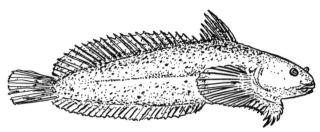

● **SEA SNAIL**   *Liparis atlanticus*

Average size 4 inches; largest 5 inches; no food value. Olive to reddish-brown with lighter and darker cloudings and dots. Sometimes crossbars on dorsal and anal fins. Shaped more like a tadpole than a fish. Has a sucking disk. Noticeable is the soft fat belly. Usually found along rocky shores.

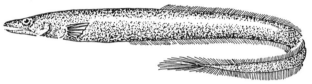

● **LONG-NOSED EEL**   *Synaphobranchus pinnatus*

Average size 14 inches; largest 22; no food value. Uniform brown, darkest below. Inside of mouth blue-black. A deep-sea Eel, unusual because of the large mouth and eyes. The mouth gaps far back of the eye. The gill openings are longitudinal on the lower side of the throat. In all other Eels the slots are on the side.

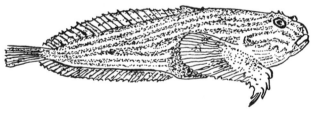

● **STRIPED SEA SNAIL**   *Liparis liparis*

Average size 5 inches; largest 10 inches; no food value. Ground tint. They come in red, green, yellow or lilac models. Most always dark striped. There never are two alike.

Lives on rocky or stony bottom. Sometimes found under rocks in pools left by the ebbing tide.

● **SHANNY**   *Lumpenus maculatus*

Average size 7 inches; largest 10 inches; no food value. Dirty yellowish, paler below. Back and sides marked with indistinct yellowish-brown blotches. Somewhat resembles a Snake Blenny except that this fish has a tail more squarely constructed.

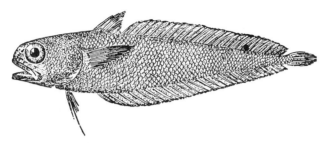

● HAKELING   *Physiculus fulvus*

Average size 10 inches; largest not known; food value not known. Light yellowish-brown with dark brown blotch on each cheek.

Lives near bottom in deep water.

● SNAKE BLENNY   *Lumpenus lumpretaeformis*

Also called Serpent Blenny. Average size 12 inches; largest on record 16 inches; food value nil.

Brownish-yellow on back with faint brown blotches, dorsal fin has oblique bars.

Related to the Rock Eel. Rare in southern waters, but believed to be common in northern deep water bottoms.

● ROCK GUNNEL   *Pholis gunnellus*

Also called Butterfish; Gunnel. Average size 6 inches; largest on record 12 inches; food value nil. Yellowish or reddish-brown above; pale cloudings on side; an oblique streak from eye to angle of jaw; has a row of 10 or 14 spots on back, spreading into dorsal fin.

Found in shoal waters mostly, preferring pebbly or rocky bottom. Quite often take refuge in clam or mussel shells.

● SHORE EELPOUT   *Zoarces anguillaris*

Average size 3 pounds; largest 12 pounds; food value fair. Recognized by dark blotches along lateral line and at base of dorsal fin.

Brings forth living young and usually gives birth in the tide waters of early spring. Goes offshore in midsummer.

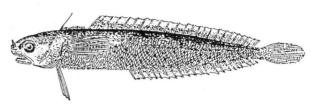

● FOUR BEARDED ROCKLING   *Enchelyopus cimbrius*

Average size about 8 inches; largest on record 16½ inches; food value fair. Back dark yellowish, sides paler, belly white dotted with brown. Lining of mouth dark purplish or bluish.

Distinguishing mark: The first section of dorsal fin consists of one ray. Has long barbels on nose. Are bottom fish, like Hake, usually found in moderately deep water. Not a rock fish. Prefer soft muddy bottom.

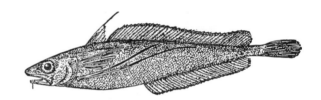

● LONG FINNED HAKE   *Phycis chesteri*

Average size 8 inches; largest on record 11 inches; food value poor. Reddish-brown above and pinkish-white below; caudal fin sooty at tip.

A deep water fish, occuring in great abundance at some spots in the Northern Atlantic; only rarely seen below North Carolina.

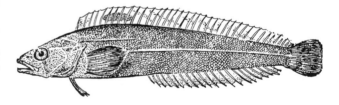

● RADIATED SHANNY   *Ulvaria subbifurcata*

Average size 7 inches; largest on record 13 inches, weighing 14 ounces, taken by Thomas A. Hussy, Myrtle Beach, S. C., Dec. 12, 1961. Back and upper sides dull brown; belly brownish, or yellow-white. Outstanding mark is large oval blotch on dorsal fin. No food value.

Falls into the same category of fishes as the Rock Eel, the Shanny and the Blenny although this is a much stouter fish than the others. Usually found under stones near low tide mark.

 # Miscellaneous Species

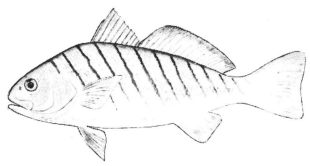

● **HILDEBRAND RARITY**   *Rhegma sp.*

Average size 2½ inches; largest not known. Dark brown, has vertical elongate spots.

A rare fish of which only one specimen has been found. This was picked up by Samuel F. Hildebrand under a rookery in the Florida Keys. Somewhat resembles a species found in Panama, except for three points involving mouth, fins and coloring.

● **BANDED DRUM**   *Larimus fasciatus*

Average size 7 in.; largest not on record. Pronounced markings run diagonally across body; usually 12 stripes of yellowish-brown over silver; fins dusky olive.

Found along surf line and tide rips in waters south of Chesapeake Bay to Galveston. Acceptable food fish but has slight iodine taste.

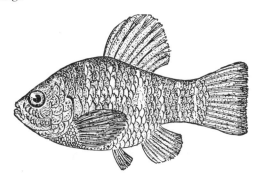

● **SHEEPSHEAD MINNOW**   *Cyprinodon variegatus*

Average size 2 inches long; largest on record 3 inches; food value none. Olive with pale greenish and yellowish-white sides; pale orange pectoral fin. Females have black spot on rear corner dorsal fin.

A flat-sided, stocky little fish with high arched back and small flat-topped head. Resembles the Mummichogs. Found in salt and brackish water.

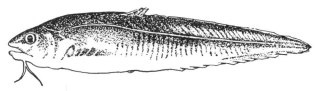

● **ALBINO CUSK-EEL**

Only specimen ever seen was 18 inches long. Silvery in color over all; two barbels beneath lower jaw. Tail tapering off to very thin edge. Diminutive dorsal fin; no other fins noticeable. Silver color shades from mottled on back to pure burnished glistening surface below. Head somewhat resembles a Croaker.

This specimen was caught by E. J. Stone of Clearwater, March 17, 1950. Has never been identified or classed in proper family since discovery. Believed to be an albino of some species. Taken from Gulf waters.

● **SAND TILEFISH**   *Malacanthus plumieri*

Also called Sandfish; Blanquilla. Average size 12 inches; largest on record 32 inches, caught by Mabel Loher, St. Petersburg, Fla., March, 1949, in the Gulf of Mexico, 50 miles offshore. Not edible.

A prettily colored fish with a series of blue variegated lines about mouth and jaws. Generally changing color to correspond with the bottom, on which it thrives. Native to the West Indies, rare on the Florida coast.

● **PELLING'S RAT-TAIL FISH**

Only one speciment known. Length 28 inches. Characteristics are a huge eye, somewhat resembling a Tarpon eye; tail tapering off to the size and appearance of a rat; narrow crimson dorsal fin, entire length of body; silvery to blue in color.

This specimen was taken from the Atlantic at Ft. Lauderdale in the fall of 1951 by L. L. Pelling of Williamsburg, Va. He was wading in the surf when the fish was washed past him. He caught the live fish with his hands.

Dr. Louis Rives, University of Miami, believes it is a deep-water specimen of the "Herring family." The mounted fish is preserved at the establishment of Joe Reese, taxidermist of Ft. Lauderdale, Fla.

23

● **MONKEYFACE BLENNY** *Cebidichthys violaceus*

Also called Blenny Eel.

Average length 10 inches; largest 30 inches. Not considered the best food, but are certainly edible. Dull or brownish-green, mottled and paler underneath. Scattered orange or reddish spots on the sides.

Identified by fleshy lump on top of the head. Has no ventral fins and a single lateral line. Anal fin has two spines in the front. These Eels are caught extensively with a stick with baited hook at the end, shoved into rock crevices. The Blenny takes hold. Native to California shores, central to northern.

● **ROCK SKIPPER** *Salarias zebra*

Average weight 6 ounces; largest on record 1 pound; food value, none. Prettily marked mostly with dark colors and usually resemble the rock shore where they live.

One of the Blenny family, related to the Cunners. This is the herbivorous member and comes into shallow, rocky spots along the ocean shore to feed on grass and sea herbs.

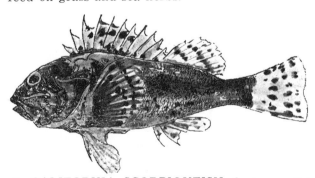

● **CALIFORNIA SCORPIONFISH** *Scorpaena guttata*

Also called Sculpin. Average length 6 inches; largest 17 inches; edible. Reddish with reddish-brown mottling. Bright pink below and small round olive spots above. Ventral fins pink, others usually dark brown.

Identified by spines atop the head and opercle. A scale fish. A common but dangerous fish caught off piers and around breakwaters. Must be handled

with care as the bony spines are coated with poisonous membranes which can inflict a painful wound. Native to many shores, particularly plentiful in the Gulf of California. Usually close inshore.

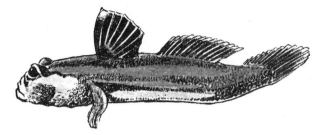

● **MUDSKIPPER** *Periophthalmus sp.*

Also called Mud Springer, Goby. Average size 8 inches; largest on record 14 inches; food value nil. Have strong pectoral fins which can be used to cling to rocks and mangrove roots. Distinguishing feature is the protruding eyes.

These little fishes can be seen around the mangrove roots at low tide, where they cling to roots and stones protruding above water. Have the power to hop or skip across mud flats bared at low tide.

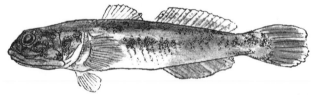

● **LONGJAW MUDSUCKER** *Gillyichthys mirabilis*

Also called Long-jawed Goby. Average length 3 inches; largest 8 inches; not edible. Olive on top, speckled, mottled or barred, becoming lighter underneath.

A baitfish with a huge mouth. Very hardy and can stand rough handling for several days. Will also survive for a limited time in fresh water. Native to Pacific, on central California coast.

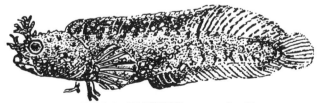

● **ROUGHHEAD BLENNY** *Acanthemblemaria aspera*

Average size 2 inches; largest 4½ inches caught by Jimmy Lunn, Hartsville, S. C. Fish taken off Surfside Pier, Myrtle Beach, S. C., Sept. 9, 1963. No food value. Dark brown to yellow with myraid of small spots.

Fairly common in coral rock formations. May be observed "sitting" at the entrance to small holes in the rock. Rests on two tiny front feet with head out of the hole.

Sea Robins, Ravens, Midshipman

THE SEA ROBBINS are a strange breed of fish. Not often caught and so considered a rarity. Although they have large pectoral fins, they spend most of their lives on the bottom of the ocean, in fairly shallow water. In natural state they glide or creep along the bottom and hide in crevices or sea grass. They pick up a tempting bait occasionally and are caught in shrimp nets.

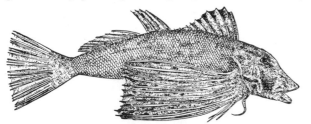

● **NORTHERN SEA ROBIN** *Prionotus carolinus*

Average size 10 oz.; largest on record 2 lbs. 7 oz. caught by Sammy Sarvis, Murrells Inlet, S.C., Nov. 23, '67, offshore. Not considered edible.

Wings are spotted and edged with blue. Top is dark colored and belly white. Legs have a yellowish tinge, mouth is rather blunt like a duck bill.

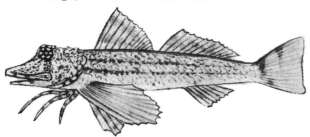

● **LEOPARD SEA ROBIN** *Prionotus scitulus latifrons*

Also called Slender Sea Robin.

Average size 5 inches; largest not on record.

Recognized by exceeding large eyes on top of head, which protrude above the body line. Two rows of dots above and below the lateral line. Overall coloring brownish-yellow. Has six legs similar to Bighead Sea Robin.

Frequents grassy flats where bait shrimp trawlers operate.

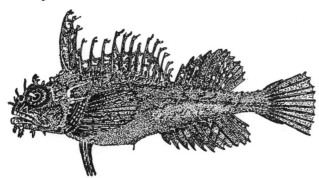

● **SEA RAVEN** *Hemitripterus americanus*

Average about 1½ pounds; largest 5 pounds. Usually reddish-brown—sometimes a bright yellow.

This is the fish which deep-sea fishermen look upon as an omen of good luck. In some localities, however, the belief is that catching a Sea Raven is an omen of foul weather.

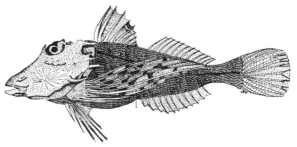

● **BIGHEAD SEA ROBIN** *Prionotus tribulus*

Also called Southern Sea Robin.

Average size 5 inches; largest on record, 12 and ¾ inches, weighing 1 pound, 4 ounces, caught by Sam Sidell in the Gulf of Mexico, near Blind Pass, St. Petersburg, Fla., 1953.

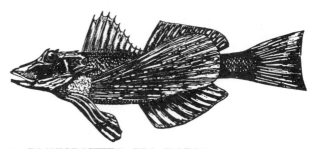

● **BLUESPOTTED SEA ROBIN** *Prionotus roseus*

Average size 5 inches; largest on record 12½ inches; weight 1 pound and 2 ounces, caught by Cecil Wilson, Bradenton, Fla. in Big Pass, Boca Grande, April 12, 1959, Not edible.

A large-finned Sea Robin of deeper Gulf waters, found mostly in the vicinity of Tortugas. A rare fish.

● **MIDSHIPMAN** *Porichthys myriaster*

Also called Singingfish, Bullhead. Average size 6 inches; largest 16 inches; not edible. Mud color or deep bronze with purplish or bluish reflections on top. Paler on sides, golden yellow underneath. A row of luminous photophores arranged in rows on the body and head, is the reason for the name Midshipman. They look like buttons on a uniform. Makes humming sound with air bladder. Native to California coast.

Its eastern counterpart, the Atlantic Midshipman, *P. porosissimus*—much the same in appearance —occurs from So. Carolina to Texas and So. America.

25

Sculpins

THE SCULPINS are a large family of fishes which may vary a great deal in coloration but are much the same in form. All of them have large bony heads, sometimes with spines. All are worthless for food. They are found in fresh water streams, along the shores of the ocean and gulf and in the deep sea of both Atlantic and Pacific oceans.

The only value of the family is for crab and lobster pot baiting. In this respect they seem to serve a purpose.

● **LONGHORN SCULPIN**
Myoxocephalus octodecemspinosus
Also called Eighteen-spined Sculpin.
Average size 8 inches; largest on record 14 inches. Highly colored and with stripe of black over dorsal fin.

● **WOOLY SCULPIN**   *Clinocottus analis*
Average size 8 inches; largest on record one foot.

● **PACIFIC STAGHORN SCULPIN**
Leptocottus armatus

Also called Armed Sculpin, Armed Cabezone, Bullhead. Average length 7 inches; largest 13, not edible.

Black, mottled olive-gray, green or brown; bordered by yellow; belly white. Dorsal is spiney with black spot at the end. Identified by the large antler-like spine on the preopercle. Scaleless body. Caught somewhat as a bait fish, and taken on hook and line occasionally. Found in brackish and fresh water.

● **DEEP-SEA SCULPIN**   *Cottunculus microps*
Average size 7 inches; largest on record 10 inches. Light grayish-brown above the lateral line; pearly-white below. Sides marked with irregular brown patches. Head is shovel-shaped and equal to two-fifths of body.
Usually found in deep waters of the continental shelf off New England.

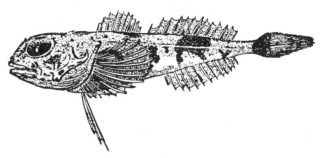

● **HOOK-EARED SCULPIN**   *Artediellus uncinatus*
Average size 2 inches; largest on record 3 inches; food value none. Skin is smooth and naked. Hook-like spines on each cheek, distinguish from other Sculpins. Two short spines on top of head. Is reddish-brown with creamy sides and dirty white belly.
Usually found in deep water with sandy or rocky bottom. Never in mud bottom.

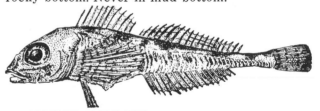

● **MAILED SCULPIN**   *Triglops nybelini*
Average size 5 inches; largest on record 8 inches; food value nil. Olivaceous above; four dark crossbars running down the sides to the lateral line and series of blackish blotches below; breast and belly are silvery-white.
The presence of a row of 45 broad plate-like scales give this fish its common name. The body is more tapering than other Sculpins.

● **CABEZON**   *Scorpaenichthys marmoratus*
Also called Marbled Sculpin, Blue Cod, Bullhead, Scaleless Sculpin. Average weight 1 pound; largest on record 25 pounds.
Reddish to greenish body, has no scales. Flaps above eyes. The largest of the Sculpins, found mostly on the Pacific Coast.

THE TOADFISH FAMILY are thick-bodied pugnacious little fishes which hide out in the grass or any receptacle they can find which allows them to stick out their mouth and snap at fish that pass by. There is nothing too large or small for them to miss a chance to grab. They can inflict a bad cut with their teeth if allowed the chance at a finger or toe.

The slime covering them is injurious so no other fish will eat one. When taken from the water they make a grunting sound with their air bladder. The last word in ugliness both in shape and by nature, no one has yet found anything to consider useful in their makeup.

See Color Pages

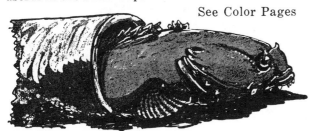

● **GULF TOADFISH**   *Opsanus beta*

Also called Dogfish. Average size 6 inches; largest on record 24 inches; food value, nil. Blackish, mud color, with extremely warty and ugly head.

The most abundant of the Toadfish on the Florida coast. They get into every old can and bottle which may rest on the bottom of shallow bays and around docks.

All head and appetite, will snap like a bulldog at any bait which comes their way and hang on. There are many instances of these fish getting into glass jars and growing to such size they cannot get out again, so spend their lives in the jar. They have strong blunt teeth.

See Color Pages

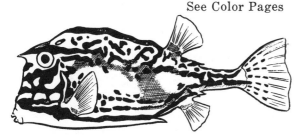

● **COWFISH**   *Lactophrys quadricornis*

Also called Rock Shellfish, Trunkfish, Platefish, Drunkenfish, Chapin. Average size 8 inches; largest 2 pounds; edible. Yellowish with spots and pale blue stripes.

There are two horns on the top of its head. A hard shell covers the fish, all but the tail. A rather appealing little fish with a sad, bovine expression. Found on grassy flats.

They may be roasted in the shell according to some authorities, and are very good. Native to Florida and West Indies.

THE CATFISH FAMILY is probably the largest group of all the fishes. There is hardly any book obtainable which lists more than a fraction of them and few scientists can recall them all.

The Cats have one thing in common, most all are scavengers and do not have scales. The majority are fresh water fish, although they migrate easily from fresh to salt water and back again.

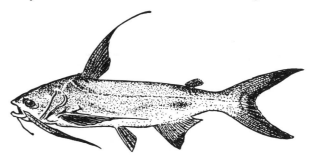

● **GAFFTOPSAIL CATFISH**   *Bagre marinus*

Also called Joe Cat, Whisker Cat. Average weight 4 pounds; largest on record 12 pounds; food value good. An elongated, silvery fish, with long dorsal and short caudal fins. Has a short skull.

A good fish which suffers from relationship with his cousin the Sea Cat. Strikes plugs readily and is a real gamefish, feeding on live minnows. Delivers a savage strike and is a hard fighter. Has a mucous film characteristic of Catfish which easily transfers to leader and fishing line. Like all Catfish has a barbed dorsal and pectoral fins.

Mostly found in open gulf water or deep channels. Caught when fishing for Trout and Channel Bass and they take the same kind of lures. To prepare these fish for eating it is necessary to skin them. The flesh is pink, or salmon-colored and quite pleasantly flavored.

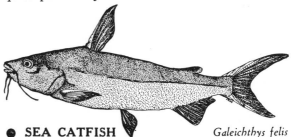

● **SEA CATFISH**   *Galeichthys felis*

Also called Oscar the Terrible. Average size 2 pounds, largest on record 8 lbs. and 8 ozs. caught by George R. Arthur Jr., 105 Diane Drive, Dunedin, Fla. Caught on west end of old Clearwater Beach bridge, Jan. 31, 1965. A sleek silvery fish with large head and long skull. Short fins all equipped with poisonous spines. No food value.

This is the pest of the waters. Picks his food from the leavings of anything. A tough customer that should never be handled with anything but a club. They have a sharp spine which can deliver a nasty wound. They are adept at twisting and throwing their barbs into anything that handles them.

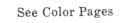

Shellfish and Batfish

See Color Pages

❶ SHORTNOSE BATFISH
Ogcocephalus cubifrons

Average size 7 inches; largest on record 14 inches; 2 pounds and 2 ounces. Caught by the Reverend John W. Baechle, Collegeville, Ind., July, 1956, in the Gulf of Mexico, near St. Petersburg, Fla. No food value.

Brownish black color with warty skin. Has angular pectoral fins shaped like feet. Slightly spotted. Mouth fair size under a thick nose, button-like.

These fish are related to the Anglerfish, but apparently have changed shape by centuries of specialization and degeneration. They are found along the shallow waters in weedy bottoms. Not caught on hook and line.

❷ LONGNOSE BATFISH
Ogcocephalus vespertilio

Found mostly in the shallow waters of the Gulf of Mexico and other tropical waters. The ventral and pectoral fins are fleshy.

They crawl around on the bottom like a toad—and this likeness is further enhanced by their warty skin. Somewhat like the Anglerfish in habits, except that the Batfish mouth is small without the long teeth. The angling spine which is put out to lure minnows is small and usually hidden by a flap of skin.

Batfish grow to a length of one foot. They have a triangular shaped head tapering to a long bony snout.

● TRUNKFISH
Lactophrys trigonus

See Color Pages

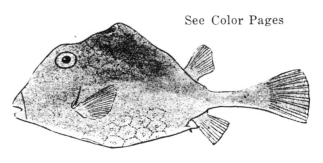

Average size 3 pounds; largest on record 8 lbs., and 22 in. long, caught by James Graham of Miami, Nov. 10, 1963 in Biscayne Bay. Food value fair.

Brownish with variegated spots of white. Tail elongated from shell.

This is a common fish of the grassy flats, in bays and river mouths. Prefer brackish water.

● COMMON SHRIMP
Peneus setiferus

Average size 2½ inches; largest is 8 inches; edible.

Grayish-white.

The beak extends back over the upper shell like a low keel, the forward part of which has a groove. The beak and feelers are extended.

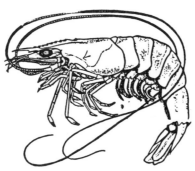

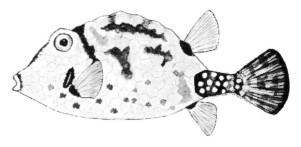

● SMOOTH TRUNKFISH
Lactophrys triqueter

Also called Drunkenfish; Platefish.

Average size 5 inches; largest 14½ inches, caught by Homeretta Gilpin, Key West, Fla. in 1961, south of Sand Key.

Round spots of yellow-white on brownish shell.

Like others of this species, the fish is encased in shell—the tail, however, is shorter and the body and fins more round.

Found on grassy flats in brackish water.

While not a fish, actually a crustacean, the Shrimp is familiar to all fishermen; millions of pounds are used each year in cocktails, salads and cooked dishes.

Native from Virginia to the Gulf of Mexico (85% of the shrimp harvested comes from the Gulf).

28

Anglers, Clingfish, Sea Moths

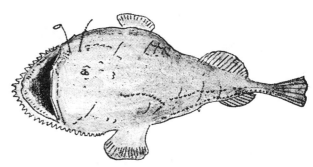

● **OCEANIC ANGLER**   *Ceratias holbolli*

Also called Deep-sea Angler.

Average size 8 ozs.; largest on record, 1 lb., 14 ozs.; length 17 inches; caught by Floyd A. Harr, Blountville, Tenn., on the fringe of the Gulf Stream near Myrtle Beach, S. C., Aug. 7, 1963. Not edible.

Specimen in British Museum is 40 inches long.

This is one of the Frogfish which live in the deep ocean. The female of the species is the mature fish while the male is a parasitic specimen which attaches itself to the head of the female for life. Color entirely black. A rare fish.

The "bait" or fishing rod of the Oceanic Angler is luminous to attract other fish in the darkness of the ocean. They are solitary fish, swimming around slowly.

● **ANGLER FISH**   *Lophius piscatorius*

Also called Goosefish, Fishing Frog.

Average size 5 pounds; largest on record 52 pounds; caught by Sidney Johnson, Winterport, Maine, near Hackett's Landing, in the Penoboscot River. Not edible.

Mud colored; skin covered with prickles; ventral fins short, enormous head and small body. An elongated tip on the first ray of the dorsal fin has a bait-like fleshy tab, which is dangled over the head to attract victims.

Eats anything coming in range of the snapping mouth. Fishes, clams, crabs and even diving birds. Usually they lie dormant on the bottom, fishing for food continuously. Native to deep water, in the North Atlantic, although the largest specimen was taken in a river.

● **SEA MOTH**   *Pegasus*

Average size 2 inches; largest not known. Food value nil. Dark brown with ridges of greens and yellows, faintly showing.

A small creature native to tropical Pacific waters. It cannot fly though it has large wing-like pectoral fins. They live for the most part on the surface of the water, hiding in bits of floating seaweed.

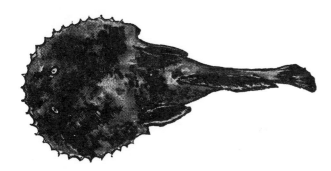

● **STIPPLED CLINGFISH**   *Gobiesox punctulatus*

Also called Rattlefish.

Average size 3 inches; largest known 10 inches. Not edible.

Has a broad, flat head and body with slender tail, tapering. Small to medium mouth with small teeth. Pectoral fins are somewhat limb-like and large. Gill slit behind the head. Two large eyes on top of head. A bony type, suction cup beneath the head.

Fish is relatively common but few are caught except by commercial shrimp fishermen fishing in shallow bays. Retiring by nature, it hides under rocks, or buries itself.

In the Far East they are dried, the head filled with pebbles and given to babies for a rattle, hence the name.

● **FLYING GURNARD**   *Dactylopterus volitans*

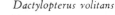

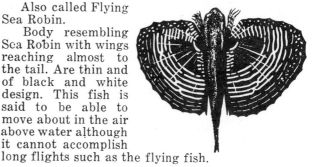

Also called Flying Sea Robin.

Body resembling Sea Robin with wings reaching almost to the tail. Are thin and of black and white design. This fish is said to be able to move about in the air above water although it cannot accomplish long flights such as the flying fish.

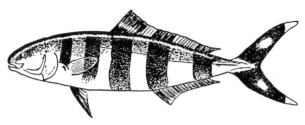

See Color Pages

● PILOTFISH
Naucrates ductor

Also called Shark Pilot.

Average size 12 inches; largest on record 24 inches. Food value poor.

Looks something like an Amberjack, except for three wide vertical dark stripes. Is cylindrical in shape, with blunt nose.

Often found in the company of off-shore Sharks, giving the appearance of piloting them. Have been observed to range out and discover a bait then swim back and forth from the Shark to the bait as if leading them on. Young Amberjack are often mistaken for Pilotfish as they are banded similarly when young.

● SHARKSUCKER
Echeneis naucrates

Average size 12 inches; largest on record 35 inches, weighing 7 lbs. 10 oz. caught by Wayne Roper, Milwaukee, Wisc., March 23, 1968, while fishing with Capt. Jerry Hefly of the Yacht Leilana, Nassau, Bahamas.

Long slender body; black lateral stripe running from tip of lower jaw through eye to base of caudal fin.

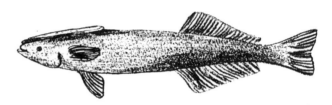

● REMORA
Remora remora

Largest specimen known 31 inches; average less than 15 inches. By means of a unique vacuum cup on top of its head, this seagoing hitch-hiker attaches itself to other fish, sea turtles, and even boats.

Color usually uniform, tan to brownish-black. Body is less elongated than that of the Sharksucker.

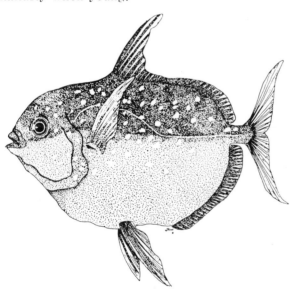

● OPAH
Lampris regius

Also called Moonfish.

Average weight 30 pounds; largest on record 106 pounds, caught by Robert T. Markle, Morro Bay, Calif., while fishing aboard the sportfisherman Mallard with Capt. Robert Gannon off Piew Piedras Blana Blancas Lighthouse, 35 miles N.W. of Morro Bay, Calif. Measurements were 44x34x9. Catch made Dec. 24, 1966. Food value poor.

An iridescent fish with scarlet fins, which attains a length of 6 feet. The silvery sheen of its body suggests the true Moonfish of the Crevalle family. However, in skeleton and construction differs considerably from the Jacks or Pompanos.

A rare visitor to the Atlantic and the Gulf coasts and when one is taken is considered quite a curiosity.

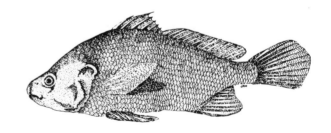

● STAR DRUM
Stellifer lanceolatus

Average size 5 inches; largest 7 inches; food value poor. Small and bony, resembling Croaker.

This is one of the few of the Croaker family which is not of commercial importance or of interest to sports fishermen. Just a dwarf specimen of the Sea Drum.

SCORPIONFISH: Widely distributed, little value, less beauty, the Scorpionfishes are carnivorous bottom-dwellers. There are hundreds of species; many so similar as to make identification difficult.

Some species (especially in the Pacific) are equipped with poisonous spines that may cause serious injury or even death. The sharp spines are dangerous even in those species that do not have venom glands.

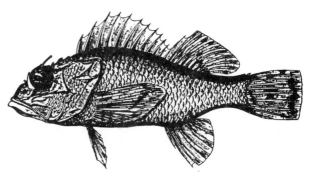

● **HUNCHBACK SCORPIONFISH** *Scorpaena dispar*

Average size 3 inches; largest 5 inches; food value, nil. Deep red color, spotted with white under head. Has regular narrow bars on pectoral and caudal fins. Mouth red inside.

A small Scorpionfish type found in the waters of Gulf of Mexico. Seldom seen by any but scientific men. A rare fish.

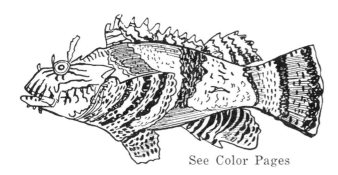

See Color Pages

● **LIONFISH** *Scorpaena grandicornis*

Average size 10 inches; largest 28 inches; food value fair. Colored with yellow bands and black stripes intermingling. No definite pattern, and changing color with background of habitation.

The Lionfish are found in all the seas. Have a large and bony head like a Sea Robin, usually of good size. They hang around rocks. They can be eaten, but there is not much meat on their bony structures. Like a rattlesnake, the Lionfish has a venom expelling spine and sac on each dorsal point.

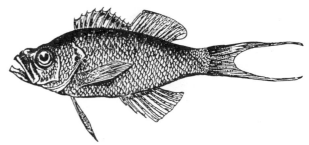

● **STREAMER BASS** *Pronotogrammus aureorubens*

Average size 6 inches; largest 9 inches; food value, nil. Pinkish on back; scales yellow margined; sides and belly silver; dorsal and caudal fins yellow.

A coral rock fish, native to the Gulf of Mexico. Not very plentiful. Those caught are taken on drop lines by deep sea fishing boats and are very rare.

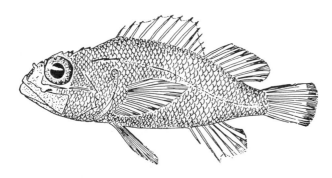

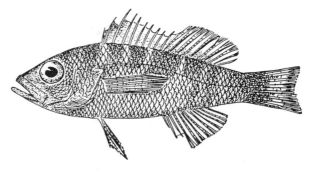

● **SMOOTHHEAD SCORPIONFISH**

Scorpaena calcarata

Average size 3 inches; largest not known. Red colored with a large black spot at posterior end of dorsal.

One of four species of Scorpaenids found in the shrimp beds off Tortugas.

● **CHALK BASS** *Serranus tortugarum*

Average size 4 inches; largest not known.

Orange color on back, becoming yellowish on sides. Nine blue vertical stripes on back and sides. All do not extend below the lateral line. A rare fish of Gulf of Mexico waters.

31

THE SWELLFISH FAMILY has the ability to inhale either air or water and swell their bodies into shape resembling a tennis ball, with a head stuck on one end and a tail on the other. They are quite common in tropical waters.

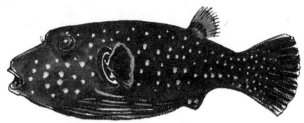

● POISON PUFFER — *Tetraodon hispidus*

Also called Maki-Maki, Deadly Fish.

Average size 8 inches; largest on record 2 feet; food value, absolutely no. Resembles the other Puffer fishes except it has a bluish-gray cast. Easily recognized by the silvery spots on back and sides and horizontal stripes on belly. Found off Hawaii.

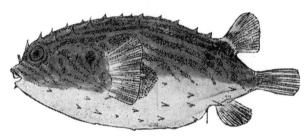

● STRIPED BURRFISH — *Chilomycterus schoepfi*

Also called Spiny Boxfish, Porcupine Fish. A rounded fish with small mouth and wide fins, variegated dark and light stripes, coated with spines.

Fairly common around the Bahamas. Ralph W. Stahl of Basin Harbor, speared a record for Great Outdoors on July 2, 1969. It was 24 in. long and weighed 33 lbs. filled with water—drained as well as possible, it still weighed 20 lbs. Food value poor.

See Color Pages

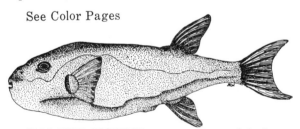

● SMOOTH PUFFER — *Lagocephalus laevigatus*

Also called Rabbitfish, Silvery Puffer.

Average size, 12 inches; largest on record, 28 inches length; 21 inches girth; weight 9 pounds, 3 ounces, caught by Ruth P. Finney, March 12, 1967 off Bean Point, Anna Maria, Fla., still fishing with shiner for bait. Food value good.

Grayish-brown, changing to silvery on belly, skin smooth. No scales.

Like the furry rabbits on land, when they multiply, they do so with reckless abandon.

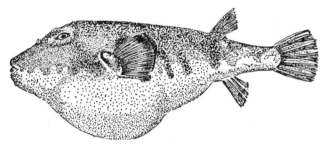

● SOUTHERN PUFFER — *Sphaeroides nephelus*

Also called Swellfish, Toadfish, Balloon Fish.

Average size 10 ounces; largest on record 4 lbs., and 8 ozs., taken by Max Obie, fishing near Kyle's Marina, North Miami, April 17, 1965. Food value good. Dark colored, mottled with green on top. Has a dark spot under the pectoral fins. They are scaleless, the skin covered with prickles.

A sluggish nibbler of the tropic seas, inhabiting the grassy flats of the bays, watching for the bits of food which they might capture. Their sharp teeth, fused together as one solid bone can clip off a barnacle or crack a small shell.

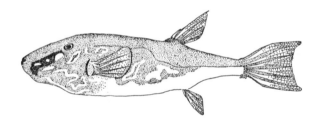

● MARBLED PUFFER — *Sphaeroides dorsalis*

Average size 4½ inches; largest not known; food value, nil.

Dorsal fin olivaceous, mottled with brown; belly white; pale yellow on lower part of side. Has pale blue penciling on cheek before gill openings.

A rare fish of Gulf of Mexico waters. Very little is known of habits or origin.

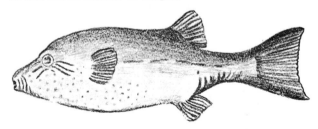

● SHARPNOSE PUFFER — *Canthigaster rostrata*

Average size 6 inches; largest not known; food value, nil. A smaller member of Swellfish family.

Usually found in West Indian waters, but taken on the Snapper banks off Tampa Bay and Pensacola.

Triggerfish and Tally

TRIGGERFISH are rounded fish primarily recognized by the three spines which erect at dorsal fin. They fold into a groove on back, but all efforts to fold them up is of no avail unless the "trigger" or one of the smaller spines is depressed which unlocks the three.

A dweller of the reefs in the Gulf of Mexico. Referred to as a leather-skinned nibbler. The small mouth makes this fish difficult to catch. However a piece of shrimp on minnow hook will do the trick. They are slow swimmers and spend much time just snoozing lazily. Their leathery skin protects them from other fish. Because of the lazy life, the fish is delicious food. Skinned and fileted, very hard to beat.

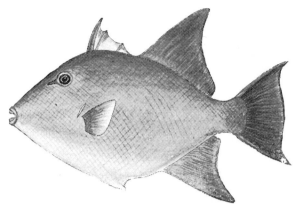

See Color Pages

● **GRAY TRIGGERFISH**   *Balistes capriscus*

Also called Common Triggerfish; Leatherjack.

Average weight 1 pound; largest on record 12 pounds and 5 ounces, caught by Al Aubrey, Staten Island, N.Y., fishing in Largo Sound, Florida Keys, March 10, 1965. Food value good.

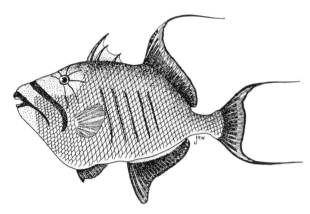

● **QUEEN TRIGGERFISH**   *Balistes vetula*

Also called Old Wife. Average weight 1 pound; largest on record 9 pounds and 3 ounces, caught by James L. Eason, Panama City, Fla., 40 miles off coast of Mexico, in 1961. Food value fair.

Yellowish on lower jowl with blue stripes from nose. Variegated lines from eye, blue fins, pinkish cast on body toward tail. Dorsal fin elongated.

● **OCEAN TRIGGERFISH**   *Canthidermis sufflamen*

Also called Great Trigger; Ocean Tally; Turbot. Average weight 3 pounds; largest on record 12 pounds; food value good.

Differs from other Triggerfish in having a deeper body and smoother scales. It is uniformly brownish or grayish, darker shading at base of pectoral fins. A wary fish usually taken in deep water—30 to 60 ft.—with hand lines. Found from New England to Gulf of Mexico.

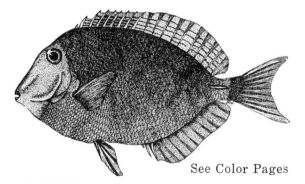

See Color Pages

● **DOCTORFISH**   *Acanthurus chirurgus*

Also called Surgeonfish, Lancet-fish; Medicos; Barberos. Average size $\frac{1}{2}$ pound; largest on record 3 pounds; food value fair.

A brown fish with 10 to 12 dark vertical stripes on body (see color plate). Color paler with blue more pronounced in fins when taken over light sandy bottom. Like the Mullet, it has a thick-walled gizzard-like stomach as it injects sand with its algal food.

● **RAZORFISH**   *Iniistius pavoninus*

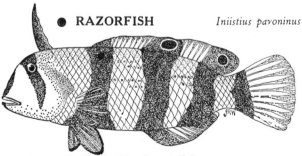

Also called Longfin Razorfish.

Average weight 8 ounces; largest on record 24 ounces; food value, good.

A large scale Wrasse, with alternate wide bands of silver and gray.

33

Flying Fish

FLYINGFISHES: This family is generally not found inshore. It is an open ocean, surface fish, considered a very fine food fish in some parts of the world. Often used as bait for Tuna and Billfishes. Most often netted at night, using a light to lure them to the net.

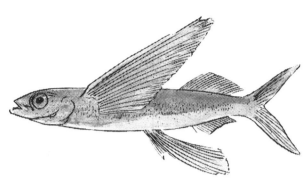

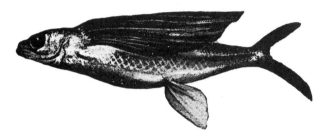

● **ATLANTIC FLYINGFISH**   *Cypselurus heterurus*
Also called Sprat.

Average size 3 inches; largest 6 inches; not edible. Pale translucent green, bright horizontal silvery band extending length of body.

The most common Flyingfish and most likely the species which supports the Caribbean bait fishery. Not generally considered edible, however in certain areas of the world it is a delicacy.

Has short single dorsal fin; extremely large mouth; deep thin body. The young have short barbels, disappearing at maturity.

● **TROPICAL TWO-WING FLYINGFISH**
Exocoetus volitans
Also called Atlantic Flying Fish or Sharpnose.

Average size 9 inches; largest on record 18 inches, food value poor. Greenish on back, shading to silver below. Ventral fins white.

The common Flyingfish of Atlantic and Gulf, which at times travels in large schools. They do not grow as large as the Pacific counterpart, but have a more rounded body and are firmer.

While they do not actually fly, it is possible for them to soar considerable distances by taking off from a wave crest and using their tail to drive ahead over the surface of the water.

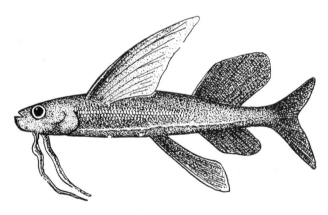

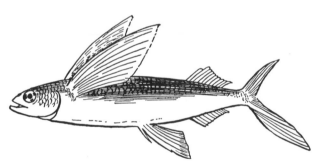

● **MARGINED FLYINGFISH** *Cypselurus cyanopterus*
Also called Bearded Flyingfish.

Like many of the 50 species of flyingfish this one is bearded only when young. All lose the barbels when adulthood is reached.

This form is characterized by two exceedingly long, fleshy and fluted barbels in the chin, which may be as long as the entire fish.

Average size 4 inches; largest 7 inches. Dark brown to black on top, yellowish to white on belly. Often found in drifting seaweed.

● **CALIFORNIA FLYINGFISH**
Cypselurus californicus

Average size 12 inches; largest on record 18 inches; food value, excellent. A silvery fish with large wing-like pectoral fins and powerful tail.

This is the largest of the Flyingfishes and inhabits all tropical seas, most abundant north of Cape San Lucas. Seen only in the summer months; it is not known where they go in winter.

Although these fish appear to fly, they actually are propelled by their tail on the surface of the water and when taking off from the crest of a wave, they can soar as far as an eighth of a mile. The ventral fins are not used as wings but as parachutes, to hold the fish from falling, until folded and the dive back into the water is accomplished.

● ATLANTIC NEEDLEFISH   *Strongylura marina*

Also called Guardfish, Long-jaws, Aguja de Casta. Average weight 8 ounces; largest on record unknown; food value, nil. Green color, silvery below; silvery-blue stripe running the length of the body.

A worthless fish of the gulf and ocean. Found in all waters where other fish live.

Although they can't be eaten and are no good for bait, the entertainment value of Needlefish is well known to natives of tropical lands.

The sign "Educated Fish" sometimes seen hanging in front of tourist attractions, indicates that a Needlefish will be put through its paces for the benefit of novices.

They have a perpetual itching of the belly, caused by minute parasites which collect on them. Thus they will jump over anything that scrapes their belly. Trainers have exhibited them jumping over sticks, or any obstacle on the surface of the water. This is enhanced by food placed on the other side of the hurdle.

● BALAO   *Hemiramphus balao*

Also called Halfbeak. Average size 6 inches; largest 12 inches; food value fair. Blue on top silvery on belly, mouth over the spear-like beak.

These little fish swim in all warm seas and are valued mostly as bait fish. They bring best results when trolled in the Gulf Stream.

● CALIFORNIA NEEDLEFISH   *Strongylura exilis*

Also called California Anchovy.

Average length 3 inches; largest 7 inches; not usually considered edible.

Metallic bluish or greenish above becoming silvery on sides and belly.

Has a short single dorsal fin but no lateral line. Very large mouth. Considered an ideal bait fish.

Most numerous in Pacific.

● ATLANTIC SAURY   *Scomberesox saurus*

Also called Skipper.

Average size 18 inches; largest on record 30 inches; food value, poor.

Dark on back, silvery on sides and belly.

A fish traveling in large schools. Leaps from the water frequently when pursued by larger fish. Spends most of life in open sea, although at times the schools come close inshore.

● HOUNDFISH   *Strongylura raphidoma*

Also called Aguja de Casta; Guardfish.

Average size 24 inches; food value, poor.

Bluish on back, silvery over belly and sides.

Has an unusually short and strong beak and solid body. Found in southern waters and as far north as New Jersey. Looks like a giant Needlefish, but is much more dangerous to a small boat fisherman.

Largest on record 40 inches, slightly over 4½ lbs., caught by Raymond E. Gaines, Palm Beach, Fla., at Juno Beach, Fla., Feb. 6, 1968, while surf casting for Bluefish.

● FLYING HALFBEAK   *Eulepterhamphus velox*

Average size 12 inches; largest 26 inches; not edible. Oddly formed with large pectorals. Has a leaping habit which approaches the Flyingfishes at times. Native to the West Indies, although sometimes found along the Atlantic Coast as far north as Cape Cod.

The largest specimen on record caught near Bay of Biscayne, Florida.

● SILVER GAR   *Tylosurus marinus*

Also called Billfish; Salt-water Gar; Garfish; Sea Pike. Average size 36 inches; largest on record, 50 inches; no food value.

Greenish, darker above with silvery sides, dull olive fins, dark bar on gill cover.

Both jaws on this Gar are the same length and long. The jaws have large teeth; the eyes are large. Sometimes mistaken for a Needlefish, but distinctly a Gar.

Stargazers

THE FROGFISHES are a curious collection of creatures, with many shapes, some only in a remote way resembling a Frog. Most of them have one thing in common, a deceptive lure which attracts tiny surface fish to their doom in the Frogfish mouth. Each of them is a replica of something else in the water, such as seaweed, a rock, a bit of shell, or anything but a fish.

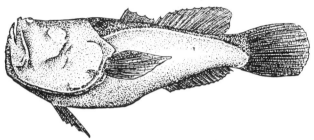

● **NORTHERN STARGAZER** *Astroscopus guttatus*

Average size 6 inches; largest recorded 11 inches weighing 1 pound 2 ozs., reported by Tommy Willis of Yaupon Beach, Southport, N.C., August 10, 1965. No food value. Dark on back, silvery on belly.

Has power to give an electric shock, with plates in top of head. Not much known about this species.

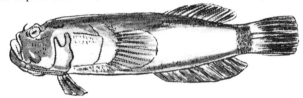

● **SOUTHERN STARGAZER** *Astroscopus y-graecum*

Also called Sand Shocker, Electric Stargazer. Average size 12 inches; largest on record 2 feet; food value none.

Drab colored with yellowish to sandy colored belly. Has several bare spots on top of head. Eyes on top of head and mouth shaped like a bullfrog.

This is a fish which causes ladies to desert the seashore. These small fish bury themselves in the sand with only eyes out to watch for any unsuspecting fish to come along, whereupon they open their big mouth and gulp the unwary creature down.

If by chance a bather were to step on the fish, especially the bare spots on the head, a vigorous electric shock would be forthcoming which often causes the victim to rise out of the water to the accompaniment of a good scream.

◐ **TORTUGAS STARGAZER** *Benthoscopus laticeps*

Average size 8 inches; largest thought to be 15½ inches; food value nil. Gray on back with many fine spots. Sides and belly ashy color.

With eyes pointing upward and mouth ready to snap at anything above, this typical bottom fish expects the next meal to come from above. A rare fish of its type and found in the Gulf of Mexico as a rule.

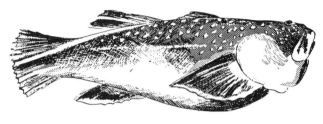

◐ **RETTBERG STARGAZER** *Astroscopus sp.*

Also called Moongazer.

Average size one pound; largest on record was caught by Roger Mock at Barnacle Bill's Fishing Pier, Topsail Beach, N. C., on Oct. 6, 1968. It weighed 6 lbs. 1 oz., and was 20 inches long.

Brownish on back with many spots, like polka-dot design. Small beady eyes. Large pectoral fins. Turned up mouth like a Stargazer.

A fish of shallow water caught in the Gulf of Mexico but probably also a fish of colder climes. First specimen discovered by Charles Rettberg in Florida waters. Seven specimens reported to Dictionary of Fishes.

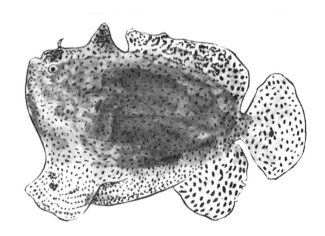

● **HAWAIIAN FROGFISH** *Antennarius nexilis*

Average size 6 inches; largest 8 inches; food value, none. Dusky colored; dorsal and anal fins covered with irregular black spots.

A native of the coral reefs and full brother to the Sargassumfish, Mousefish and others. Likes to hang around the heavy beds of seaweed and grass. This species is rather common at Honolulu. There are about 65 recognized species of this grotesque fish found in all tropical & some temperate waters.

Pincushion Fish

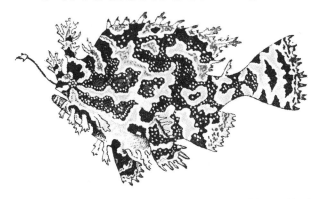

● **SARGASSUMFISH** *Histrio histrio*

Also called Mousefish. Average size 5 inches; largest on record 15 inches, taken by Capt. A. F. Wetherell, Daytona Beach, Fla. Nov. 30, 1957. Not edible.

A mottled and odd shaped fish, which may have a dozen different colors according to the background of its habitat at the moment. Mostly green and yellow.

A close cousin to the Angelfish, this little fellow lives among the floating beds of seaweed in the tropical waters of America. As the seaweed floats so goes the fish and may wind up most anywhere there is an ocean current.

● **PACIFIC LIONFISH** *Pterois volitans*

Average size 10 inches; largest on record believed to be 2 feet; food value poor. Highly colored with vertical bars of alternating black and yellow. Dorsal fin spines have white bands.

This is one of the Scorpionfish family, found in tropical Pacific waters. They must be handled carefully as each one of the spines has a poison secreting sac which is capable of inflicting a painful sting. They have a large bony head and small amount of flesh on the bodies.

Seldom stray far from the rock crevices which they call home. This is usually in a coral reef. Sometimes caught on a bait intended for Grouper.

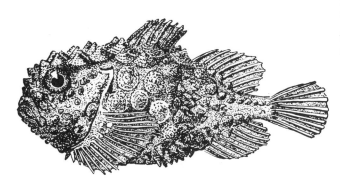

● **ATLANTIC SPINY LUMPSUCKER**
Eumicrotremus spinosus

Also called Spiny Lumpfish.

Average size 2 pounds; largest not known; food value poor. Brownish color all over.

Similar to common Lumpfish, except the body is covered with hard spines.

Feeds on seashore life, such as jellyfish and invertebrates without protective shell.

The young are camouflaged with a mottled coloring which blends with sea grass so they are hard to find. Make excellent specimens for amateur aquariums.

Native to the Atlantic on both coasts. Have been found on the North American coast from the New Jersey shore to Key West. Mostly found on rocky bottoms.

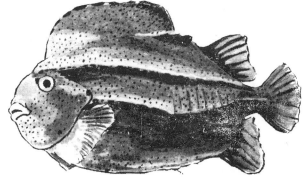

● **LUMPFISH** *Cylopterus lumpus*

Also called Lumpsucker; Seagoing Basketball.

Average size 3 pounds; largest on record 20 pounds, caught by John K. Nelson, Gerrittsen Beach, Brooklyn. N. Y., near Orient Point, L. I. Not edible.

Vary in coloration, some green, others brown and still others reddish. Has a sucker on ventral surface. The skin is covered with tubercules.

This is considered an Arctic fish, although they come south in the winter. A slow swimming fish with a habit of anchoring itself to stones or pilings. Lays a large mass of eggs on the bottom which are cared for by the male until hatched.

Filefish

SLOW SWIMMING FILEFISH with rough leathery skins are common in all warm seas. They have a single dorsal fin which consists of a single long stout spine, in some cases with serrated edge. They are greatly compressed laterally with a single gill slot. They never grow to a large size but specimens of 5 pounds have been found. Usually they will weigh a bit over a pound.

Found mostly around barnacle-encrusted pilings, where they nip off the small barnacles with their strong canine teeth. Because they do not move away from danger and are apparently very clumsy these fish are often called Foolfish. The Filefish are often confused with Triggerfish, which also are slow swimming and have a small mouth.

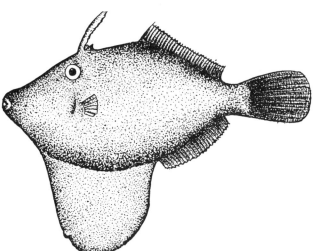

● **FRINGED FILEFISH**   *Monocanthus cieliatus*
Average size, 6 inches; largest 12 inches; no food value. Can be distinguished by the dark spot on flap. The only member of the Filefish family which has the pouch on belly.

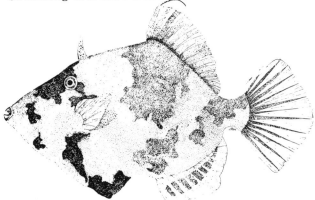

● **FANTAIL FILEFISH**   *Stephanolepis spilosomus*
Covered with small spots, have softer dorsal fin and no spine. Average size 8 inches; largest on record 26½ inches, caught by Mrs. L. T. Van Denberg, Merrill, Iowa, in waters adjacent to West Palm Beach, Fla. Recorded Feb. 1954. Barely edible.

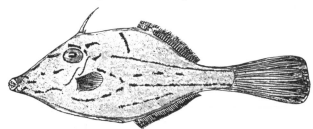

● **DOTTEREL FILEFISH**   *Alutera ventralis*
Also called Tortugas Filefish.
Average size 10 inches; largest on record 28 inches, caught by William Turk of Pompano Beach, Fla. in waters adjacent to that city.   Recorded March 31, 1960. Barely edible.

Drab colored with very small scales and scattered darker blotches. A rare Filefish, taken from waters of Tortugas, Cuba and Florida East Coast.

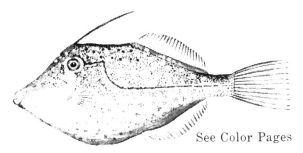

See Color Pages

● **ORANGE FILEFISH**   *Alutera schoepfi*

Average size 12 inches; l a r g e s t 19½ inches, caught by Charles Coe of Philadelphia while fishing near Wildwood, N. J. Reported Feb. 1, 1964 and recorded at Pilger's Sports and Hobby Shop.

Has a square tail and elongated spine on head. Widely distributed from Maine to Texas.

This fish has been observed to spend hours in the water, head down and tail up. In this position the appellation "Foolfish" is applied.

With a very small mouth equipped with sharp teeth the short barnacles on pilings are easily clipped off. While the fish appears to be eating all the time it is always as thin as a piece of paper.

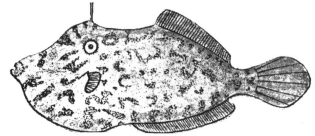

● **UNICORN FILEFISH**   *Alutera monoceros*
Average size 12 inches; largest on record 24 inches; food value, poor. Bony-plated fish with dark pattern in splotches of color. Recognized by single spine standing over eye.

Occasionally straggles to the fishing grounds of Gulf of Mexico area but more common in the West Indies.

Coral Reef Fish

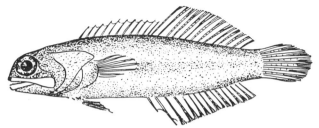

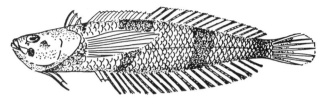

● **DUSKY JAWNESTER** *Opisthognathus whitehurstii*
Also called Rock Nester.
Average size 1½ inches; largest 2 inches; no food value. Gray and olive colored, with horizontal bands of the two shades blending in a light, hazy manner. A careful scrutiny will detect 7 bands of gray on a background of olive.
Dig in sand about coral. Have sharp teeth and can carry a large amount of sand in their mouths for use as a sand screen when enemies approach.

● **BANDED JAWFISH** *Opisthognathus fasciatus*
Also called a Coral Mason.
Average size 3 inches; largest 5 inches; no food value.
Has a mottled appearance with 8 (sometimes 1 more or less) blotches of darker shade.
Found on gravelly bottom near the shore. Burrows and then builds an edifice of sand and some kind of adhesive which forms a cement. The little Mason houses can be seen often in the sandy bottom.

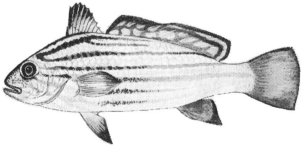

● **CUBBYU** *Equetus acuminatus*
Average size 10 inches; largest not on record.
Fairly elongated body with fins like the Jackknife fish, except the spiny dorsal is not large. The soft rayed dorsal is similar. Slight yellowish coloring on nose and lower lip, spotted dorsal and six dark stripes on a silver background running horizontally from gill cover to caudal.
Usually found on reefs in Gulf waters. They have been taken up to 2 pounds, but no authentic records. Popular fish in Cuban market.
Acceptable food fish.

● **SADDLE STARGAZER** *Heteristius rubrocinctus*
Average size 2 inches; largest 5 inches; no food value. Yellowish-cream color background with 4 stripes (some have 3) vertically. These are brownish-black.
A sandy bottom digging fish with speed.

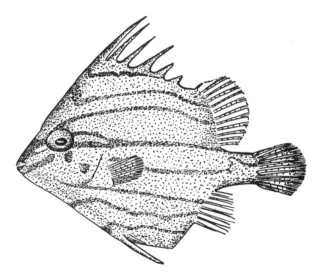

● **JAMBEAU** *Parahollardia lineata*
Also called Coral Beauty.
Average size 4 inches; largest 6 inches; no food value. Rose colored with fins orange tinted, body has 8 longitudinal bars of an erratic pattern.
Usually found in the coral bottoms of Fla. Keys.

● **HIGHFIN GOBY** *Gobionellus oceanicus*
Also called Ocean Goby.
Average size 12 inches; largest not known; food value, poor.
Variably colored fish of the coral rocks in Gulf of Mexico and as far north as South Carolina.

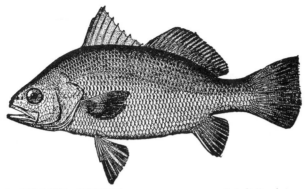

● **SILVER PERCH**   *Bairdiella chysura*

Also called Mademoiselle, Butterfish, Sand Perch. Average weight 1 lb.; largest on record 1 lb. 12 oz. caught by Jesse Morgan, New Orleans, La. June 24, '63, from Fisher's Pier, Ft. Myers Bch., Fla. Food value good. A silvery little panfish with slight shading of blue on top of white belly.

One of the most abundant of panfish in the bays bordering on the Gulf of Mexico shores. They are the joy of Midwestern visitors to Florida, who catch them by the bucketful. Most always referred to as "Butterfish."

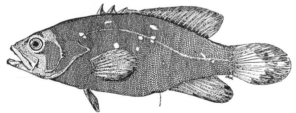

● **SOAPFISH**   *Rypticus saponaceus*

Average size 10 inches; largest 14 inches; food value, nil. Recognized by the excessive amount of soap-suds like mucous they exude when handled.

Live for the most part in old Conch shells and about crevices in coral bottom or rock. More numerous on the Florida Keys and Bahama Islands than Gulf of Mexico.

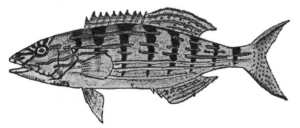

● **SAND PERCH**   *Diplectrum formosum*

Also called Coral Snapper.

Average size 8 oz. Edible. Dark vertical bars and longitudinal stripes of bluish-green; eye piped with yellow.

An avid bottom feeder, found the year around throughout the tropical waters, usually near live coral.

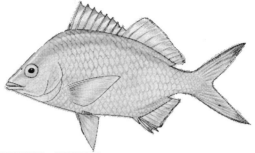

● **SILVER JENNY**   *Eucinostomus gula*

Also called Mojarra or Sand Perch.

Average weight about 12 ounces; largest on record 2 pounds, 12 ounces, caught by Ginette Adnot, Lake Park, Fla., on Mar. 18, 1965. Food value good.

Coloring of gray beginning at dorsal fin gradually brightening to silver over rest of the body, growing very light around belly.

The Silver Jenny of southern waters, is closely related to the White Perch found in South Carolina waters and has the same habits. They are very gregarious and found chiefly in brackish tidal waters.

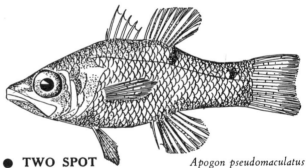

● **TWO SPOT CARDINALFISH**   *Apogon pseudomaculatus*

Also called Apogon.

Average size 3 inches; largest not known.

Reddish color, with a black spot on each side, below dorsal fin. Found in Gulf, Cuban and Atlantic coast waters.

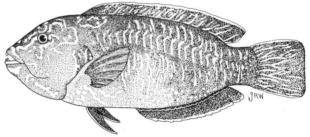

● **PUDDING WIFE**   *Halichoeres radiatus*

Also called Doncella. Average weight 1 pound; largest on record, unknown; food value fair.

This is one of the larger Parrotfishes. Can be identified by a fleshy lump on the forehead, increasing in size with age. Native to West Indies, but has been seen as far north as Chesapeake Bay.

● **BLUEBACK HERRING** *Alosa aestivalis*

Also called Alewife, Glut Herring, Summer Herring, Blackbelly, Kyack.

Average size 5 inches; largest 12 inches and 16 ounces in weight. Food value poor.

Dark blue above; sides and belly silvery. Bluebacks and Alewives are often confused. The most experienced guides often cannot recognize the difference. However there is one infallible mark. The lining of Bluebacks is black. Other Herring of the same general appearance are smoky-gray.

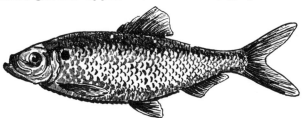

● **ALEWIFE** *Alosa pseudoharengus*

Also called Big-eyed Herring, Wall-eyed Herring, Spring Herring, Sawbelly, Gray Herring, Golden Shad, Skipjack, Bang, Greenback.

Average size 4 ounces; largest on record reported by Paul Hinds, Bayside Fishing Headquarters, St. Petersburg, Fla., April, 1959 at 16 ounces weight and 11¾ inches length. Food value poor.

Gray-green or blue-green on back and upper sides; silver below. A small dark spot behind upper angle of the gill cover. This little keeled and sawbellied fish is one of the most numerous bait fishes of the ocean. Usually appear in spring in great numbers from Canada to Florida.

● **ATLANTIC MENHADEN** *Brevoortia tyrannus*

Also called Mossbunker, Bony-fish, Whitefish, Bugfish, Fatback, Pogy.

Average size 8 inches; largest 18 inches; food value nil. Bluish above, sides silvery with strong brassy luster.

A bait fish which is found along the Atlantic coast in great numbers in summer. They are caught with nets and used as bait and chum. Beeause of the strong oil content are ground up for chum to attract larger fish such as Tuna.

● **TIDEWATER SILVERSIDE** *Medidia beryllina*

Also called Whitebait. Average size 2 inches; largest 6 inches; food value, poor.

Greenish-blue on back, silvery on sides. A carnivorous fish, of small size, traveling in great schools near the shores of tropical and semi-tropical waters. As a rule they are not considered much as food.

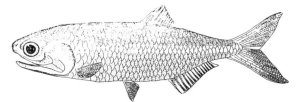

● **BAY ANCHOVY** *Anchoa mitchilli*

Also called Glass Minnows.

Average size 2 inches; largest 5 inches; food value poor. Olivaceous with narrow silver stripe.

A bait fish, numerous about piers and inland waters in smaller sizes. Large schools in Gulf of Mexico.

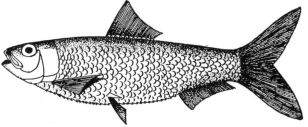

● **SCALED SARDINE** *Harengula pensacolae*

Also called Pilchard.

Average size 3 inches; largest 8 inches; edible.

Silver on sides; dark green to smoky-gray on back. Abdominal cavity smoky-gray.

Belly is keeled; sharply pointed.

Numerous bait fish in southern latitudes in winter and spring. Sometimes seen as far north as Cape Cod in warm weather. Most numerous in the Florida Keys.

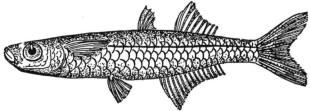

● **ATLANTIC SILVERSIDE** *Menidia menidia*

Average size 2½ inches long; largest 3 inches; food value nil.

Waxy, translucent, thickly punctuated with black on top of head; dots on edges of scales.

Small Bait Fish

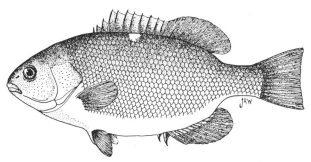

● **OPALEYE**　　*Girella nigricans*

Also called Black Perch, Green Perch, Blue-eyed Perch, Bluefish, Catalina Perch, Button Perch, Blue Bass, Greenfish.

Average length, 7 inches; largest on record, 17 inches; edible. Greenish in color, becoming paler below; eye opalescent blue; young have whitish blotch on either side of back.

Identified by three spines and 12 soft rays on anal fin. Usually found about rocky shores.

Native to central California coast.

● **GIANT KELPFISH**　　*Heterostichus rostratus*

Average length 10 inches; largest on record, 16 inches. Not desired as food, but edible.

Color ranges from brown to green or purplish and varies widely. Usually barred or blotched.

Extremely long dorsal fin marks this fish. The ventral fins have only one spine. Lower jaw projects. Tail is forked. A common fish around the kelp beds on Pacific coast. Native to Pacific, British Columbia to lower California.

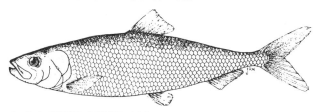

● **PACIFIC HERRING**　　*Clupeaharengus pallasi*

Average length 8 inches; largest 18 inches; edible. Pinkish-purple above, becoming silvery on sides and below.

Identified by a single short dorsal fin in the middle of the back. No scales on head and no lateral line. A schooling fish, taken throughout the Pacific for canning.

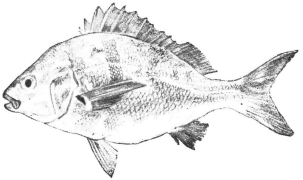

● **SARGO**　　*Anisotremus davidsoni*

Also called Perch, Black Croaker, China Croaker.

Entirely metallic-silvery in color with a grayish tinge above, plain silvery below; back, head and sides have vague dark blotches. Band on side from tip of ventral to fourth spine in dorsal. Rarely taken by sportfishermen, and then usually in the summer and fall. Native to Pacific waters.

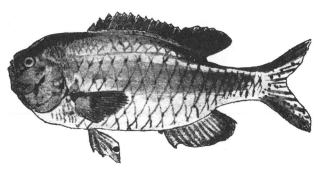

● **BLACKSMITH**　　*Chromis punctipinnis*

Also called Black Perch, Blue Perch, Kelp Perch. Average length 4 inches; edible.

Dark slate above becoming lighter on underparts. Tinged with blue everywhere; small dark brown spots on back. A member of the Damselfish family; rather a rare fish, usually found around kelp rocks.

Native to all tropical waters.

● **WHITEBAIT SMELT**　　*Allosmerus elongatus*

Also called Smelt, Surf Smelt, Small Fry, Perlin.

Average length 9 inches; pale preenish—almost colorless; silvery stripe along side. Has 15 to 17 anal rays and a large mouth.

Taken in surf with dip nets or small hand seines. Native to California coast.

Small Surface Fish

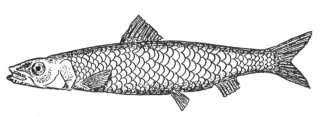

● **ATLANTIC ROUND HERRING** *Etrumeus sardina*

Average size 8 inches; largest on record 12 inches; food value fair.

Olive-green above with silvery sides and belly.

One of the rare members of the Herring family. An elongate specimen of the common Herring. Found on both Atlantic and Gulf of Mexico coasts.

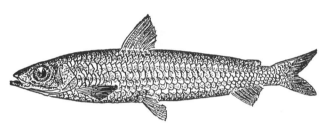

● **PACIFIC ARGENTINE** *Argentina sialis*

Also called Herring Smelt.

Average size 12 inches; largest on record 18 inches; food value fair.

Back is brownish; sides silvery with brassy luster; belly white.

Smelt-like fish with large pointed nose. Has large eyes. Jaws are toothless but tongue armed with small teeth. A deep water fish.

● **HALFMOON** *Medialuna californiensis*

Also called Blue Perch, Blue Bass, Medialuna.

Average size 8 ounces; largest on record 1 pound and 8 ounces or 12 inches in length. Food value good. Slaty-black with bluish luster, becoming whitish or mottled below.

Identified by three spines and 19 to 20 rays in the anal fins. A nibbler of seaweed, found around rocks and submerged wrecks. Their diet is mostly algae; are considered herbivorous. Make excellent panfish, favored as baitfish.

Native to rocky coasts of the Pacific, on the central and southern shores of California.

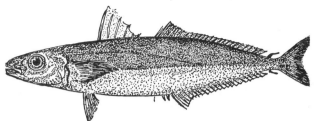

● **MACKEREL SCAD** *Decapterus macarellus*

Average size 10 inches; largest on record 13 inches; food value fair.

Slate-blue above; silvery below; small black spot on margin of gill cover. Of the Pompano family. Has a series of 31 keeled shields, largest on peduncle, larger than ordinary scales. A warm water fish, usually found in the Atlantic.

● **PEARL FISH** *Carpus bermudensis*

An interesting little fish that lives only inside the sea cucumber, comes out at night to forage. Rarely exceeds seven inches and usually average three to five inches.

The flesh is largely transparent with some pearly or silver-colored patches behind the head.

Uses the sharp pointed tail to gain entry into anal opening of the sea cucumber. Instances of three to four fish living inside one sea cucumber have been reported.

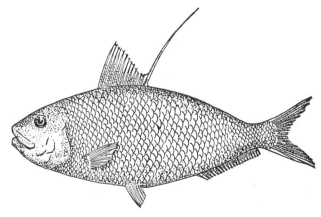

● **ATLANTIC THREAD HERRING** *Opisthonema oglinum*

Average size 5 inches; largest 12 inches; food value poor.

A surface feeder, not found in large numbers. Usually found in warmer waters, although occasionally straying north of Virginia.

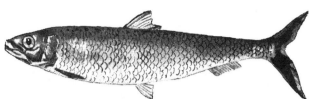

● SURF SMELT *Hypomesus pretiosus*

Also called Surf Fish, Nightfish, Perlin, Silver Smelt. Average length 3 inches; largest 10 inches; edible.

Pale greenish, becoming silvery on sides and below. Identified by absence of scales on head and a dorsal fin composed entirely of rays.

Usually caught in the surf; in quantity mostly in the summer months. Used as bait extensively.

Native to colder waters of Pacific.

● PACIFIC SARDINE *Sardinops sagax*

Also called Pilchard, California Sardine.

Dark green to blue above with many small dots, shading into silver below. Identified by single short dorsal fin. Mouth opening at tip of head, neither jaw projects. Scales have spines which can be felt when finger is drawn across.

An important Pacific fish, netted throughout the ocean and sometimes found in adjacent oceans to Pacific. Primarily canned.

● JACKSMELT *Atherinopsis californiensis*

Also called Silverside, California Smelt, Horse Smelt, Blue Smelt. Average length 4 inches; largest 18 inches; edible.

Grayish-green to green above with bluish tinge. Sides and belly silvery. Metallic band tinged with blue extends length of body.

Identified by two dorsal fins well separated. First has weak spines, second soft rays. Even jaws.

The most caught of the Smelts on the California coast. Occurs in large schools. Sports fishermen take them with snag lines, which are lines with hooks attached at intervals, pulled through a school concentrated by chumming. Somewhat of a live bait fish also. Native to the Pacific.

● DEEPBODY ANCHOVY *Anchoa compressa*

Also called Garfish, Billfish.

Average size 10 inches; largest 36 inches; not edible. Green above, becoming silvery below. Bluish band along the side of body.

Narrow jaws are greatly prolonged in a snipe-like beak.

Native to the waters of Pacific.

● CALIFORNIA GRUNION *Leuresthes tenuis*

Average length 4 inches; largest 7 inches; edible.

Green or grayish-green above, silvery below. Bright silver band tinged with blue extends length of body.

The absence of teeth in the mouth distinguish this fish from the Topsmelts. Also the upper jaw has the capability of being drawn out to form a tube. Front of dorsal is just back of vent.

The remarkable spawning habits of Grunion make this fish quite interesting to the amateur. They swarm onto the beaches of lower California in the dark of the moon at high tide. The fish swim up on a wave, spawn on the beach and then catch another wave to go back. At this time fish-hungry persons slaughter millions of them on the beaches. The spawning period ranges from March to August, most of which is protected by law.

Native to Pacific.

● TOPSMELT *Atherinops affinis*

Also called Little Smelt, Least Smelt, Rainbow Smelt, Bay Smelt.

Average length 4 inches; largest 12 inches; edible. Blue-gray to clear green above, becoming silvery below; bright silver band bordered above with bright blue or purple; extends length of body.

Identified by top of upper jaw projecting slightly over tip of lower. First dorsal fin is directly over vent. Often taken with baited hooks or snag lines.

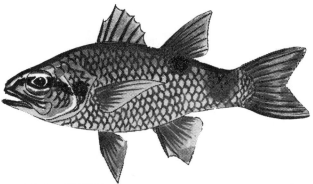

● FLAMEFISH   *Apagon maculatus*

Average size 4 inches; largest 6 inches; food value poor. Bright red in color with dark blotches at base of tail.

A Florida Gulf Coast reef fish, found quite often on the coral bottom.

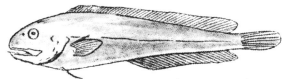

● KEY BROTULA   *Ogilbia cayorum*

Only measurement of average size known is that of Charles M. Breder, Jr., who gives the figure 2.33. Believed to be a stray from deep water. Specimen noted here was taken in Florida Keys.

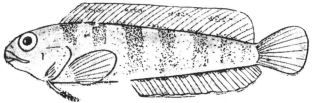

● STRIPED BLENNY   *Chasmodes bosquianus*

Average size 4 inches; largest 6 inches; food value, poor.

Usually colored a variegated pattern blending with the seaweed or grass which forms their natural protection. Feeds on small shellfish.

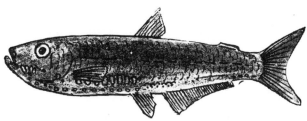

● PEARL SIDES   *Maurolicus pennanti*

Average size 2 inches; largest 3 inches; food value, nil. A silvery looking fish.

Found almost entirely on the open sea; rarely close to shore. Its appearance is associated with storms and violent water eruptions.

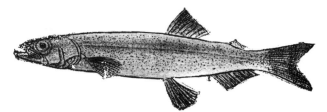

● CAPELIN   *Mallotus villosus*

Average size 6 inches; largest 12 inches; food value excellent.

Mouth rather large, body elongate, covered with minute scales. A northern salt water fish, found on both coasts.

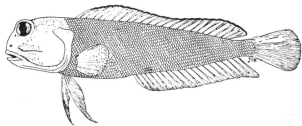

● FLORIDA JAWFISH   *Gnathypops maxillosa*

Average size under 5 inches; largest not established; food value, poor.

A silvery to black fish of the Gulf. Known only on the Florida West Coast and the shores of Cuba, this is a relatively little known species.

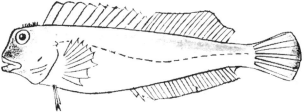

● MOLLY MILLER   *Blennius cristatus*

Average size 4 inches; largest not known; food value, poor.

A small fish found in Florida waters and as far south as Brazil.

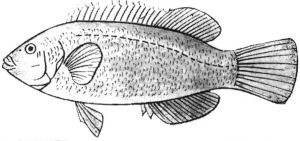

● CUNNER   *Tautogolabrus adspersus*

Average size 12 inches; largest on record 15½ inches; food value, good.

Dark colored, fairly large scales.

A fairly common fish of the eastern coast.

Butterfish and Relatives

THE BUTTERFISH FAMILY is found throughout the southern waters to Brazil. They are a panfish which often are the stock in trade of small dealers. In Baltimore they will be found hawked about the streets as also in Charleston, S. C., and other Atlantic cities.

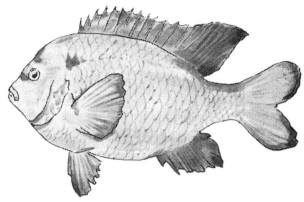

● GARIBALDI *Hypsypops rubicunda*
Also called Garibaldi Perch, Ocean Goldfish, Demoiselle. Average length 6 inches; largest 14 inches; edible. Uniformly bright in color. The young have blue spots.

This is a fish well known to visitors of aquariums. One of the most brilliant of ocean fish. Caught only incidentally by sports fishermen. Usually found around rocky shores. The largest of the Damselfish.

● SOUTHERN HARVESTFISH *Peprilus alepidotus*
Also called Whiting. Average size 4 inches; largest on record 12 inches; food value, excellent.

Bluish above, bright silvery below. Dorsal fin edged in black.

They take a hook, a very small hook baited with bits of clam or softshell crab. Are also caught in nets in some areas. The flavor is rich and delicate as Pompano and highly prized as a food fish.

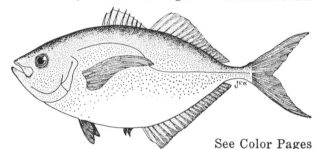

See Color Pages

● BUMPER *Chloroscombrus chrysurus*
Also called Casabe.

Average size 4 inches; largest 10 inches; food value poor. Greenish above, sides and belly golden, inside of mouth black.

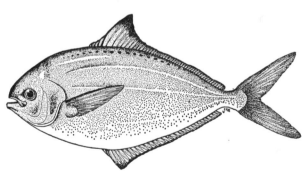

● BUTTERFISH *Poronotus triacanthus*
Also called Dollarfish, Sheepshead, Pumpkinseed, Starfish.

Average size 4 inches; largest on record 9 inches; food value, good.

Usually abundant on Atlantic coast in July and they seem to come and go when the Mackerel do. The young seek shelter in the vicinity of stinging jellyfish, which is apparently to protect them from larger fishes, although they themselves sometimes fall victim to the stinging tentacles of these sea creatures.

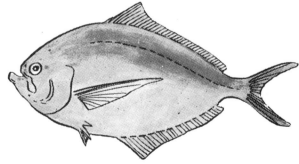

● POMFRET *Brama rayi*
Average size 6 inches; largest not known; food value, nil. Silvery sides to dark on back.

A small fish of the open seas, only rarely seen. Another Pomfret, seen more often is identical in shape with this fish. but of red color. Found on the Gulf of Mexico Snapper banks.

Rainbow-hued Fish

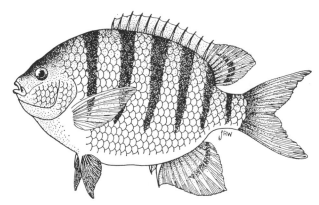

See Color Pages

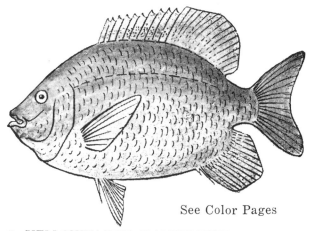

See Color Pages

● **SERGEANT MAJOR**   *Abudefdul Saxatilis*

Also called Cockeye Pilot.

Average weight 6 ounces; largest on record 24 ounces; food value good.

Stripes are a bright yellow and black.

An abundant species of small fish which gathers in swarms around docks, pilings and tide rips on coral or rock bottom. They can change color if necessary to accommodate themselves to surroundings.

Spend their time nibbling barnacles from the pilings. Although quite small on the whole, they make an excellent little panfish. Can be readily caught with a small hook and a bit of oyster for bait.

● **YELLOWTAILED DAMSELFISH**
                    Microspathodon chrysyrus

Average size 5 inches; largest 8 inches; food value fair. Dark bodied with brilliant yellow tail.

Feed on organic debris. Found mostly in Gulf of Mexico.

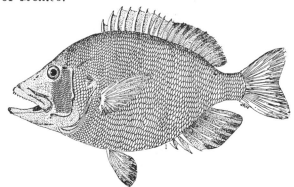

● **BUTTER HAMLET**   *Hypoplectrus unicolor*

Also called Midget Sea Bass.

Smallest of Sea Basses, seldom more than 10 inches long. Small food value.

Brightly colored with pattern varying according to location. Combinations of blue, yellow or brown. Found on rocky or sandy shores of Atlantic and Gulf coasts.

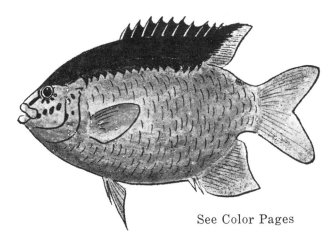

See Color Pages

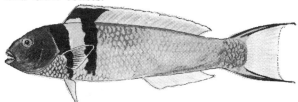

● **BEAUGREGORY**   *Eupomacentrus leucostictus*

Average size, 4 inches; largest 7 inches; food value poor.

Yellow on belly and blue on back, large scales.

An aggressive little fish of the tropics. They usually appropriate any large empty shell for their nests and will defend themselves against the attacks of any size enemy. They make fine aquarium fish.

● **BLUEHEAD**   *Thalassoma bifasciatum*

Average size 5 inches; not a food fish.

The smallest of the Wrasse family and the most colorful. Has solid blue head and tail with greenish body. Two wide black bands circle the body at the gill cover and edge of pectoral fin.

Native to waters from Florida Keys to West Indies.

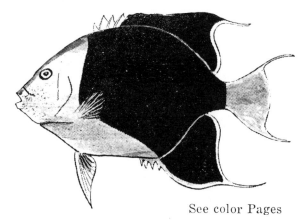

See color Pages

● **ROCK BEAUTY** *Holacanthus tricolor*

Average weight 1 pound; largest on record 3 pounds; food value fair.

As indicated by the scientific name, has three colors. Center of fish is black, nose and tail alternate in yellow and scarlet.

A small-mouthed nipper of barnacles and shellfish about the piers and wrecks of clear gulf or ocean water. Usually found where Angelfish are seen.

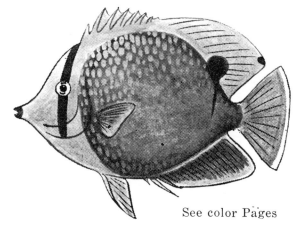

See color Pages

● **SPOTFIN BUTTERFLYFISH** *Chaetodon ocellatus*

Also called Coral Fish.

Average size 5 inches; largest on record 10 inches; food value poor.

A prettily colored fish with silvery body and yellow fins edged with green at the tail; a band of black from dorsal to gill cover across the eye.

A very aggressive and graceful fish of the coral reefs. Their great activity and defensive coat of scales enable them to hold their own in the struggle for existence.

● **MOORISH IDOL** *Zanclus cornutus*

Also called Kikikihi.

Average weight 10 ounces; largest on record 2 pounds; food value fair.

Strikingly marked with black and white, broad stripes. Dorsal fin long and sweeping.

Strictly speaking the Moorish Idol is the lone member of its family. However they are most always found in company with the Angelfishes, therefore are associated with this group. Most prevalent in Pacific waters, but specimens occasionally picked up in all warm waters.

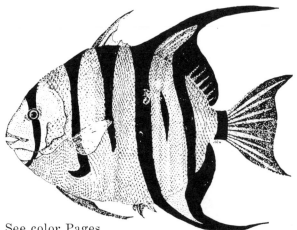

See color Pages

● **ATLANTIC SPADEFISH** *Chaetodipterus faber*

Average weight 20 ounces; largest on record 9 pounds, 1 ounce, caught by Mrs. John Brooks, 1310 Washington St. Myrtle Beach, S. C., fishing in Murrells Inlet using shrimp for bait. May 30, 1965.

Food value good.

Prominently marked by vertical bars of black and silver. As the fish grows older the markings fade. An abundant fish in certain localities about piers and bridges. Always nibbling at the barnacles and along shell-encrusted seawalls. If a small hook is used and bits of oyster or clam flesh is the bait, they can be caught. They are expert bait stealers.

Butterfly Fish

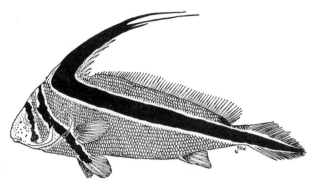

● **JACKKNIFE FISH**   *Equetus lanceolatus*

Average size 10 inches; largest on record 16 inches; food value fair.

A rarity among the Drum tribe in western Gulf waters, but seen more often around the Florida Keys. The stripe is black. Unmistakable in shape and coloring for identity.

The striking appearance of this fish, seen ocsionally from the bridges and causeways of the Florida Keys overseas highway is an important tourist attraction. They are also featured residents of aquariums in Florida cities.

● **SAILFIN TANG**   *Zebrasoma veliferum*

Also called Api. Average weight 14 ounces; largest on record 3 pounds. Dark background, brownish-black with diagonal silvery-white stripes around body. Two large fins, dorsal and anal.

A cross between the Butterflyfish family and the Doctorfish tribe. This fish, however, is a true Tang, recognized by the lancet on each side of the tail. These sharp spines can cut their way through nets and make plenty of trouble for a larger fish which might swallow this fellow.

The beautiful fins are graceful in the water. Often referred to as "My Doctor With a Scarf".

● **STRIPEY**   *Microcanthus strigatus*

Average weight 12 ounces; largest on record 3 pounds; food value good.

Unmistakable black and silver horizontal stripes.

One of the Butterflyfish, hanging around the rocks and reefs, with other Angelfish of the same type. Have a very small mouth which indicates they live on parasites. Pacific fish abundant around Australia.

● **BANDED BUTTERFLYFISH**   *Chaetodon striatus*

Average size 5 inches. Largest not on record.

Outstanding among the Butterflyfish in that the black bands running vertically around the body are pronounced. First thru the eye, then thru the pectoral fins and third just back of anal fins. Caudal is rounded and matches the dorsal and soft anal fins. Entire fish tinged in yellow.

Has a tiny mouth and seldom, if ever, caught on hook and line. Can be netted in vicinity of coral reefs, over sand bottom. Makes a good aquarium fish. Hardy. Live well in captivity.

Angelfish

THE ANGELFISH are one of the most beautiful and highly colored fishes of the Florida reefs. They are carnivorous fishes although not often taken on hook and line. Are exceedingly active and their quickness of sense and motion enable them to maintain themselves in the close competition of existence among the coral reefs. These brilliantly colored fish are members of the Butterflyfish *Chaetodontidae* family.

They take most any bait resembling small crabs or shellfish. They eat tiny barnacles and minute marine growth. Have very small mouths.

Average size of Angelfishes 10 inches; largest 24 inches, food value, fair.

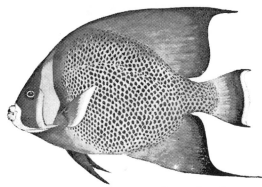

See color Pages

● **GRAY ANGELFISH**   *Pomacanthus arcuatus*

The commonest of the Angelfishes. Under side of pectorals are bright yellow. The young show light vertical crossbands.

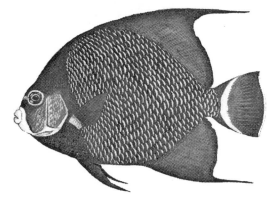

See color Pages

● **FRENCH ANGELFISH**   *Pomacanthus paru*

The bright yellow edges of the velvety black scales easily separate this fish from the Gray Angelfish, which never shows yellow on body. (Note, the yellow on under side of pectorals of Gray Angelfish is entirely hidden as fins fold against body.)

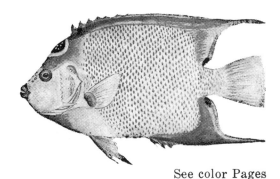

See color Pages

● **QUEEN ANGELFISH**   *Holacanthus ciliaris*

One of the most beautiful of marine fishes. Has a generous dab of blue at base of head. Grows to 2 feet in length. Largest ever taken is not recorded.

Primarily a West Indian species, reaching Florida in the Keys.

Color is predominantly blue and yellow. Fins are bright lemon color all over. as differing from the yellow-tinged fins of the Gray Angelfish. Juvenile specimens show marked blue stripes running vertically across body.

Especially popular in aquariums where they stand out because of their brilliant coloring.

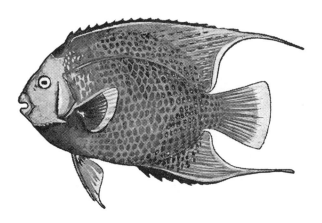

● **BLUE ANGELFISH**   *Holacanthus bermudensis*

This group has several spines on the gill covers. They are the largest and showiest of the Angelfishes. Common on the Florida coast.

50

Sea Perches

THE SEA PERCH FAMILY are comparatively small, silver fishes of shallow water. They are originally from the Pacific coast and few specimens have been taken elsewhere. They are viviparous by nature and bear only a few well developed young at a time. The little fishes, from the time of delivery, are able to maintain themselves in the surf where they are born.

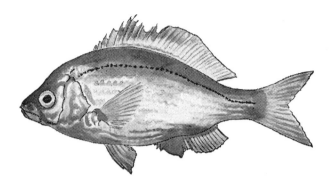

● **SHINER PERCH** *Cymatogaster aggregata*

Average size 4 inches; largest 6 or 7 inches; edible.

Silvery with dusky back. The sides have a series of broken vertical bars formed by clusters of dark points on the scales; between these bars are three light yellow bars. The males are almost black in the spring. The rather high spiny portion of the dorsal fin (the highest spine longer than the highest ray) serves to identify. The scales are also large (less than 50 to a row on the lateral line). Tail is only moderately forked.

These small Perch are rather common along the shore line of the California coast, especially in bays and on sandy bottom.

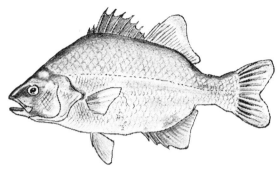

◐ **WHITE PERCH** *Rocus americana*

Also called Silver Bass, Sea Perch, White Bass.

Average weight 1 pound; largest on record 4 pounds, 4 ounces; food value, good.

Ordinarily the back is olivaceous but also varies to a dark green; sides have a brilliant silvery sheen and are usually marked with a pale longitudinal streaks. Mouth is small but head is large in relation to size of the body.

They inhabit the tidal areas of the coast, most abundant about the coast of South Carolina. They range between salt and fresh water, and are perfectly at home in brackish water. Often they work their way up streams and become landlocked in headwaters or ponds. They cannot reproduce, however, unless returned to salt water for some period of the life cycle. Shrimp, crabs and insects are the food most preferred. They will respond to still fishing, casting or trolling.

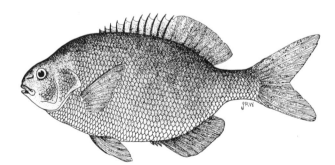

● **BLACK PERCH** *Embiotoca jacksoni*

Also called Surf Fish, Bay Perch, Porgy, Blue Perch.

Average size 5 inches; largest 14 inches; edible. Usually found in shades of brown, although this is highly variable. Sometimes tinged with blue, green, red or yellow. Identified by thick reddish-brown lips. Dorsal spines are much shorter than dorsal rays.

Rather rare fish, although sometimes found in fair numbers with other Perch.

Native to Pacific.

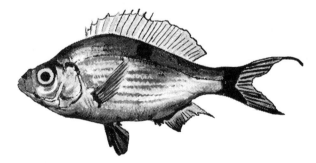

● **PINK SEAPERCH** *Zalembius rosaceuus*

Average length 4 inches; largest 8 inches. Not edible.

Red-rose in color with silver reflections. Two distinct chocolate-color spots on the back, the first and larger below the end of the soft dorsal.

Identified by spiny part of dorsal being higher than rayed part. Has a somewhat deep head, rather blunt; deeply forked tail.

Usually found in deep water, rarely in shallow water. Most common in depths to 20 fathoms.

Native to Pacific, central to southern area.

Sea Perches

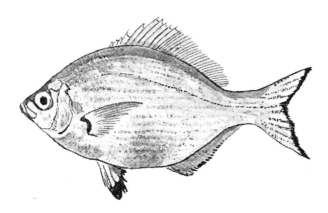

● KELP PERCH *Brachyistius frenatus*

Average length 4 inches; largest 8 inches; edible.

Dark olive in color, greenish-brown spots above with small dark spots at the base of each scale. Bright copper-red below. Fins are reddish.

Has a slender, pointed head and deeply forked tail. The spiny and rayed parts of dorsal are of equal height. Relatively large scales, about 40 in row along lateral line. Not common for fishermen, but often seen in aquariums where the bright color makes it noticeable.

Native to the Pacific, from British Columbia to Mexico.

● WALLEYED PERCH *Hyperprosopon argenteum*

Also called Silver Perch, Surf Perch.

Steel-blue in color, becoming silvery on sides and belly, sides have faint bars, which fade soon after death. Pectoral fins black tipped.

Has an oval or compressed body; very large eye. The largest dorsal spine is higher than any of the soft rays. Usually found along the sandy beaches.

Native to Pacific.

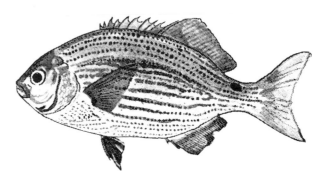

● STRIPED SEAPERCH *Embiotoca lateralis*

Also called Blue Perch, Rainbow Perch, Squawfish, Crugnoli.

Average length 6 inches; largest on record 10 inches and weighing 24 ounces. Taken from waters of Gulf of Mexico by Ben Arons, 1957. Edible.

Has horizontal blue stripes with dull orange and blue along rows of scales. Head has several blue spots and streaks. Colors fade after death.

Usually found along rocky shores and most plentiful in Pacific waters. Protected by closed season in California, May 1 to July 15.

Best bait are clams, cut bait or mussels.

Native to Pacific, mostly colder waters.

● BARRED PERCH *Amphistichus argenteus*

Also called Sand Perch, Surf Perch, Silver Perch. Average length 6 inches; largest 18 inches; edible.

Silver, tinged with bluish or grayish above. Silvery on the sides and belly; usually barred and spotted. Sometimes silvery streaks on the sides.

A popular surf fishing catch. Taken in large numbers all year, except closed season in California May 1 to July 15. Not a true Perch, but a distant relative. Bears its young alive.

Found on sandy coast.

Native to the Pacific, mostly Southern Calif.

● RUBBERLIP SEAPERCH   *Rhacochilus toxotes*

Average size 7 inches; largest 18 inches. Desirable food.

Silvery on sides. Back has a bluish tinge. Pectoral fins are yellowish. Other fins tipped with black. Lips white or pink.

Identified by exceedingly thick lips. Forward edge or spiny portion of dorsal fin is the lowest.

One of the leading commercial fish of the Pacific. Taken on clams, mussels and cut bait.

Native to Central and Southern California.

● PILE PERCH   *Rhacochilus vacca*

Also called Split-tail Perch, White Perch, Porgee, Forktail Perch and others.

Average size 8 inches; largest 16 or 17 inches; edible. Blackish, or brownish-grey with a silver luster on top, which becomes even more silvery on the sides and belly. At various times in the fish's life there are dark blotches showing on the back and sides. The fins are always dusky.

Positive identification is made by the sharply elevated first dorsal rays, about twice as long as the last dorsal spine. Also this Perch has a deeply forked tail.

Fishing season for this important West Coast food fish is good all year, except for the California state law on closed season. Quite often they appear in numbers with purse seine catches of sardines.

Native throughout the Pacific and seen mostly from Alaska to Mexico on the American West Coast.

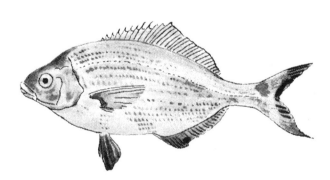

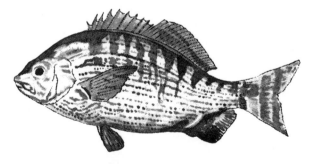

● WHITE SEAPERCH   *Phanerodon furcatus*

Also called Split-tail Perch, Porktail Perch, White Surffish.

Average size 5 inches; largest 12 inches; edible.

Silvery with dark hue above. Anal fin has a dusky spot. Identified by deeply forked tail and uniformly slender body taper.

An important commercial fish in California. Some estimates are as high as 40 per cent of total Perch catch. Common along sandy shores.

Native to Pacific, Vancouver Island to Southern California.

● RAINBOW SEAPERCH   *Hypsurus caryi*

Also called Striped Perch, Bugara.

Average length 6 inches; largest 12 inches; edible. Striped horizontally with red, orange and blue; has irregular streaks of orange and blue on the head; fins are brightly colored. Identified by the count of 24 soft rays in anal fin.

Caught by surf fishermen and dock fishermen with pile worms, clams or mussels as bait.

Parrotfish, Wrasse

THERE ARE MANY VARIATIONS of Parrotfish, all highly colored. The Blue Parrotfish is the largest of the family and the only fish which attains such large size. Most Parrotfishes are small and not worth much as food or game. The prominent teeth of most Parrotfish are whitish or rosy colored.

They live around coral reefs, feeding on barnacles and crustaceans. Most of them change colors as they grow older.

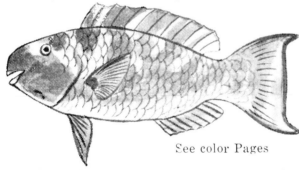

● **PURPLE PARROTFISH**　　*Scarus coelestinus*
Also called Midnight Parrotfish.
This fish is dark purple, nearly black all over, with bright blue markings on the head. Light bars show when the fish is excited or frightened.

See color Pages

● **BLUE PARROTFISH**　　*Scarus caeruleus*
Average weight 4 pounds; largest on record, 24 pounds and 12 ounces. Caught by Dr. Richard A. Gilbert, at Durado Beach, Puerto Rico, March 28, 1954, spearfishing. Edible.
Can be identified by a fleshy lump on the forehead, increasing in size with age. Native to West Indies, but has been seen occasionally as far north as Chesapeake Bay.

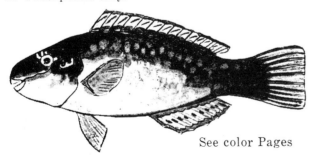

See color Pages

● **SPOTFIN PARROTFISH**　　*Sparisoma axillare*
Brilliantly colored member of the genus, abundant in Gulf waters, seen mostly at Key West.

See color Pages
● **RAINBOW PARROTFISH**　　*Scarus guacamaia*
One of the largest of the Parrotfish. Predominately green and orange with margins of median fins blue; unscaled part of head and chest, dull orange. In large adults the colors are brighter and may range to almost uniformly blue.
Found in tropical West Atlantic waters, around the Bahamas and Fla. Keys, south to Argentina.

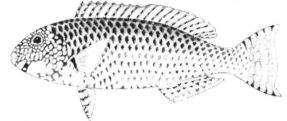

● **MUD PARROTFISH**　　*Sparisoma flavescens*
Also called Viega Colorado.
Average size about 10 inches; largest not on record.
Mottled effect on head, pinkish on belly, yellow edged tail. Large scales, tinged in brown above, pink below; pectoral fins black spot at base, yellowish toward edge.
This is one of the most common of the Parrotfishes, especially around the flats of eel grass in Key West vicinity. They take any small bait. Poor quality as food fish.

● **SPOT WRASSE**　　*Lepidaplois albotaeniatus*
Average size 8 inches; largest 15 inches; food value good. Bright red with longitudinal stripes of silver. Black spot at base of dorsal fin. Fins and tail edged in yellow.
A rare species of Wrasse, which exceeds others in food value. While most members of this family have soft flesh, the Spot is solid and firm. Feeds on mollusks and shellfish.

Squirrelfish Family

THE SQUIRRELFISH FAMILY is known in most parts of the world as Soldierfish and are found in the Pacific, Atlantic and Gulf of Mexico in equal number. Never very plentiful except possibly around Puerto Rico or the Hawaiian Islands.

As a rule the flesh is soft and although edible, most of them are not choice eating. They do make up in color what they lack in market value. Noted especially for their large eyes and bright red cast. Because so many bigger fish choose them for food, they are both timid and fast. During the day they stay pretty well hidden.

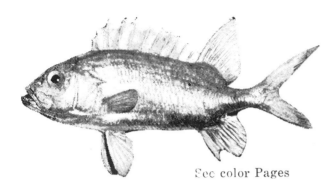

See color Pages

● **SQUIRRELFISH**   *Holocentrus ascensionis*

Also called Red Squirrelfish, Soldierfish.

Average weight 2 pounds; largest on record not established; food value, good.

A pink or reddish fish with large eyes which are dark. Inhabiting the offshore reefs of the tropics, they are a timid fish by nature, hiding mostly in daytime and out at night. They spend most of their life in rocky crevices. Most of the larger fish prey on them for their food.

Take a hook readily, especially night fishing and they are comparable to Red Snapper as a food fish, although the flesh is a bit softer than Red Snapper.

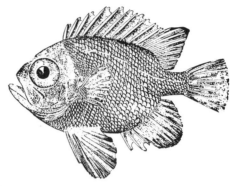

● **SHORT BIGEYE**   *Pristigenys alta*

Average weight 1 pound; largest on record was caught by Francis R. Lunsford, U.S. Airforce, Charleston, S. C., fishing aboard Capt. Jack Murray's MUSTANG III about 34 miles off shore. Length 13⅝ in.; weight 2 lb. 8 oz.

Brilliant red color all over with unusually large protruding eyes. A striking fish in color. The brilliant red blends with the green of the gulf waters to make the fish appear gray and less conspicuous.

These fish are considered rare in American waters, however Emery C. French of Destin, Fla., has observed a considerable number coming in with Red Snapper on the Destin deep-sea fishing boats.

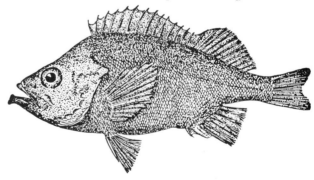

● **DEEPWATER SQUIRRELFISH**

Holocentrus bullisi

Also called Whitestriped Squirrelfish.

Average size 6 inches; largest 12 inches; food value, fair.

Usually bright colored corresponding to the area of the bottom they are residing in. This fish is quite noticeable by the white stripes running laterally on the side in perfect pattern.

● **REDFISH**   *Sebastes marinus*

More often called Rosefish or Ocean Perch. Also called Norway Haddock.

Average size 15 inches; largest 24 inches; food value, good. Reddish colored.

A deep water fish not too happy in warm water. Migrates deep and north when water gets warm. Unusual in that the eggs are kept in a pouch within the female and the young emerge alive. Feeds on shellfish.

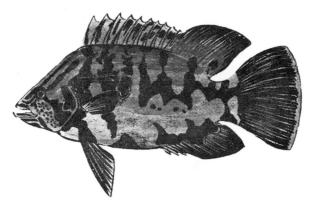

● TRIPLETAIL   *Lobotes surinamensis*

Also called Chobie, Black Perch, Flasher, Sea Perch, Buoyfish, Sunfish.

Average 5 pounds; largest on record was caught by Herman H. Schwartz, Rochester, N. Y., fishing in intercoastal waters off Palm Beach, Fla., on Feb. 5, 1969. Length 33 in.; weight 27 lbs. 5 oz.

Dull black, silvery-gray sides and belly. Young fish mottled with yellow or grayish irregular spots.

An open water fish, occasionally taken in inside waters, but prefers shady spots where the water is cooler, or deep wrecks. They like to lurk around weed rafts, driftwood, channel buoys or any object beneath which they can hide.

They like live shrimp, crabs and such bait and will take a hook readily.

Caught mostly still fishing, only very rarely do they take a trolled lure.

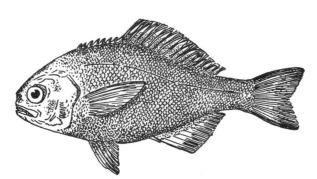

● BARRELFISH   *Palinurichthys perciformis*

Also called Logfish; Rudderfish; Black Pilot.

Average size 8 inches;. largest on record 12 inches; food value, fair.

Blackish-green on top paling to bluish on belly; mottled with darker dots a n d bars; can change color with surroundings.

Sometimes seen hanging around drifting wreckage or barrels, hence their name. They feed on the barnacles attached to drifting wood.

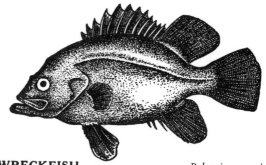

● WRECKFISH   *Polyprion americanus*

Average size 10 pounds; largest not established; food value, good.

Dark on top, yellowish to lighter on belly.

Usually found in open water around drifting wreckage or barnacle encrusted pilings. They can attain a length of 6 feet and are usually found on the surface.

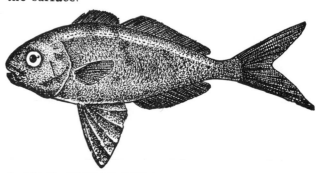

● MAN-OF-WAR FISH   *Nomeus gronowi*

Average size 4 inches; largest 8 inches; no food value. A friend of the Portugese Man-O-War, the stinging jellyfish that drifts on tropical waters. Will be seen lurking in the vicinity of the tentacles, to feast on other unfortunate fish which might become trapped.

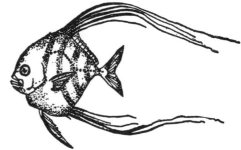

● THREADFISH   *Alectis ciliaris*

Average size 3 inches; largest on record was caught by Edith Aubry, Staten Island, N. Y., on Mosquito Banks off Key Largo, Fla., on Feb. 6, 1969. Weight 1 lb. 8 oz.

Distinguished by long trailing threads from dorsal and anal fins. Found in all warm seas throughout the world. Belongs to the Crevalle family. Some icthyologists believe it to be the young of the African Pompano.

Bright Hued Fishes

GOATFISHES: Worldwide in distribution, but found mostly in tropics. They are distinguished by their long barbels and two widely separated dorsal fins. During feeding, the barbels are raked rapidly across the bottom or thrust into the mud in search of food. Four species are found in Western Atlantic. The two most common are:

● **YELLOW GOATFISH**   *Mulloidichthys martinicus*

Body shape similar to Red Goatfish. Average size 12 in.; weight 1 lb. Yellow strip from eye to tail fin distinguishes this fish.

● **SPOTTED GOATFISH**   *Pseudupeneus maculatus*

Snout more elongated than Yellow Goatfish. Three spots along lateral line; color sandy to reddish.

Sufficiently abundant in 1879 to warrant opening a fishery to harvest them. In 1882 a billion and a half dead Tilefish were sighted. Their sudden demise was due to an abnormal intrusion of cold water which upset the delicate balance necessary for survival. A decade later they began to reappear. The fishery was gradually reestablished.

Found along the outer edge of the continental shelf from Maine to Chesapeake Bay in water deeper than 25 fathoms.

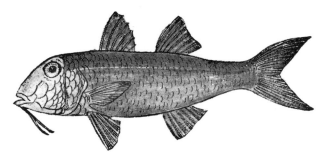

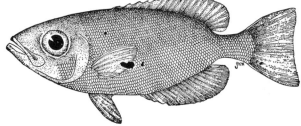

● **RED GOATFISH**   *Mullus auratus*

Also called Surmullet, Red Mullet.

Average size 6 inches; largest 14 inches; food value, good.

Scarlet color becoming crimson where scales are removed. Side has two distinct yellow bands. Sides of head silvery lustre.

Found in all the warm seas but mostly on the Red Snapper banks of the Gulf of Mexico. Often the entrails of Snapper and Grouper will contain these fish, which apparently are a source of diet for large reef fish.

Seldom caught and not abundant enough to be considered as a food fish. The flesh is white and tender, however, and in the Mediterranean countries is much sought after as food.

● **BIGEYE**   *Priacanthus arenatus*

Also called Catalufa, Comico, Toro.

Average size 12 inches; largest on record 22 inches; food value, good.

A bright red with striking blue on upper jaw. Fins yellowish tipped.

Ordinarily a fish found in the West Indies and south to Brazil, specimens have been taken at various points on the Gulf of Mexico coast, particularly about the Tampa Bay area.

Very little is known of this fish by habit except that when present on the reefs will take a bait intended for Red Snappers. They present a remarkable change of colors when they are taken from the water and expire. The flesh is firm and flaky and of good flavor.

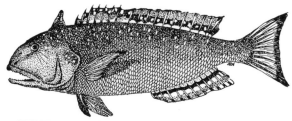

● **TILEFISH**   *Lopholatilus chamaeleonticeps*

Average size 20 pounds; largest on record 50 pounds; food value, excellent.

A colorful fish—back and upper sides bluish to olive green, changing to yellow or rosy on sides. Belly bright rose with white midline.

● **HAWKFISH**   *Paracirrhites forsteri*

Average size 6 inches; largest 10 inches; food value, fair. Abundant in Hawaiian Islands.

Several models of fish. One has red spots, another is black-sided and a third has dark rings. All are the same in general appearance.

Natives of the Grouper banks, they nibble away at the bait intended for Grouper and Snapper.

Hogfish and Threadfish

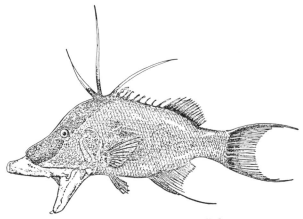

See Color Pages

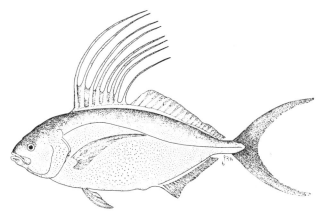

◉ HOGFISH　　　　　　　　　　*Lachnolaimus maximus*

Also called Captain, Perro Perro, Capitaine.

Average weight 2 pounds. Largest on record, 20 pounds, caught by Mrs. Florence Renny, St. Petersburg Beach, from a deep-sea fishing boat off Johns Pass, in 1957. Food value good.

Bright colors. Can frequently change coloring to match background. Mostly mottled reddish mixed with amber and white. Easy to recognize by elongated snout and large mouth. Three streamer type dorsal spines are outstanding characteristic.

Living mostly on bottoms of the Gulf of Mexico coral reefs, this fish is found singly or in pairs. Rarely found around bare coral sand but common where there are coral fans. They feed in daytime on mollusks and shellfish.

Will take any bait on still fishing line which would attract Grouper. Especially fond of shrimp.

◉ ROOSTERFISH　　　　　　　*Nematistius pectoralis*

Also called Papagallo.

Average weight 6 pounds; largest on record 114 lbs., length 5 feet, 4 inches, girth 33 inches, caught near La Paz, Mexico, June 1, 1960 by Abe Sachheim. Food value fair.

Purple on the back, sides golden; indigo-blue crossband on snout, another on forehead; dorsal spines banded with alternate blue-black and white.

This is one of the most stately and beautiful fishes of the warm waters. Something like a giant Angelfish with streamers. The brightly colored rays give it a most striking appearance.

They take a bait only occasionally and are very cagey. Considered a rare catch in the Gulf of Mexico. Found in Pacific.

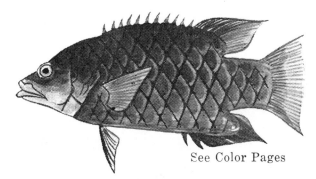

See Color Pages

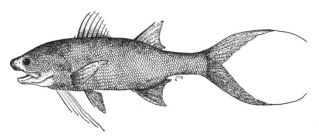

● SPANISH HOGFISH　　　　　　*Bodianus rufus*

Also called Ladyfish.

Average weight 1 pound; largest on record 8 lbs. Food value fair.

Handsomely colored as the common Hogfish, with reds predominating. Reaches a length of 2 ft.

Found under same conditions as the common Hogfish. Greatest difference is this species has an entirely different shaped dorsal and mouth.

● ATLANTIC THREADFIN　　　*Pollydactylus octonemus*

Average size 5 inches; largest on record 16 inches in length; one pound and 9 ounces weight, caught by Barry Lynn Farmer off Juno Beach Fishing Pier, Florida East Coast. Recorded Dec. 10, 1960. No food value.

Light olivaceous, belly whitish, pectoral black in adult.

A family of tropical fishes inhabiting the waters of Atlantic and Gulf coasts in large part, elsewhere rare. Usually found on sandy bottom and in shallow water. They take a hook fairly easily baited with cut mullet or crabs. Not very plentiful.

Pompanos

POMPANOS and their cousins the Jacks look so much alike it is hard to distinguish them, but their resemblance ends there. The Pompano is considered the finest of all food fish, while Crevalle Jack is about the poorest.

The Pompano is a fighting, flashing gamefish of the first caliber, rising to artificial lures or live bait. They are strong and tenacious for their weight, putting everything into their fight for freedom.

Most Pompano are taken close to shore, preferably in sloughs and swash channels where sea fleas and small shellfish are likely to be found.

Most popular of fishing methods is "duding." This is the using of a small feather jig called a dude, attached to a short leader and light line. The action is to drop the lure straight down and then cause it to flip off the bottom at regular intervals in imitation of a sea flea or shrimp.

Pompano, of course, like their native food such as hermit crabs and other small shellfish.

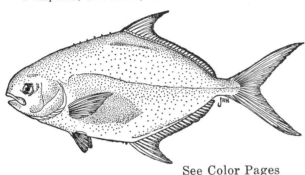

See Color Pages

● **FLORIDA POMPANO**   *Trachinotus carolinus*

Also called Carolina Pompano, Cobbler.

Average size 2 pounds. Silver and pale blue above, golden below. A record Pompano was reported from "Moonhole", Bequia, St. Vincent, W.I. A 16-yr. old boy, Arnold Hazell caught a 9 pounder on Sept. 9, 1968.

Food value excellent.

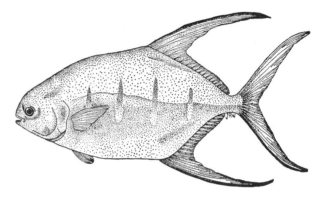

● **PALOMETA**   *Trachinotus goodei*

Also called Old Wife, Longfin Pompano.

Average size 2 pounds; largest on record 8 pounds; food value good but not comparable to Florida Pompano.

Much the same coloring as the Florida Pompano, except that it has longer fins. Distinguished by 4 narrow vertical bars. Found mostly in the Bahamas and vicinity of Puerto Rico, only rarely are specimens caught on Florida Coast.

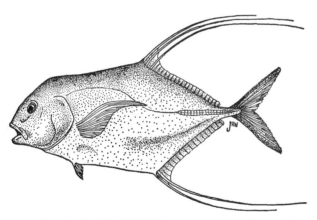

● **AFRICAN POMPANO**   *Alectis crinitus*

Average 2 to 4 lbs. Largest on record reported March '69. Paul H. Grier, Bethesda Md., in the MET Tournament caught a 42 pounder.

Silvery body with bluish-green above. Soft rays of the dorsal fins up to 4 times length of body in young. Shorter in maturity due to wear and tear— may be twice the length of body.

Native to both sides of Atlantic from temperate to warm waters, it is quite a fighter. Usually taken trolling. Some consider it a fine food fish, especially smoked.

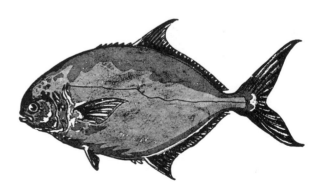

● **PERMIT**   *Trachinotus falcatus*

Also called Round Pompano.

Average size 3 pounds; largest on record 20 lb. 2 oz. caught on a fly rod in the 1969 MET Tournament by Norman Duncan of Miami. Food value good.

Blue on upper sides, top of head darker blue, rest of body silvery with deep golden reflections.

Crevalle Family Jacks

ROVERS OF THE OCEANS and preying upon everything they can find, the Crevalles are the murderous fishes of the deep. Most of them travel in schools, others are lone wolves.

They will attack any other fish which can be eaten, and strike any kind of lure which resembles a fish. The whole family is low on food value for humans. They are strong, oily and the flesh is dark with blood. Only by bleeding when first caught and treating as smoked fish are they considered palatable. Prepared in this way, however, and labeled "Southern Salmon," they are quite good.

Few fish in the ocean possess the bulldog strength and endurance of the Crevalles.

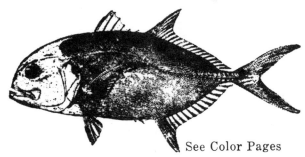

See Color Pages

● CREVALLE JACK — *Caranx hippos*

Also called Cavalla, Horse Crevalle, Skipjack, Toro, Jack, Pompano, Ulua.

Average size 5 pounds; largest on record 50 pounds even set by Jack McDonald, West Palm Beach. Taken from the Atlantic Ocean in 1957. Food value poor.

Light olive on back, shading to grayish-gold on sides and yellowish on belly. A distinct black spot on gill covers; broad forked tail.

A savage fighter and rightfully called the bulldog of the sea for the stubborn fight put up when hooked. Many anglers call the Crevalle the strongest and toughest of all fish. They are constantly on the move and anglers seldom hunt them in particular. They are taken usually while fishing for other fish. They travel in schools, and one strike is usually the signal for all lines to be busy at the same time. A fair sized Crevalle can put up a 20-minute fight which will leave the fisherman amazed that one fish of the size he has on the line could make such an effort to escape.

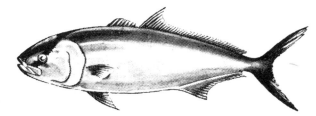

● AMBERJACK — *Seriola dumerili*

Also called Cavalla, Horse Crevalle, Skipjack, Toro, Jack, Ulua.

Average weight 18 pounds; largest on record 138 pounds and 8 ounces; set by Harry C. Winslow, 315 Lester Road, Springfield, Penna. He fished at Alligator Light near Islamorada, Florida Keys, with Capt. Henry Clifford out of Bud 'n' Mary's Dock. Hook and line, cut bait. Food value, fair.

They are greenish on the back, sides reddish to silvery. The Amberjack has little fear of man and his works, roaming the seas and inspecting fishing boats and coral reefs with equal impartiality. They feed entirely on live small fish, most anything from Mullet to Grunts.

Outstanding trait of the Amberjack is curiosity. Whenever one is hooked the entire school will follow the battling fish to the boat. Another bait presented by fishermen is quickly snapped up and the whole school can be caught by always having one fish left struggling in the water.

● ATLANTIC MOONFISH — *Vomer setapinnis*

Also called Moonfish.

Average size 12 inches. Largest not on record.

Bears a close resemblance to Lookdown except the dorsal and anal fins are not elongated. Pronounced curve in the lateral line. Pelvic fin, tiny, almost non-existant. Vague shading of rainbow colors at gill covers, otherwise uniform silvery color.

Another of the Jack family with flesh of oily and strong characteristic. Not recommended as a food fish.

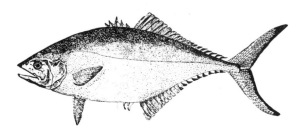

● LEATHERJACK — *Oligoplites saurus*

Average size 8 ounces; largest on record 2 pounds; food value, poor.

Back is light greenish, sides silvery, leathery skin. Has a small spine which can protrude and give a painful wound.

The small member of the Jack family. Used sometimes as bait when other bait fish not available. A very fast swimmer and found in open water.

● **PACIFIC POMPANO** *Palometa simillima*

Also called Butterfish.

Average length 5 inches; largest 11 inches. Considered a delicacy.

Dull green, shading into bright silvery below. The entire fish gleams in iridescence.

Deep thin body, no ventral fins; long low dorsal; anal fin of same length and shape.

This is not a true Pompano, but a *Stromateidae*, of the small Butterfish family. Pompanos and Jacks have the same general characteristics.

They are caught with small hooks and cut bait.

Native to the Pacific. British Columbia south to Lower California.

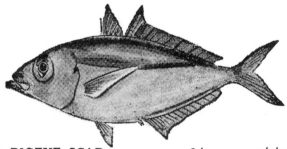

● **BIGEYE SCAD** *Selar crumenopthalmus*

Also called Goggle-eye.

Average weight 6 ounces; largest on record 1 pound; food value, fair.

Gray-black on top, sides dusky. Easily identified by the large eyes.

A common school fish, found to considerable extent around bridges and piers. They are sometimes used for Tarpon bait. Will strike at any small bait such as shrimp, glass minnows, etc. Could only be considered sport on the lightest tackle.

Range world-wide in temperate and tropical seas.

● **RAINBOW RUNNER** *Elagatis bipinnulatus*

Also called Spanish Jack. Average size 4 lbs., largest on record 30 pounds and 15 ounces, as listed

in the International Gamefish Association record book. Food value, good. Back is olive-green with bright blue horizontal stripes and light yellow tail.

This is considered the rarest of the Jacks. They range the Grouper-populated reefs in solitary splendor. Only once in a great while is one caught and then always trolling. They are very swift.

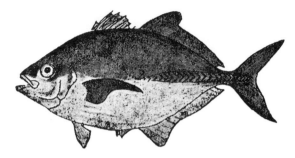

● **HORSE-EYE JACK** *Caranx latus*

Also called Goggle-eye, Crevalle, Jack.

Average size 3 pounds; largest on record 35 pounds; food value, poor.

Large eyes. Blue on back and gilt-silver below. Fins dusky.

Roams the Gulf Stream and the reefs in schools, usually small. Not a common fish like the Jack Crevalle, although sometimes seen in sizeable numbers in mid-summer. Occasionally stray in fresh water.

● **YELLOWTAIL** *Seriola dorsalis*

Also called White Salmon, Amberfish.

Average size 10 pounds; largest on record 105 pounds and 12½ ounces, caught by M. A. Yant, Bahia de Topolobampo, Mexico, April, 1955. Food value, excellent.

A close relative to the Amberjack. Steel-blue above, shading into bluish-silvery sides. An irregular brassy or yellowish stripe extends along the sides, from the eye to the tail.

This is one of the finest gamefish of the Pacific and should not be confused with the Yellowtail of the Florida Coast, which is a much smaller fish of the Snapper family. Like the Amberjack they are taken mostly trolling or still fishing in deep water.

The Yellowtail is so important on the Pacific coast that large tournaments like the San Diego Yellowtail Derby is run in their honor.

Crevalle Family Jacks

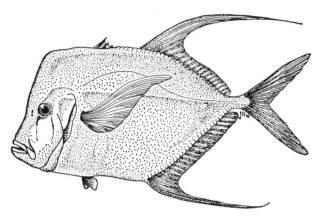

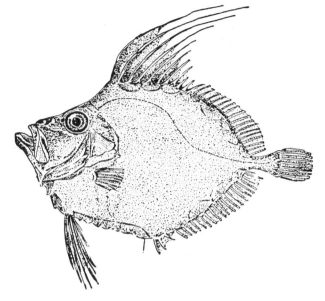

● **LOOK DOWN** *Selene vomer*

Also called Moonfish, Blunt-nosed Shiner, Jorabado, Old Man of The Sea; Silver Moonfish.

Average weight 2 pounds; largest on record 30 pounds; food value, poor.

Uniform silvery color.

Quite often these fish are caught trolling in the Atlantic Ocean. They are rare in Gulf waters. Will strike most anything they can catch. Considered to be a member of the Jack family and the flesh is of like oiliness.

● **JOHN DORY** *Zenopsis ocellatus*

Average size 6 inches; largest 8 inches; food value, poor. Plain silvery with black lateral spot.

A small Butterfish type of the Atlantic and Gulf. Considered a rare fish in the southern waters. Only a few specimens found south of New Jersey.

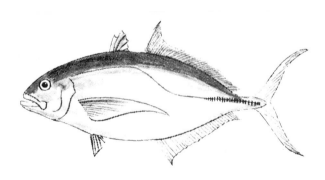

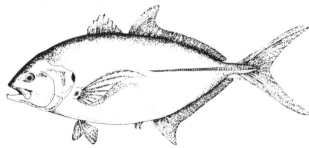

● **YELLOW JACK** *Caranx bartholomaei*

Average weight 8 pounds; largest on record 25 pounds; food value, good when smoked.

Body greenish-blue, silvery-gilt below—fins yellow. A similar fish, the Bar Jack is distinguished by a deep purple stripe running the length of back through lower side of caudal fin. Long pectoral fin. Found mostly in the Florida Keys, but occasionally caught in all Gulf waters as well as tropical Atlantic Ocean areas. They strike at trolled baits and put up a lusty fight.

The flesh is strong and is only palatable when smoked or cured in some like manner.

● **BLUE RUNNER** *Caranx crysos*

Also called Hard-tail Jack, Yellow Jack, Yellow Mackerel, Runner.

Average size 1 pound; largest on record 6 pounds; food value, fair.

Greenish on back and upper sides, shading into a yellowish-silver. Fins almost colorless.

This fast and hard striking little Jack is numerous all the year in the bays and channels of southern waters. They mostly run with schools of Mackerel or Bluefish and when they're biting it is possible to catch a great number.

Almost always caught trolling, for they feed on live top bait such as Sardines and Menhaden. At times they attack schools of these fish with such force the water boils for quite some time as they gorge themselves. Are excellent bait for Sharks.

Albacore, Bonito

MACKEREL FAMILY HEAVYWEIGHTS, these are the thick bodied fish. The stubbornest, fighting-est, tackle-rippingest fish in the ocean. All of them are solid muscle and game throughout. Not so much for food but all for thrills in catching.

● **ATLANTIC BONITO** *Sarda sarda*

Also called Boston Mackerel, Frigate Mackerel, African Bonito, Little Tunny, Boneater, Bloater, Bonejack, Skipjack.

Average weight 4 pounds; largest on record 26 pounds, 8 ounces, caught by Gino Cappelletti, Wellesley, Mass., fishing in the Atlantic near Miami, Fla., Jan. 1, 1967. Not considered edible except as smoked or steam processed and canned.

The flesh is dark and oily. Quite bloody. Bluish steel above, shading off to silvery sides which become white on belly. Dark stripes run obliquely down and forward from back to lateral line.

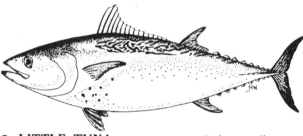

● **LITTLE TUNA** *Euthynnus alletteratus*

Also called Blue Bonito, Little Tunny, Frigate Mackerel, Tuna, False Albacore.

Grows to about 20 lbs.

Bluish above and belly silvery, several oblique wavy stripes above lateral line, none below.

This pelagic fish, the Little Tunny as it is frequently called, is closely related to the Bonitos.

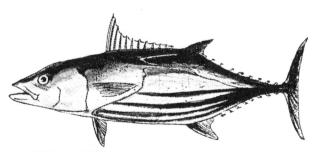

● **SKIPJACK TUNA** *Katsuwonus pelamis*

Also called Arctic Bonito, Ocean Bonito, Striped Tuna, Watermelon, Victor Fish.

Average weight 3 pounds; largest on record 39 pounds and 15 ounces, caught near Walker Cay, Bahamas, Jan. 21, 1952 by Frank Drowley. Food value, poor.

● **BLACK SKIPJACK** *Euthynnus lineatus*

Average weight 5 pounds; largest 25 pounds; edible. Flesh is dark and should be smoked or baked. Blue to violet above with greenish reflections. Noticeable stripes on back distinguish from other Tuna-like fishes.

Common throughout the Pacific. Large catches are taken in Mexican waters. They take a trolled lure readily. An active fighter for sports fishing.

Commercially they are canned. The California tuna law forbids the canned product being labeled Tuna.

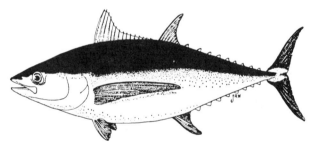

● **ALBACORE** *Thunnus alalunga*

Also called Long-finned Albacore, Long-finned Tuna Abrego, Alilonghi, German.

Average weight 18 pounds; largest on record 69 pounds, caught by P. Allen, near St. Helens, April 7, 1956. Food value excellent.

Dark blue on top, shading to light blue below. Belly silvery-white. Has unusually long pectoral fins which are nearly half as long as the fish.

If it were not for the long pectoral fin, it would be hard to distinguish this fish from the Bluefin Tuna.

Has been observed and recorded in both Pacific and Atlantic. Said to have been seen as large as six feet in length.

Rare on the North American coast north of Florida, yet the fish has been known to occur in Massachusetts waters.

A very handsome species of the Tunny family.

Tuna

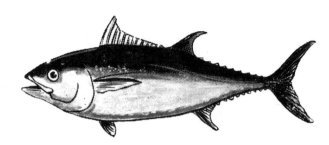

● BLUEFIN TUNA   *Thunnus thynnus*

Also called Giant Mackerel, Leaping Tuna, School Tuna; average 30 pounds; largest reported to Great Outdoors 977 pounds caught by Don Hodgson in St. Ann Bay, Nova Scotia, Sept., 1950. Food value good.

Dark blue on back, shading to bluish-gray above lateral line. Silver-gray blending into silvery sides and belly. Tail and dorsal fins are dark blue.

Found in all the warm seas of the world. Pelagic in habits. Has been taken as far north as northern Newfoundland and as far south as the Caribbean.

There is a strong belief the Bluefin Tuna spawns in the vicinity of the Bahamas. Large numbers gather there early in summer.

In California the Bluefin Tuna is known as "Leaping Tuna" and a much sought after gamefish.

Pacific Tuna attain 250 pounds in weight. Off the European coast they have been recorded to 500 pounds. On the North American shores they become monsters, with a top of 1,800 pounds now on record.

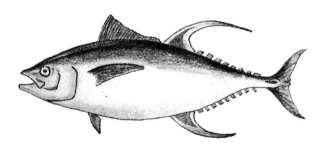

● ALLISON TUNA   *Neothunnus allisoni*

Average weight 50 pounds; largest on record 269 lbs., 8 ozs., with 53-inch girth and measured 6 feet, 9 inches in length, caught near Hanolei, Hawaii, May 30, 1962 by M. Salazar. Food value, excellent.

Also called Tuna, Yellow-finned Tuna, Long-finned Tuna, Yellowfin. Note, the Yellowfin Tuna (*Thunnus albacares*) is almost identical to the Allison, and many experts believe they are the same fish. The Yellowfin is a Pacific Coast version. The Allison Tuna has a longer dorsal.

● YELLOWFIN TUNA   *Thunnus albacares*

Average weight 125 pounds; largest on record 265 pounds, caught by J. W. Harvey, Makua, Hawaii, July, 1937. Edible.

Metallic dark blue above, shading into silvery gray below. When first caught, generally a golden yellow, iridescent band along the side.

Distinguished by eight finlets following both dorsal and anal fins.

An excellent sports fish, taking readily to trolled feather jigs. Caught with live bait or trolling.

They travel in schools throughout the Pacific sometimes covering great distances in a day.

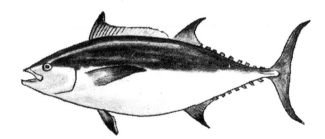

● TUNNY   *Thunnus secondodorsalis*

Average size 200 pounds; largest verified 710 pounds. Believed to attain a weight of more than 1,500 pounds. Edible.

Dark blue above, with a polished steely glint. Usually silver on the belly, with various markings of yellow. There are often tints of green, pink and other hues on the sides.

This is one of the largest gamefish and much sought after. Believed to rove on the European shore in a great migration around the Atlantic, as distinguished from the Bluefin Tuna, an Atlantic shore line resident. There is considerable debate on the family and relationships in the Tunny classifications.

However it is well established they feed on Mackerel and Squid and reproduce in southern waters.

MACKEREL ARE CONSIDERED one of the world's most important food fishes. Found in every ocean and sea of the world, there is still much to learn about their life span. Restless, roving fish, which can never be kept in captivity. Preyed upon by all other fish, they sometimes spawn in such quantity as to supply all other deep-sea fish and humans, with food throughout the year.

● **ATLANTIC MACKEREL** *Scomber scombrus*
Also called Common Mackerel, Bull's-eye Mackerel, Tinker Mackerel, Northern Mackerel.
Average weight 1½ lbs.; largest on record 15 lbs. 8 oz. caught by Radonna C. Sears, Mooresville, Ind., fishing from the CAPT. RUDY off Miami, Fla., May 15, 1968. Food value excellent.
Metallic, steel-blue above lateral line, with a brassy or golden sheen and light green cast. Irregular, wavy, blackish-colored transverse bars above lateral and silvery below.
They travel well offshore in large schools.

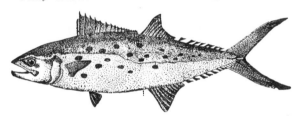

● **SPANISH MACKEREL** *Scomberomorus maculatus*
Also called Spotted Speedsters.
Average weight 28 ounces; largest on record 18 pounds and 3 ounces, caught by Ralph Helpbringer, Pasadena, Calif., fishing in Los Friles Bay near La Paz., Mexico, May 17, 1966. Food value excellent.
Dark bluish-brown on back with golden spots both above and below the lateral line. Silvery on the belly. Staple food fish of southern waters.

● **PACIFIC MACKEREL** *Scomber japonicus*
Also called Blue Mackerel, Greenback Mackerel, Striped Mackerel, American Mackerel.
Average length 20 inches; largest on record 25 inches, 6 pounds, 4 ounces; edible.
Dark green to blue above with metallic reflections shading into silvery on sides and below, wavy bars down back.
Has a very high first dorsal, separated widely from a smaller dorsal. Small scales, easily brushed off. A plentiful fish in the Pacific.

● **KING MACKEREL** *Scomberomorus cavalla*
Also called Kingfish, Cero, Cavalla, Sierra.
Average weight 8 pounds; largest on record 82 lbs. caught by George Heine of Jupiter, Fla., in May of '68, reported by Red Marston of the St. Petersburg Times.
Dark on back, shading to silvery on sides and white on belly.
The great King Mackerel is a migratory fish which travels through the Gulf waters in spring and fall, providing anglers with unexcelled fishing for six weeks. They usually appear off the Texas coast in June. The schools are large and fishing is frequently heavy and exciting.

● **SNAKE MACKEREL** *Gempylus serpens*
Average size 30 inches; largest 44 inches; food value, fair.
Somewhat resembling the Atlantic Mackerel in coloring. A deep water fish known from New York to Brazil only as a rare find. Seldom are found with the inshore schools.

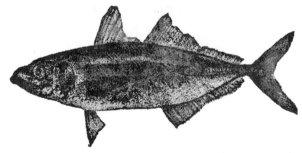

● **JACK MACKEREL** *Trachurus symmetricus*
Also called Horse Mackerel.
Average weight 1 pound; largest on record 4 pounds, length 22 inches; edible.
Iridescent green above, sometimes with bluish luster; often mottled with lighter and darker shades; silvery on sides and belly.
The two dorsal fins are close together and about the same height. There are bony shields along the entire length of lateral line.

Snappers

CRAFTY, CHOOSY, INTELLIGENT as fish go, Snappers are the aristocrats of smaller fish. Plentiful everywhere in warm water, they never travel in large schools but rather in bunches. There is an old saying among fishermen that "You can only fool a Snapper once"

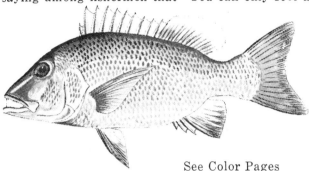

See Color Pages

● CARIBBEAN RED SNAPPER Lutjanus campechanus

Also called Acara Aya, Pensacola Snapper, Pensacola Red Snapper, Mexican Snapper, Pargo Colorado.

Average weight 7 lbs.; largest on record 36 lbs. 8 oz. caught by Daniel Kostomay of Cincinnati, Ohio, in the Gulf off Destin, Fla., Oct. '68. Food value excellent.

Deep brick-red all over, except shading to a paler red on belly and throat. Fins also red.

This is a deep water fish, taken mostly by commercial fishermen in waters of the Atlantic and Gulf. Seldom caught on anything but stout hand lines. Some of the best Snapper bottom is 200 to 300 feet deep. When a school is located they usually bite fast and the catch is heavy.

Natural food is small fish, crabs and shrimp. Cut mullet is excellent bait for them.

Rock bottom is best Red Snapper fishing. Range is from the Florida coast to West Indies and Brazil.

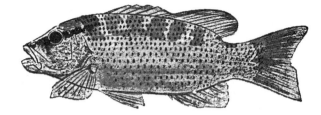

● GRAY SNAPPER   Lutjanus griseus

Also called Mangrove Snapper.

Average weight 7 pounds; largest on record 59 pounds and 8 ounces, reported by Bill Stevens of Johns Pass, Fla., in 1957. Food value excellent.

Bronze-green above, shading into brassy-red on sides and light gray on belly, interspersed with darker markings on scales. Sure to be recognized by the dark streak which runs from nose across eye and fades toward dorsal fin. Looks like a bluish-black slash. This is the wisest and most alert member of the Snappers and you can include most of the other fish in that category also. While they are quite numerous in bays and bayous, especially around mangrove studded islands, are not easily caught.

It is a fact that around the docks at Key West, a properly presented live shrimp bait will catch one Snapper out of a school or sometimes two, but that's all. The rest of the school immediately get wise when they see what happened to their brothers.

See Color Pages

● DOG SNAPPER   Lutjanus jocu

Also called Jocu, Pargo Colorado.

Average weight 2 pounds; largest on record 110 pounds; food value, good.

Olive colored above, shading into reddish cast on sides and still lighter on belly. Copper cast over entire body and very faint bars.

Found in fairly deep water, around reefs. Very fond of hanging around wrecks. Caught in southern waters mostly in fall and winter but along the Texas coast are taken all summer. Rare in middle Gulf but more or less common in the northern Gulf Stream. They are caught still fishing.

● SCHOOLMASTER   Lutjanus apodus

Also called Sea Lawyer, Black Snapper, Caji.

Average weight 2 pounds; largest on record 8 pounds; food value, good.

Reddish-brown on back, shading into an orange cast on sides. Reddish tint and deeper orange below. Broad greenish-white vertical bars from back to lower part of sides.

One of the most beautiful of the Snappers. Has rather large scales and a very large canine tooth on either side of upper jaw.

Abundant on reefs and bottoms where Grouper and Grunts are found.

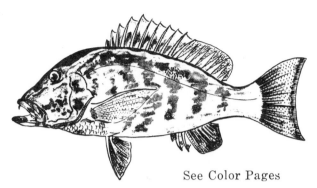

See Color Pages

● LANE SNAPPER
Lutjanus cyanopterus

Also called Spot Snapper, Red-tail Snapper, Biajaiba, Silk Snapper.

Average weight 12 ounces; largest on record 8 lbs., even, caught by R. K. Hawkins, Ft. Pierce, Fla. Dec. 30, 1964.

Rose colored, shading off to silvery with an olive cast. Series of deep golden stripes along sides. One of the smallest members of the Snapper family.

This beautifully colored Snapper is abundant in shallow water, in company with Grunts and similar shore fishes. Usually a solitary fish, not often in schools. Quite frequently are found around wharves and river mouths, inlets.

They are fond of small crabs and shrimp and take a hook readily. Caught still fishing.

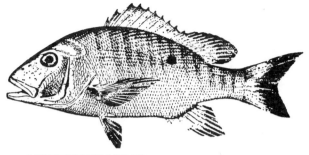

● MUTTONSNAPPER
Lutjanus analis

Also called Muttonfish, Pargo, Reef King.

Average weight 4 pounds; largest on record 32 pounds; food value, excellent.

Back orange-red to salmon colored. Has black spot on either side of back near juncture of hard and soft dorsal. Prominent, narrow blue streak from nostril to eye.

An important food fish of the Havana markets, and found in limited numbers throughout the Gulf of Mexico and Atlantic in sub-tropical waters. Often confused with the Red Snapper, although this is a different fish. The Muttonsnapper is admittedly good food, but Red Snapper brings the highest price.

They are caught still fishing over the reefs with cut bait, much the same as Grouper and Grunts. Quite often a popular method is to drift over likely spots. The Muttonsnapper will dart out and snatch a bait which passes close to him.

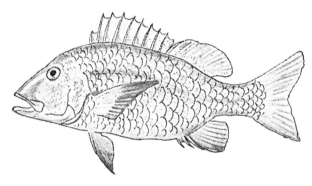

● CUBERA SNAPPER
Lutjanus cyanopterus

Average size 6 pounds; largest on record 104 pounds, caught by Arthur S. Jones, West Palm Beach, Fla., while fishing aboard the boat Blue Sea off Jupiter Inlet in July, 1952.

Reddish tinge, shading to dark on fins.

Somewhat resembling the Mangrove Snapper, except that head markings differ. Large canine teeth in both jaws; on the roof of the mouth is a crescent-shaped patch of very small teeth having a short, if any, backward stem to the crescent.

Native of the West Indies and Bahama Islands.

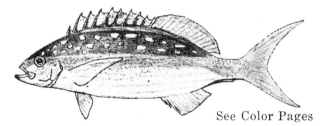

See Color Pages

● YELLOWTAIL SNAPPER
Ocyurus chrysurus

Also called Yellowtail, Rabirubia.

Average under 12 inches in length in Florida, and five pounds is a good-sized fish. In other parts of the world they grow to huge dimensions. Largest on record weighed 111 pounds, measured 5 feet, 2 inches in length and had 38-inch girth, caught in the Bay of Islands, June 11, 1961 by A. F. Plem. Food value excellent. Pronounced *delicious* by seafood fanciers.

Variable coloring. Usual color grayish-blue with yellow spots and lines. A broad yellow stripe from snout to tail. Lower parts of body rosy. Fins yellow. Has deeply forked tail. Top of head has no scales.

Very abundant in Florida in channels and among the keys. Usually found in medium depths in inlets and lagoons. Feeds day and night on smaller fishes, crabs and shrimp.

They will take most any bait offered which looks as if it is alive. Put up a good fight for their size.

Porgies

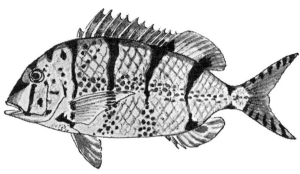

● **GRASS PORGY** *Calamus artifrons*

Average weight 8 ounces; largest on record 18 ounces; food value, good. Resembles the Saucereye Porgy in coloring without the big eyes. Inhabits the grass beds of Florida coasts, especially the Florida West Coast.

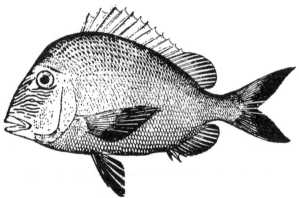

● **LITTLEHEAD PORGY** *Calamus proridens*

Average weight half pound; largest on record 3 pounds; food value, good. Silvery, with bright reflections above, much brighter than other species. Each scale above middle of side has a spot of blue at base. These form longitudinal streaks. Spots on lower part of body pale orange. Mostly found in Florida Keys, moderately common in Gulf waters.

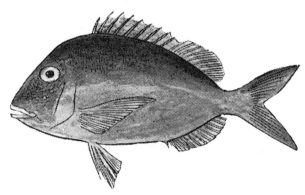

● **SAUCEREYE PORGY** *Calamus calamus*

Also called Pez de Pluma.
Average size 12 ounces; largest on record 16 lb.

2 oz. caught by F. A. Bailey off Charleston, S. C., on July 23, 1968. Food value excellent.

Silvery with bluish reflections. Base and central portion of each scale is golden. These form longitudinal stripes. Between them are pearly stripes.

Very plentiful around Key West, and found in some quantity in all tropical waters.

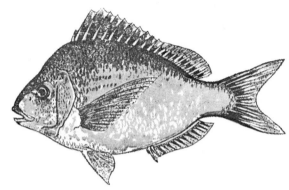

● **JOLTHEAD PORGY** *Calamus bajonado*

Average weight 2 pounds; largest on record 21 inches, 6½ lbs., caught by Mrs. J. T. Kirby off Boca Raton in March '69. Food value, good.

Has a large head with heavy upper jaw; a stripe of vivid lavender-purple follows the line of deeply slanting profile. A deeper water fish with larger mouth, so can be taken with larger hooks. Otherwise the same as other Porgies.

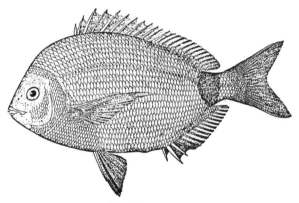

● **SPOTTAIL PINFISH** *Diplodus holbrooki*

Also called Spotail Porgy, Pinfish, or Spot.

Average size 8 ounces; largest on record 2 lbs. 1 oz. caught off Topsail Beach, N. C., by Mrs. Carolyn Ferguson of Liberty, on June 1st '69. Somewhat resembles common Pinfish, yet has deeper body and firmer flesh.

Found along our South Atlantic and Gulf coasts from Cape Hatteras to Cedar Key, Fla. Considered excellent panfish.

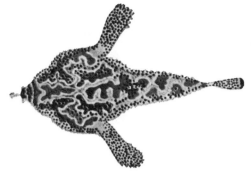

SHORTNOSED BATFISH

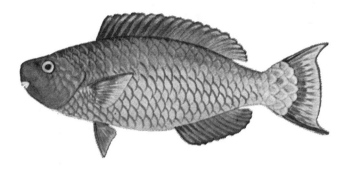

BLUE PARROTFISH

STRIPED BURRFISH

SCHOOLMASTER

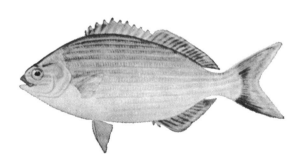

BERMUDA CHUB

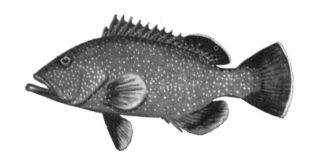

CONEY

GULF TOADFISH

INSHORE LIZARDFISH

I

RED GROUPER

SHEEPSHEAD

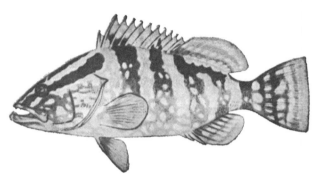

NASSAU GROUPER

SPOTTED WEAKFISH

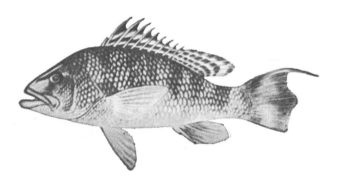

BLACK SEA BASS

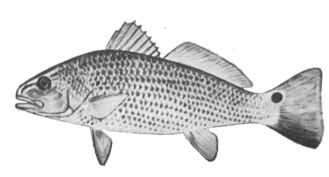

RED DRUM
(Channel Bass)

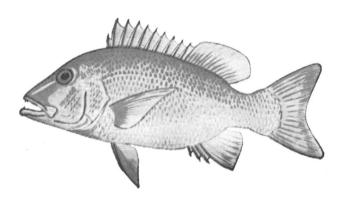

CARIBBEAN RED SNAPPER

BLACK DRUM

Color Plates by Courtesy of Marine Studios, Marineland, Fla.

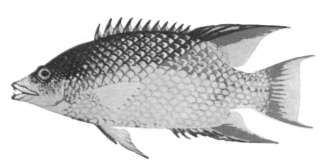

SPANISH HOGFISH

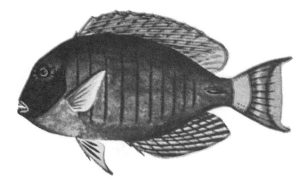

DOCTORFISH

SHARKSUCKER

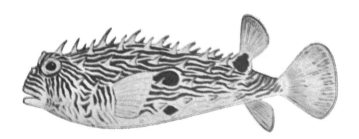

SPINY BOXFISH

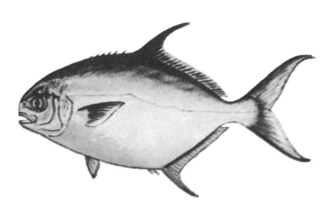

FLORIDA POMPANO

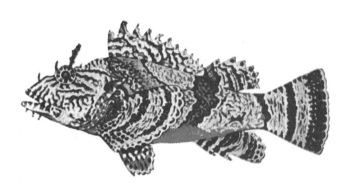

LIONFISH

COWFISH

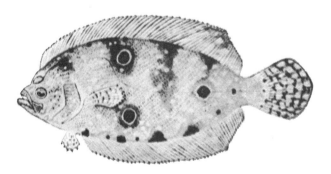

GULF FLOUNDER

SPOTTED MORAY

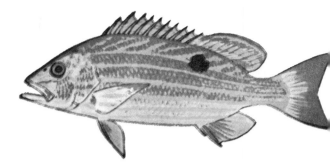

LANE SNAPPER

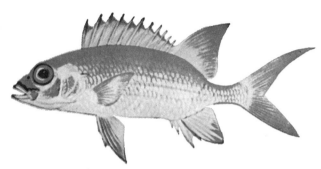

SQUIRRELL FISH

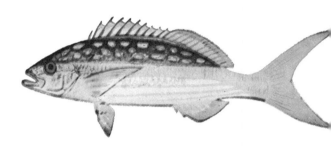

YELLOWTAIL SNAPPER

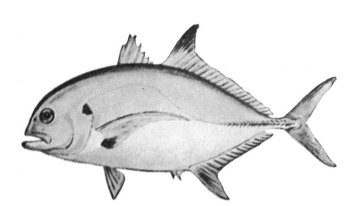

CREVALLE JACK

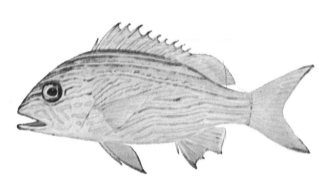

FRENCH GRUNT

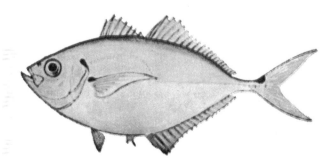

BUMPER

BLACK MARGATE

Color Plates by Courtesy of Marine Studios, Marineland, Fla.

YELLOW-TAILED DEMOISELLE

GRAY TRIGGERFISH

RAINBOW PARROTFISH

FILEFISH

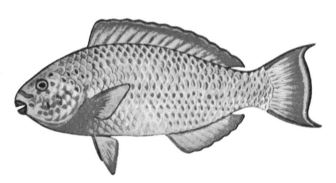

SPADEFISH

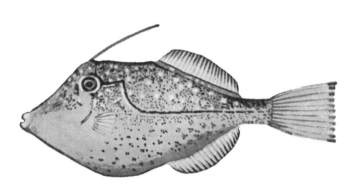

ORANGE FILEFISH

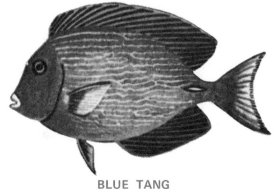

BLUE TANG

TRUNKFISH

Color Plates by Courtesy of Marine Studios, Marineland, Fla.

V

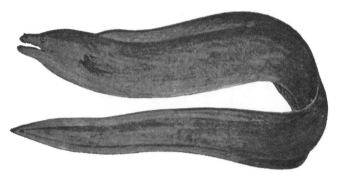

GREEN MORAY

PORKFISH

STRIPED MULLET

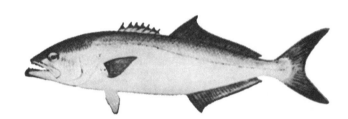

BLUEFISH

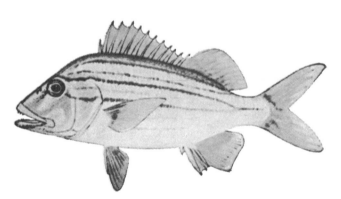

MARGATE

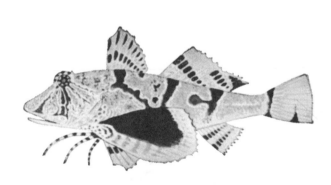

SOUTHERN SEA ROBIN

SERGEANT-MAJOR

HOGFISH

Color Plates by Courtesy of Marine Studios, Marineland, Fla.

YELLOWEDGE CHROMIS

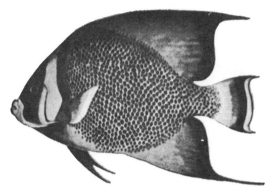

GRAY ANGELFISH

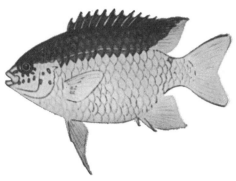

BEAU-GREGORY

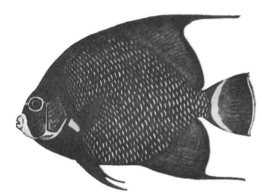

FRENCH ANGELFISH

SPOTFIN BUTTERFLYFISH

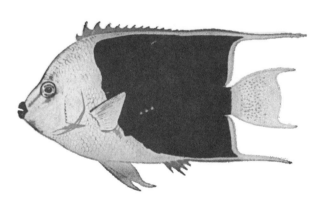

ROCK BEAUTY

FOUR-EYED BUTTERFLYFISH

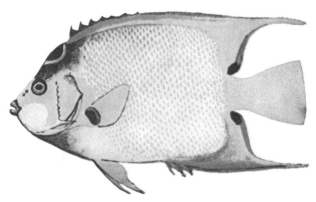

QUEEN ANGELFISH

Color Plates by Courtesy of Marine Studios, Marineland, Fla.

GRAY SNAPPER

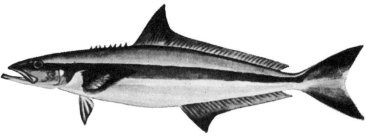

COBIA

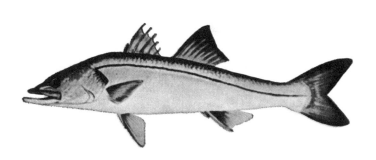

SNOOK

WHITE GRUNT

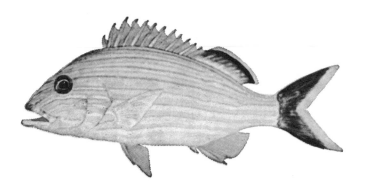

BLUE-STRIPED GRUNT

SOUTHERN WHITING

SPOTTED JEWFISH

ATLANTIC CROAKER

Color Plates by Courtesy of Marine Studios, Marineland, Fla.

● **SCUP**   *Stenotomus chrysops*

Also called Northern Porgy, Common Scup, Fair Maid, Maiden, Paugy, Scuppang, Ironsides.

Average weight 12 ounces; largest on record 3 pounds; food value, excellent.

Brownish on back, silvery below and white underneath. Fins mottled with darker markings.

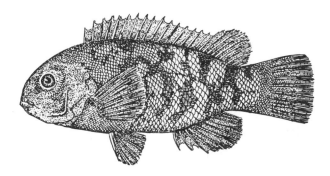

● **TAUTOG**   *Tautoga onitis*

Also called Blackfish, Black Porgy, Bergolls, Salt Water Chub, Moll, White-chin, Oyster Fish.

Average weight 2 pounds; largest on record 21 pounds and 6 ounces, caught by R. N. Scheafer of Cape May, N. J., June 1954. Food value, good.

Mottled greenish or brownish body, with irregular blackish bars or blotches. At times, blackish without blotches. Like a few other species of fish, the Tautog is able to change color to correspond with that of environment.

This is a large Wrasse which is abundant along rocky shores, mostly of the Atlantic. Preferring places where the tide runs strong. Has powerful jaws which can crush a clam or a crab with equal facility.

Like a Sheepshead is difficult to hook, the fish takes short quick nips at a bait which causes fishermen to say: "Jerk before he bites." They will not look at an artificial lure and their natural foods of mussels, clams and such kind of shellfish must be matched. Usually oysters make ideal bait, if other smaller fish are not about to steal it.

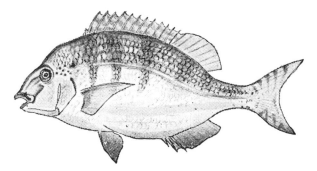

● **SOUTHERN PORGY**   *Stenotomus aculeatus*

Average weight 12 ounces; largest on record 8 pounds and 13 ounces; 26 inches in length; by Paul Streeter, Fort Lauderdale, Fla., May 19, 1955. Edible.

Has a band from forepart of cheek to the tail; cheek is bright yellow; fins are marked with black. Delightful eating panfish. Feeds mostly on small mollusks, very fond of shrimp. Fights determinedly for a short time, then gives up. Found on grass banks. Native from Cape Hatteras, throughout the South Atlantic and Gulf.

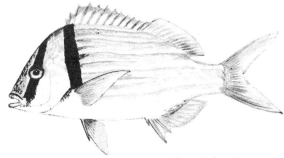

See Color Pages

● **PORKFISH**   *Anisotremus virginicus*

Also called Catalineta.

Average weight 1 pound; largest on record believed to be 4 pounds; food value, good. A strikingly colored fish of bright yellow with black stripes.

These fish always run in small schools and are fast striking when bait is cast among them. They are the prey of many larger fish and elude their enemies by darting in and out of coral rocks. Most always found where coral and rock bottom is honeycombed with caves and holes. They belong to a fast swimming group, mostly traveling together in unison as they swim.

While not always caught as the prime object of the fishing trip, there are many fishing spots on the Florida Keys where anglers fish for Porkfish entirely.

Caught still fishing and take most any bait acceptable to Sheepshead or other bottom feeding fish, such as cut bait and shrimp.

Range throughout the tropics, most numerous over coral reef bottoms.

● **WIDOW ROCKFISH**   *Sebastodes enomelas*
Also called Widow Rock Cod, Widow, Zipola,
Viuva. Average length 6 inches; largest 14 inches.
Dusky, olive-tan above, becoming creamy or
whitish below, everywhere tinged with reddish or
pink. Edible.
Five pairs of lower spines on head, one near
nostrils. Small mouth with lower projecting jaw.
Second anal spine is noticeably longer than third.

● **TREEFISH**   *Sebastodes serriceps*
Also called Gopher, Gopher Rock Cod.
Average length 6 inches; largest 14 inches;
edible. Dark olive above shading to yellowish below. Has 6 to 8 black bands across body. Tinged
with red on front and lower part of body.

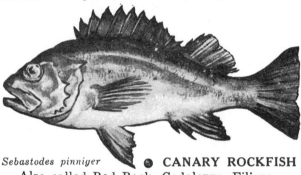

Sebastodes pinniger   ● **CANARY ROCKFISH**
Also called Red Rock, Codalarga, Filione.
Average size 9 inches; largest 30 inches; edible.
Olive-gray blotched with orange or yellow
above; becoming white below. Occasionally a black
blotch at different places on the body. Fins bright
orange. Distinguished from Vermillion Rockfish in
that the scales under jaw of this fish are smooth to
touch, whereas in the Vermillion they are rough.

● **VERMILLION
ROCKFISH**   *Sebastodes miniatus*
Also called Red Rock Cod, Salmon Grouper,
Red Snapper, Bar Rancho, Barrachon, Racha.
Average length 12 inches; largest 36 inches;
edible. Vermillion above shading to pink on sides
and light red below. Black dots on back. There are
three obscure orange stripes radiating from the
eye. Lining of mouth red.
The lower jaw projects slightly and has a knob
on the end. Three pairs of lower spines above the
eyes.

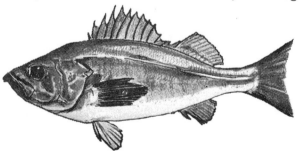

● **CHILIPEPPER**   *Sebastodes goodei*
Also called Rock Cod, Red Rock Cod.
Average length 10 inches; largest 22 inches;
edible. Pinkish-red on top, shading to pink below.
A narrow pink stripe extends the length of the
body at the lateral line.
Identified by a broad convex space between the
eyes. There are no spines on top of the head. Has a
projecting lower jaw. The lining of abdomen is
white, with black dots. This is the most important
of the Rockfish family.

● **CHINA ROCKFISH**   *Sebastodes nebulosus*
Also called Cefalutano, Gopher, Gopher Rock
Cod.
Average size 8 inches; largest 16 inches; edible.
Blackish to blue-black. Speckled everywhere
with yellowish to whitish dots, tinged with blue.
Usually found in waters too deep for sports
fishermen.

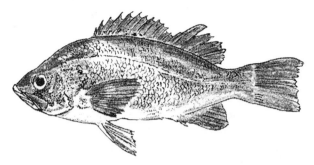

● **BLACK ROCKFISH** *Sebastodes melanops*

Also called Black Rock Cod, Bluefish, Black Bass, Cherna, Negro. Average size 9 inches in length; largest 20 inches. Edible. Back almost solid black, becoming paler on sides, ranging to dirty white below with dark fins.

Identified by broad convex space between the eyes. Different from the Priestfish, which is erroneously called Black Rockfish because of all white abdominal cavity.

● **BLACK-AND-YELLOW ROCKFISH**
Sebastodes chysomelas

Average size 6 inches; largest 15 inches, edible. Highly prized. Dark olive-brown to black above, shading to yellow below. Obscure dark stripes radiate from eyes. Has five pairs of strong spines above the eye. The broad pectoral fins have thick rays. A rarity of the Rock Cods, and seldom found in any quantity. Exceptionally fine food.

● **STARRY ROCKFISH** *Sebastodes constellatus*

Also called Spotted Rock Cod, Chinafish, Scacciatle, Red Rock Cod. Orange to vermillion, shading into yellowish below. Sometimes has brownish blotches. Body is covered with many small dots.

Native to the Pacific.

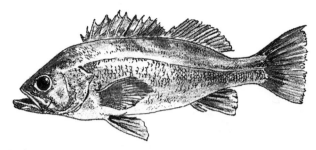

● **YELLOWTAIL ROCKFISH** *Sebastodes flavidus*

Also called Yellowtail, Rock Cod, Gialota.

Average length 8 inches; largest, 24 inches. Edible. Grayish-brown on top, shading to white below. Sides finely spotted with yellow. Caudal fin is yellow.

Noticeable projecting lower jaw and convex space between the eyes are identifying features.

Native to Pacific, Vancouver Island to lower California.

● **GREEN-SPOTTED ROCKFISH**
Sebastodes chlorostictus

Also called Red Rock Cod, Bolina, Chucklehead, Cernie, Chinafish. Average length 6 inches; largest 15 inches; edible.

Identified by pink flesh color above, becoming whitish below. Fins are pink. Irregular yellowish-green splotches on back. Has knob at tip of lower jaw. Six pairs of spines on top of head.

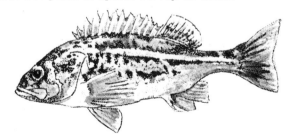

● **GREENSTRIPED ROCKFISH** *Sebastodes elongatus*

Also called Red Rock Serena, Rainha, Strawberry Rock. Average length 5 inches; largest on record 12 inches. Edible. Green basic color, suffused with pink or red. Four green irregular horizontal stripes, with lower part of the body becoming white. A slender-bodied fish. There are three spines on top of the head. The lateral line of pale pink.

Not too common and represents a small part of the catch in the Pacific.

71

Sea Bass Family

● **BLACK SEA BASS**   *Centropristes striatus*

Also called Bass, Black Will, Blackfish, Bluefish, Black Harry, Hannabill, Black Perch, Rock Bass, Rockfish, Talywag. Average size 2 pounds, largest on record 8 pounds, caught by H. R. Rider, Nantucket Sound, in May, 1951. Food value good. Flesh soft, will not keep long without ice.

Mottled black, interspersed with lighter colored white markings.

They are caught mostly on patches of rock surrounded by grass bottom, often in large numbers around wrecks. Sometimes as deep as 250 feet.

Method of angling is still fishing with lead and hook rigged as for Grouper or bottom fish.

They eat barnacles, crabs, small fish, shrimp or most anything, any type of cut bait is suitable. No artificial lures are successful fishing for these fish.

● **GOLDEN-STRIPED BASS**   *Grammistes sexlineatus*

Also called Pigmy Grouper, Little Big Mouth.

Average weight half pound; largest on record 4 pounds; food value, good. Difficult to eliminate bones in preparation.

A dwarf Grouper found in the coral reefs where Red and Black Grouper are plentiful. A very common fish in the islands of Pacific and about reefs of Caribbean. Has six golden stripes on a nearly black background. These stripes increase in number as the fish grows larger and on the largest fish might number a dozen.

● **KELP BASS**   *Paralabrax clathratus*

Also called Rock Bass, Cabrilla.

Average weight slightly less than a pound; largest on record 6 pounds; food value, excellent.

Mottled bluish-black on top, shading off to white on belly. Has a typical square tail of the Sea Bass but without the soft appendage of the Atlantic Sea Bass.

Kelp Bass are quite common on the Pacific Coast and rarely found on the Atlantic, however occasional specimens have been taken. They spend their time in the kelp and sea grass beds of the ocean, feeding on smaller fish and such shell fish as might be attached to grass and rocks.

Many experts consider the Kelp Bass as the Pacific equivalent of the Atlanic Sea Bass. Both species have the same soft flesh and almost identical flavor.

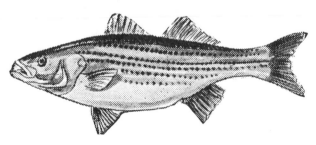

● **STRIPED BASS**   *Roccus saxatilis*

Also called Greenhead, Linesides, Squid Hound, Rock Bass, Rockfish, Striper, White Bass.

Average weight, inside waters, 5 pounds; in the ocean 15 pounds; largest on record, hook and line, 73 pounds, caught in Vineyard Sound, Mass., Aug. 17, 1913 by C. B. Church. Excellent Food.

Greenish-olive on back, shading into greenish-silver on sides with brassy cast and light silver on belly, dark horizontal stripes of a greenish cast run from head to tail just below lateral line.

A leading game fish of both Atlantic and Pacific Coasts. No matter what the fishing, the Striped Bass will go for the bait. Equally popular in plug casting or fly fishing, the Stripers are game to the core. They like worms, crabs, mullet, shrimp, clams, squid or eels and will strike most any natural looking artifical bait. Like Channel Bass they run mostly in swash channels and mouths of rivers.

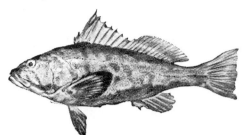

● **SAND BASS**   *Paralabrax nebulifer*

Also called Johnny Verde.

Average length 8 inches; largest 20 inches; edible. Greenish-gray with traces of irregular vertical dusky bands on side of body; under parts white or pale gray.

Region below the eye has small round golden spots. Distinguished from Kelp Bass by the spiny portion of dorsal, higher than rayed part. Three spines at anal fin front edge. Found over sandy bottom, or in bays.

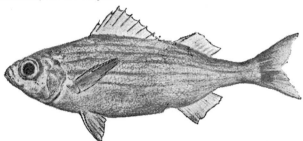

● **SALEMA**   *Xenistius californiensis*

Also called Big-eye Bass.

Average length 8 inches; largest 14 inches; edible.

Blue to green with iridescent reflections above, becoming silvery on sides and belly; 6 to 8 orange-brown horizontal stripes on sides and belly.

A fish on the rare side, taken only occasionally on hook and line, chiefly in spring and summer, mostly off the California coast in the vicinity of San Diego.

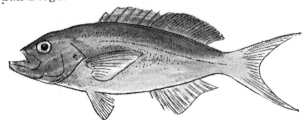

● **CREOLE FISH**   *Paranthias furcifer*

Also called Rabirubia, Catalufa.

Average weight 12 ounces; largest on record 3 pounds; food value, good.

Bright red with three small violet spots. Sides faint oblique streaks. Dorsal has longitudinal blackish streak.

Found in southern waters, both Atlantic and Pacific. Feed in small schools several feet above reefs, dart away to hide at first approach of danger —making any catch rare.

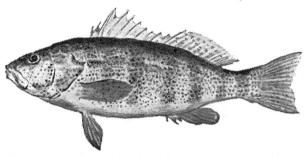

● **SPOTTED SAND BASS** *Paralabrax maculatofasciatus*

Largest on record 8 lb. 12 oz. caught by Harvey L. Simms fishing on Brushy Creek, Alabama, July 12, '68.

Greenish or olive-brown above, becoming whitish below. Has 6 vague dusky bars extending down the sides from the back. Small brownish spots cover the head, fins and body.

Spiny and soft portions of dorsal fins being connected. Third spine appreciably longer than rest.

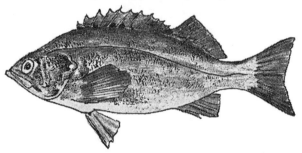

● **BLUE ROCKFISH**   *Sebastodes mystinus*

Also called Black Rockfish, Priestfish, Black Rock Cod, Blue Perch, Nervi, Black Snapper, Black Bass.

Average length 8 inches; largest 20 inches; fine eating. Slaty or bluish-black on upper body; lower body is paler with white belly. Intermittent lighter and darker blotches on sides. Body cavity has a solid black lining. Identified by broad convex space between the eyes. Important sport fish on Pacific coast.

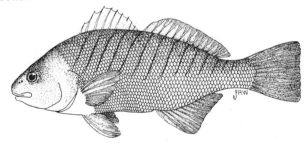

● **SPOT**   *Leiostomus xanthurus*

Also called Lafayette.

Average size 8 inches; largest on record 3 pounds; food value, good. Brownish-silver color with a head like a Croaker and a spot just behind the gill edge; has light diagonal stripes.

Prefers sandy bottoms of Gulf of Mexico.

73

Sea Bass

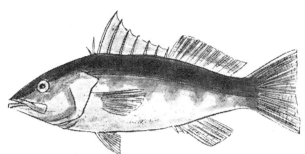

● WHITE SEA BASS *Cynoscion nobilis*

Also called Catalina Salmon, Pacific Squeteague, Sand Bass, Sea Trout.

Average weight 20 pounds; largest on record, 83 pounds and 12 ounces, caught near San Felipe, Mexico by L. C. Baumgardner, March 31, 1953.

Steel-blue above, shading into silvery-blue on upper sides. Sides silvery and white below.

Identified by lower projecting jaw. The largest and most important of the Croaker family.

As a gamefish, this fish ranks high on the list. A native of the Pacific coast, specimens have been found in many waters of the world including the Gulf of Mexico. Although universally dubbed a "Bass" this fish is really not a Bass but a Weakfish. It is a west coast edition of the Sea Trout.

These fish are caught mostly trolling and they are found around the edge of seaweed or kelp beds. By keeping in hiding themselves, they dart out like a Barracuda when a trolled bait passes.

They feed on Herring, Anchovies, Flyingfish, Sardines and other small bait fish. Like all fish of their family they also like shrimp.

Spoons, squids, feathered jigs and strip bait are considered best.

Found usually in fairly shallow water and native to the warm waters of the western hemisphere. Most plentiful in southern California.

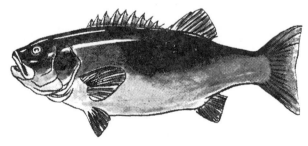

● GIANT SEA BASS *Stereolepis gigas*

Also called Black Sea Bass, Giant Bass, California Black Bass, Pacific Jewfish, California Jewfish.

Average size 200 pounds; largest on record 551 pounds, caught by G. Pangorakis, Galveston Bay, in June, 1937. Food value good.

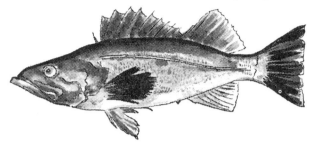

● BOCACCIO *Sebastodes paucispinis*

Also called Rock Cod, Grouper, Salmon Grouper.

Average weight 3 pounds; largest on record 18 pounds. Good food fish.

Olive to dusky brown on top, shading into dull orange, reddish on the sides, then pale pink to white below. Flushed throughout with red. Sometimes black splotches on body.

Identified by broad convex space between the eyes; a greatly projecting lower jaw.

One of the most important fish and the best known of the Rockfish on the California Coast.

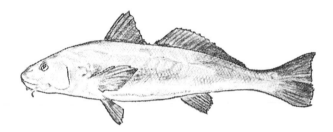

● CALIFORNIA CORBINA *Menticirrhus undulatus*

Also called California Whiting, Corvina, Surf Fish. Average length 18 inches; largest 20 pounds; edible; sooty-gray to steel-blue on back, shading to gray on sides and white below; fins dusky.

Tip of snout projects beyond tip of lower jaw; short fleshy barbel at tip of lower jaw; has large pectoral fins. A popular gamefish taken almost entirely in the surf, using sand crabs for bait. A bottom fish found on sandy beaches.

Native to California coast.

● ORANGEMOUTH CORVINA *Cynoscion xanthulus*

Also called Yellow Mouth or Yellowfin Corvina. Average size 14 to 18 inches weighing ¾ to 4 lbs.

There is some confusion regarding the name Corbina vs. Corvina. The Orangemouth Corvina is found only in the Gulf of California and the Salton Sea. Col. James E. Long, Sr., reports the Salton Sea was stocked with these fish and that the largest verified catch was 27½ lbs. taken by Leonard Johnson of Victorville, on May 26, 1968

Salton Sea Corvina have a different color, being of a bronze hue, due to color of water of Salton Sea. Gulf of California Corvina vary from steel blue on back to white on belly. Both fish have distinctive yellow mouth and yellow fins.

Pacific Coast Favorites

MALE

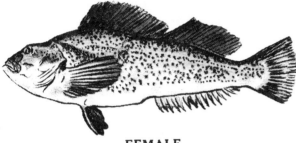

FEMALE

● **KELP GREENLING**   *Hexagrammos decagrammus*
Also called Rock Trout, Rockfish, Bluefish.
Average size 8 inches; largest 20 inches. Edible.
Brownish or grayish of various shades, sometimes with a slate-blue ground color. Female has round reddish-brown spots. Male has zigzag markings.
Long dorsal fin has 21 spines. No canine teeth are present. Another identifying mark is the presence of five lateral lines.
A very desirable sports fish, taken at irregular intervals all year from waters of the Pacific, Mexico to Alaska.

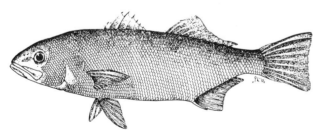

● **QUEENFISH**   *Scriphus politus*
Also called Kingfish, Herring, Tomcod, Shiner, Sea Trout. Average length 6 inches; largest 12 inches; edible.
Bluish above, shading into silvery on sides and underparts. Fins yellowish; base of pectorals dusky.
Large lower jaw projects slightly beyond tip of upper; two widely separated dorsal fins, which identifies it from all other Croakers. Has no barbels on lower jaw.
Usually caught from piers or boats in shallow water. Shiners or cut bait are used. Most plentiful in the vicinity of Los Angeles, California.

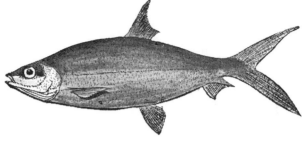

● **MILKFISH**   *Chanos chanos*
Also called Awa.
Average size 24 inches; largest on record not known; food value, good.
Silvery in color, snout depressed, no teeth.
Has wide distribution. Found on sandy shores, mostly on the Pacific. Known from Arctic to the Hawaiian Islands and to the Indian Ocean.

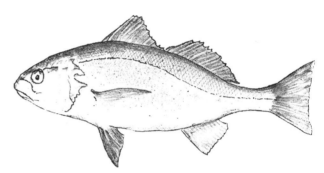

● **WHITE CROAKER**   *Genyonemus lineatus*
Also called Tomcod, Shiner, Herring, Carbinette, Chenfish, Kingfish.
Average weight 10 ounces; largest 13 inches; edible. Silvery with brassy luster, becoming lighter below; faint wavy lines follow rows of scales backwards; fins, except ventrals, normally yellowish; small black spot at upper and inner corner of pectoral base.
Identified by several small barbels on lower jaw; front dorsal has 12 to 15 spines.
Taken by sportsmen with all types of bait and tackle. Large numbers are caught on the Southern California coast. A schooling fish roaming widely in warm waters.

● **NORTHERN ANCHOVY**   *Engraulis mordax*
Average size 12 inches; largest 18 inches. Edible.
Deep blue on back and sides, becoming abruptly silvery on belly.

Groupers

THE GROUPER FAMILY is a large and prolific one inhabiting the tropical and semitropical seas from Brazil to the Carolinas. They are considered one of the most important of American fishes and furnish a large quantity of the seafood served on American tables.

They range from the great Jewfish, weighing over 700 pounds to the Red Hind, averaging 2 pounds. Some members are active and others sluggish and slow-moving, some are dull-colored and others have brilliant markings. All are good to eat. Mostly they are taken by still fishing in deep water,

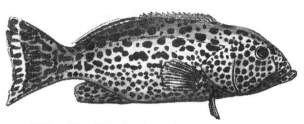

● **YELLOW-FIN GROUPER** *Mycteroperca venenosa*

Also called Rockfish, Bonaci, Spotted Grouper, Princess Rockfish.

Average size 6 pounds; largest on record 50 pounds, even, caught by an unidentified angler aboard the deep-sea fishing boat, "Admiral Too", out of Cortez, Fla.

Olive-green and bluish below. Sides and back blotched with light green. Body and head covered with orange-brown spots. Inside of mouth orange. Pinkish on breast. Fins edged with yellow.

The Rock Grouper, sometimes referred to as a separate species, is believed to be the same fish as the Yellow or Yellow-Fin. The Rock Grouper is usually caught in deeper water. Inasmuch as the only difference is coloration, this is a natural transition of depth.

These fish are caught on the Atlantic side of Florida mostly, ranging all the way from the Florida Keys to the northern boundary of South Carolina.

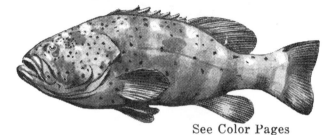

See Color Pages

● **JEWFISH** *Epinephelus itajara*

Also called Giant Sea Bass, Great Grouper.

Average size 50 pounds; largest on record, 735 pounds caught in Tampa Bay in 1958 by Jim Renner using a CO-2 speargun. Food value excellent, especially the smaller sizes. Brownish to black on top shading to yellow on the belly. Head and back covered with small black spots. Front half of dorsal low, back dorsal, rounded and shortly rayed.

The giant tackle buster hangs around old wrecks and pilings. Take any kind of bait.

While these giant fish are not usually classified as a "gamey" species they certainly provide opportunity for a fisherman to exert all his muscle to get one off the bottom. They immediately sulk when hooked and use all their energy in pulling straight down.

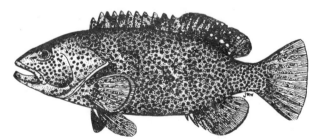

● **ROCK HIND** *Epinephelus adscensionsi*

Average weight 4 pounds; largest on record, 103 pounds even, caught by Phillip Stone, Tampa, Fla., while fishing on the "Flying Fisherman" out of Hubbard's Pier, Pass-a-Grille, Fla., April 23, 1967. He was fishing in the Gulf of Mexico at a depth of 128 feet.

Reddish-brown cast with olive blotches along sides and back; whitish blotches with pinkish cast over entire body. Head and lower part of body covered with orange spots. This is a valued food fish, commercially important and one of the most beautifully patterned of the Groupers. Primarily a reef fish.

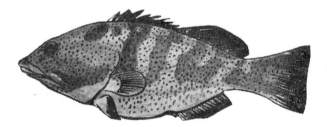

● **RED HIND** *Epinephelus guttatus*

Also called Calico Grouper, Coney Grouper, Polka Dot Grouper. Average size 2 pounds; largest on record, 67 lbs., caught by W. L. Bracknell, Miami, Fla., fishing in the Atlantic near Miami, on March 25, 1967. Excellent food.

Reddish-brown shading to darker on back and spotted all over with small scarlet dots. Fins lemon-olive and spotted. Tail-fin margin rather straight with rounded corners. Top of head narrow between the eyes. These fish are not too common on the Florida coasts, however they are found in both the Gulf and Atlantic waters.

The species is fairly abundant around Cuba and found in the markets of Havana in some quantity. They are usually caught in fairly deep waters, over the reefs.

The Groupers

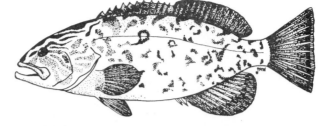

● GAG
Mycteroperca microlepis

Also called Black Grouper along Fla. West Coast.

Average size 5 pounds; largest on record not officially determined.

Brownish-gray, greenish tint. Sometimes uniform brownish over all. The dorsal fins are dusky green, edged in white. Black tail fin has bright blue patches and is edged in white. Ventral and pectoral fins dusky. Dorsal fins dark olive. Fish taken from shallow water will be of lighter color than those of deeper water.

The Gag is increasing in popularity with fishermen about the Florida Keys, where most of them are caught. These fish are not too plentiful anywhere.

Highly esteemed as a food fish, the off-shore, tourist fishing boat crews usually keep an eye out for these fish when they come aboard.

● SPECKLED HIND
Epinephelus drummondhayi

Also called Kitty Mitchell Grouper.

Average size 5 pounds; largest on record 55 lbs., caught by Richard H. Lash Sr., Jan. 21, 1967, in the Gulf of Mexico, off Mobile, Ala. Food value good.

A true Grouper with the shape of a Giant Grouper (Jewfish) yet miniaturized to the size of a large Snapper. The coloring is more elaborate than any other Grouper. A myriad of brownish, whitish and pink dots and dashes. The fins are identical to a Black Grouper.

This species is comparatively rare, appearing only at isolated areas. Most plentiful on the coral bottoms surrounding the Florida Keys and also found on the Snapper fishing grounds in the vicinity of Pensacola. Never in any quantity, but occasional strays are taken when Snapper fishing.

This speckled fish was once rejected in favor of the black or red snapper; then a Mrs. Kitty Mitchell found them to be delicious and requested that fishing captains bring the speckled to her boarding house. They did—tagging them with her name. So goes the story of how the fish got its name.

● SCAMP
Mycteroperca phenax

Average size 8 pounds; largest on record 17 lbs., caught by Richard H. Lash Sr., Panama City, Fla., Nov. 21, 1967, in the Gulf of Mexico near Southwest Pass of the Mississippi River. Food value excellent, considered the best by many experts; considered a rare catch on the Florida coast.

Probably the most treasured catch of the deep-sea fishermen, and always a prize when taken on the open party fishing boats in the Gulf of Mexico waters.

Some commercial fishing families who operate deep-sea fishing fleets — and a restaurant ashore, have capitalized on the delectability of the Scamp by having their fishermen save all of these fish to serve in the restaurant.

Most connoisseurs will agree that the Scamp is about the best food fish to come out of salt water, except possibly the Pompano.

● WARSAW GROUPER
Epinephelus nigritus

Average weight 20 pounds; largest on record 500 pounds, caught by Capt. Anderson of Panama City in 1961. Blackish in color when alive, turns brown when dead.

Usually caught in deep water. Fights strongly when hooked and darts for a rock hole, trying to stay in its pressure zone. When pulled up, the bladder inflates.

The Groupers

● BLACK GROUPER
Mycteroperca bonaci

Average size 8 pounds; largest on record 67 pounds, caught by Richard H. Lash Sr., Dec. 4, 1967, in the Gulf of Mexico, near Panama City, Fla. from the vessel Poly K., and reported by James L. Eason.

There are actually two related forms of the Black Grouper. One found in deep water and one in shallow water. The deep water fish is seldom seen and rarely enters the coastal waters.

Deep water fish have small dark patches, close set; shallow water fish have dark splotches, larger —and with a squarish shape.

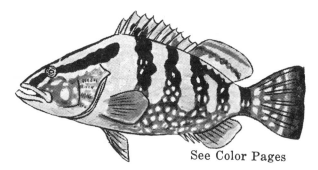

See Color Pages

● NASSAU GROUPER
Epinephelus striatus

Also called White Grouper, Gray Grouper, Rockfish.

Average weight 8 pounds; largest not officially known.

The Nassau Grouper is extremely variable in coloration. Ranges from solid white phases to solid grayish-brown phases. Most often found with four irregular, dark vertical bands on sides, each enclosing small whitish spots. There is a stripe starting at the snout and running through the eye to the base of the dorsal fin. Usually a square jet black patch at the root of the tail. All the fins are colored like the body, except the dorsal and tail fins which are bordered with a narrow pale yellow patch.

These fish are stubborn fighters, using their bulky weight to best advantages. Usually found in rock grottoes, but they are also seen over sandy bottom—and have the ability to change color to match any environment.

78

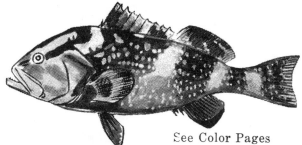

See Color Pages

● RED GROUPER
Epinephelus morio

Average size 6 pounds, largest on record, 35 pounds even, caught by Lt. Paul E. Liles, USN., Feb. 2, 1968, fishing in the Gulf of Mexico offshore from Pensacola. He used mullet for bait.

Olive-gray, clouded with pale olive, reddish jaws, salmon cast over body. Colors fade when they die.

This is the most common of all fish taken by fishing boats in the Gulf of Mexico. They bite readily and are caught in great numbers when a school is located. As a food fish the Red Grouper is a standby, comparable to commercial fish taken anywhere.

Typical bottom fish of the reefs, seldom, if ever rising to the surface. They have bladders that are adjusted to depths they inhabit and when hauled in these bladders often expand and burst. They offer little resistance when hooked and are not considered a "gamey" fish.

Most of these fish are caught off shore, but they are also taken in deep water channels in bays and harbors. While they prefer squid there is hardly any type of cut fish they will refuse.

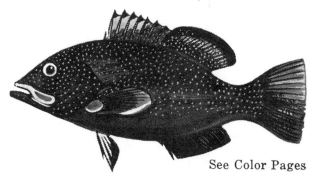

See Color Pages

● CONEY GROUPER
Cephalopholis fulva

Average size about 1 pound.

This is a fish with many color phases. Most important identification is the myriad spots covering the entire body and tail. The fish itself is on the dark reddish side and the spots yellowish. Often confused with the Red Hind.

Caught all year around in southern waters, but always a rarity.

Seldom, if ever, seen in the commercial markets, but often in mounted specimens, inasmuch as the colorful exterior makes a fine display. A very good food fish, matching the quality of the Red Hind.

Florida Grunts

THE GRUNT FAMILY is possibly one of the most numerous and useful of all the tropical fishes. Never sensational, they are the bread and butter of the fish world and always good to eat.

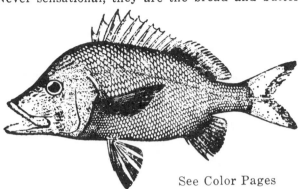

See Color Pages

● **WHITE GRUNT**   *Haemulon plumiere*
Also called Black Grunt, Boar Grunt, Boca Colorado, Cachicata, Ronco, Ronco Grande, Squirrelfish, Key West Grunt, Flannel-mouth Grunt.

Average size 1 pound; largest on record, 6 pounds; food value, good.

Bluish-gray above, with a light brownish cast, base of upper scales bright bronze. Numerous narrow, light clear-blue stripes on head. Inside of mouth colored bright reddish-orange.

This common White Grunt is the most numerous and important of all the Grunts. The name is derived from the ability to make a deep, muffled, grunting sound which can be heard some distance above water.

These fish ordinarily do not strike at artificial bait, but are caught at times on feathers and small spoons and plugs, trolled deep.

Still fishing is the best method of fishing, with cut bait on fairly large hook. Natural foods are shrimp, crabs, and all manner of small fish. They strike readily on cut bait.

● **COTTONWICK**   *Haemulon melanurum*
Also called West Indies Grunt; Comical Grunt; Caesar Grunt.

Average size 10 inches long; largest on record 13 inches, reported by W. H. Kroll, Key West Aquarium, Key West, Fla. Dec. 5, 1953.

Eyes are bright glossy blue, an unusual shade. Ground color of fish on sides is dark olive, almost black. The lateral line running from just above the mouth to tail is most prominent. Belly golden yellow. Mottled with silver at lower jaw and nose and above the anal fin. Tail is golden yellow, slightly edged with black. Native to the West Indies.

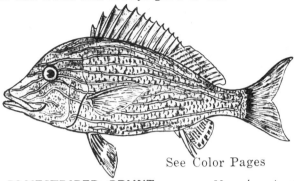

See Color Pages

● **BLUESTRIPED GRUNT**   *Haemulon sciurus*
Also known as Yellow Grunt, Blue Grunt.

Average length 8 inches; largest on record 23¼ inches; weight 8 pounds even. Girth 17 inches. Caught at Roosevelt Roads, Puerto Rico, June 3, 1966, by Mrs. E. O. Raulerson Jr. Edible.

Deep blue body color with narrow yellow stripes. Fins are dusky or nearly black. Inside of mouth is bright red.

This is one of the most plentiful of the Grunts. Ranking next to the White Grunt in numbers. Referred to by reef fishermen as the most accomplished of bait stealers. This because they are found in such quantities where larger hooks are used for the big-mouth Grouper.

They make a nice panfish and are worth while for anglers who are interested in spending the day on the fishing grounds and just like to catch something.

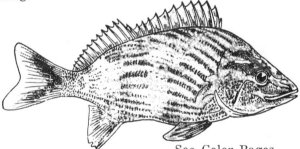

See Color Pages

●**FRENCH GRUNT**   *Haemulon flavolineatum*
Also called Yellowstriped Grunt, Open-mouthed Grunt, Ronco Contenado.

Average size 8 inches; largest 14 inches; food value, good.

Ground color gray-blue. Longitudinal yellow or brassy stripes above the lateral line. One stripe crosses the others running from the head to end of dorsal base. Fins bright yellow. Corner of mouth black. Black spot on gill cover.

They feed chiefly at night on small spineless fish. A choice meal for all gamefish, they spend most of their lives hiding out. Will grab at a baited hook, especially if it has a bit of clam or oyster as bait. Not very plentiful.

Found about coral patches and especially in vicinity of ledges and rock crevices in the ocean bottom.

 # Margates and Grunts

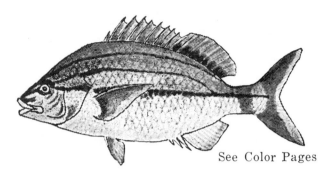

See Color Pages

● **MARGATE** *Haemulon album*

Also called Margaret Grunt, Marketfish. Red-mouth Grunt.

Average size 1½ pounds; largest on record 10 pounds; food value, good.

Usually a light pearl-gray, has longitudinal lines most distinct on upper sides. Fish may turn greenish when caught. Lips yellowish.

Usually a deep water fish, except when feeding. They like to pick up sea fleas and small crabs from the bottom. Are caught in large enough quantities for market, although not as good a fish as Grouper. Do not keep too well.

Still fishing is the only method of catching. They have a large mouth and take a good sized hook. Cut bait or shrimp.

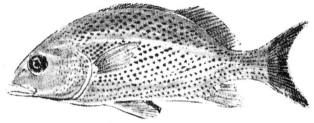

● **SPANISH GRUNT** *Haemulon macrostomum*

Also called Ronco Blanco, Ronco Prieto, Brown Grunt, Ronco, Bastard Margate.

Average size 2 pounds; largest on record 21 pounds; food value, good.

Gray with iridescence or shading. Scales have small brown spots which form wavy streaks below the lateral line. Black spot on gill cover. Fins dark gray. Mouth lining bright red.

They live in water fairly shallow, around reef bottoms. Found both in schools and singly. School mostly in summer, their spawning time. Quite often taken about channel inlets.

While they are good food, have a tendency to spoil quicker than other fish if not gutted when caught and placed on ice. These fish are quite plentiful around Key West and many fishermen call them Key West Grunts. Others refer to them as Red Mouth **Grunts.**

● **BLACK GRUNT** *Haemulon bonariense*

Also called Hoarse Muffle, Snorer, Blower, Corocoro.

Average weight 4 ounces; largest about 12 inches; edible.

Brownish above, fading to lighter below. Has typical Grunt mouth and big eye. One long spine on leading edge of anal fin. Usually 11 to 12 spines in dorsal. Spine section higher than rayed section, which is rounded on top.

A shallow water fish, most common along the coasts of Cuba.

Sold commercially, although not considered anything of a delicacy.

Native to West Indies and Florida Keys.

See Color Pages

● **BLACK MARGATE** *Anisotremus surinamensis*

Also called White Margate, Pompon.

Average size 2 pounds; largest on record 15 pounds and 8 ounces; caught by John R. Serna, Palm Bay, Fla. in Fort Pierce Inlet, April 6, 1966. Length 27¾ inches. Lure, yellow bucktail. Food value good.

Colors of Margates subject to rapid change. The Black Margate has heavy large scales, large eyes and dark markings on the body and fins. The general color is silvery. Margate Fish is usually very light, almost pearl-gray. Dark spots on the scales form wide spaced longitudinal lines, most distinct on upper sides.

Mostly a deep water fish, except they range into shallower reefs when feeding. Have all the characteristics of the Grunts in food. Will take most any bait readily.

Pinfish and Pigfish

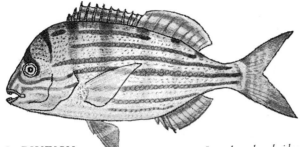

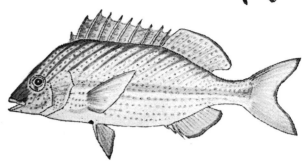

● **PINFISH**   *Lagodon rhomboides*

Also called Shiner, Sailors Choice, Bream, Cho-by, Chopa Sina, Porgy, Scup, Spanish Porgy.

Average weight 8 ounces, largest on record 3 pounds and 8 ounces, reported Nov. 11, 1929 by Arnold (Specs) Loher. Food value, fair. Colored by alternating bars of pale blues and yellows. Has distinctive black spot behind gill cover. A common fish found in quantities in all southern waters around grassy flats and about docks. Used extensively as a bait fish for Tarpon and Grouper fishing.

● **PIGFISH**   *Orthopristis chrysopterus*

Also called Piggie.

Average weight 12 ounces; largest on record, 4 pounds and 2 ounces, set by Emmett E. Baker, Laurinberg, N. C. Caught off Murrells Inlet, S. C., June 9, 1963, on a deep-sea fishing boat. Food value, good.

Usually a light blue and silver striped nose with brown spots on snout. Has a blue streak on side of upper lip. Mouth whitish inside. Dorsal fin spotted with bronze; tail yellow, dusky tipped.

A hardy fish and in ordinary conditions one of the most plentiful of panfish on the shores of the Gulf of Mexico. The fish which has a hundred uses, not the least of which is the finest Tarpon bait on the books.

● **SAILORS CHOICE**

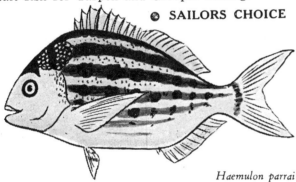

Haemulon parrai

Also called Ronco; Bastard Grunt.

Average weight 12 ounces; largest on record 3 pounds; food value, good. Especially noted because of a single spot. Other markings are changeable.

Common panfish of the Grunt family, caught in most all the inshore spots of gulf and ocean fishing.

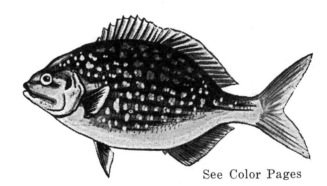

See Color Pages

● **BERMUDA CHUB**   *Kyphosus sectatrix*

Also called Rudderfish, Chopa.

Average weight 1 pound 8 ounces; largest on record 11 pounds and 14 ounces, caught off Jensen Beach by Anthony R. Letteriello and reported to John Crawford of Snook Nook Bait and Tackle, Jensen Beach, Fla., Nov. 28, 1962; food value good.

Vary in color, but generally dark with faint stripes on sides or checkered in a pattern of white and steel-gray. Have the ability to change color rapidly. It is possible to see this by watching the fish for a short time.

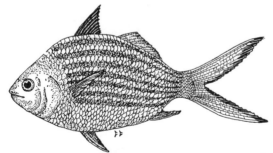

● **STRIPED MOJARRA**   *Diapterus plumieri*

Also called Sand Perch, Goat, Sand Brim, Irish Pompano.

Average size about 10 oz. going to around 2 lbs., reaches about a foot in length.

They are easily recognized by deeply forked tails. Little biological information on this species. Food value good, but a little on the bony side. Also used as bait.

A plentiful fish, especially in the waters of Atlantic, where great numbers of them gather on coral reefs. Sometimes considered as a gamefish in larger sizes and when hooked will put up a strong fight.

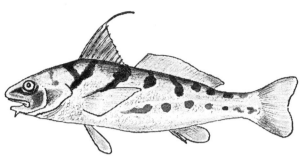

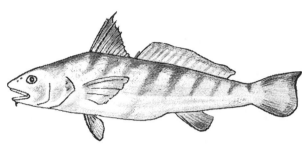

● **NORTHERN KINGFISH**   *Menticirrhus saxatilis*

Also called Northern Whiting.

Average size 1 pound; largest on record 5 pounds; food value, good.

Grayish-silver with irregular dark bars running obliquely forward and down, except the anterior bar which runs from nape backwards, forming v-shaped blotch.

This member of the "Three Whiting Brothers" ranges farther north than the Southern Kingfish, though area overlaps to a great extent; Southern Kingfish range from New York to Texas; Northern from New York to Florida.

They are a bottom feeding fish, preferring crustaceans. Spend most of their time exploring gulf and ocean swash channels for food. This is where they are caught by surf fishermen.

Make a nice little gamefish to while away the hours until the big Reds or Blues come along.

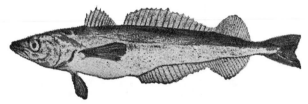

● **PACIFIC HAKE**   *Merluccius productus*

Also called Whitefish, Haddock, Butterfish, Mellusa, Mulsette.

Average length 12 inches; largest 36 inches; edible.

Metallic-blackish or silvery-gray above, shading to silvery below. Lining of mouth black.

Has two sets of dorsal fins, first is short and composed of spines. Second dorsal is matched by the anal fin, both deeply notched near the tail. No barbel on lower jaw. Loosely-attached scales.

A migratory fish traveling in large schools from Alaska to the Gulf of California. A Cod-like fish but not as good eating—coarse, watery flesh.

● **SILVER HAKE**   *Merluccius bilinearis*

Also called New England Hake or Whiting.

Similar in appearance and habits to Pacific Hake. Found from Newfoundland to Cape Cod, south as far as Bahamas, in deep water.

Average weight 4 lbs.; largest on record at Great Outdoors, 48 lbs., caught by Larry Keck, Brielle, N.J., March 17, '67, fishing off Brielle.

● **SOUTHERN KINGFISH**   *Menticirrhus americanus*

Also called Barb, Bermuda Whiting, Bullhead Whiting, Gulf Kingfish, Gulf Whiting, Sand Whiting, Sea Mink, Sea Mullet, Sea Smelt, Silver Whiting, King Whiting, Surf Whiting.

Average weight 14 ounces; largest on record 3 pounds.

Grayish-silver above, shading into lighter below. Belly white, marked with obscure shadings along back and sides which at times are in the form of bars. The entire body has a bronze cast.

This is the most important of the three principal species of Whiting found on the American Atlantic and Gulf coast. Ranges from New York to Texas and is plentiful in the South, known as Southern Whiting.

A bottom fish, they live on small shellfish. Frequent the same waters as Croakers and Channel Bass.

Caught mostly by surf casters. They are numerous in swash channels along the Gulf Beaches.

● **ATLANTIC TOMCOD**   *Microgadus tomcod*

Also called Frostfish.

Average weight 1½ pounds; largest on record 8 pounds; food value, good.

Olive or gray above, shading into yellowish below. Variegated splotches of coloring on sides. Found from Virginia to Labrador.

A young brother to the Cod and cousin to the Pacific Tomcod, *microgadus proximus*, which ranges from Alaska to Central California.

Can be caught with surf rigs. Also travel up into brackish water creeks. Not plentiful enough to be important commercially.

Croakers

IMPORTANT TO SPORTSMEN are the Croakers, without them the art of surf fishing would be unknown. Throughout the length and breadth of the American shore line, the Croakers leisurely explore the surf and adjacent channels. Because they are so handy to fishermen who like to have two feet on dry land, the Croaker is held in deep appreciation.

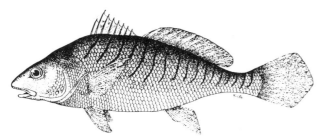

● **ATLANTIC CROAKER**   *Micropogon undulatus*

Also called Chut, Grunter, Crocus, Rocodina.

Average weight 1½ pounds; largest on record 6 pounds; food value, excellent.

Brassy above, lighter below, middle part of body has short irregular, dusky, vertical bars crossing the lateral line. Many dark brown spots on side of back, irregularly placed.

The Croakers derive their name from the peculiar croaking sound made by both males and females.

They are usually found on sandy bottom in swash channels near the beaches, beyond the line of breakers. Inlets and lagoons are favorite places.

● **BLACK CROAKER**   *Cheilotrema saturnum*

Also called Chinese Croaker, Surf Fish, Black Perch, Blue Bass, Black Bass.

Average size 7 inches; largest 15 inches; edible.

Bluish or dusky with coppery reflection above; silvery below with dark specks; vague pale band across body from front of second dorsal to ventral fins.

Identified by extension of snout over lower jaw. Has no barbels on lower jaw, two stout spines at front of anal fin.

A sports fish, although not plentiful. Illegal to sell commercially. Taken usually from piers or in bays.

Native to Pacific, mostly around the Mexican coast.

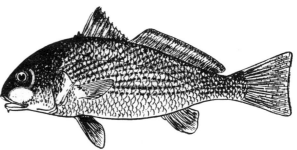

● **YELLOWFIN CROAKER**   *Umbrina roncador*

Also called Yellow-finned Roncador, Yellowtail.

Average size one pound; largest on record 3 lbs., 13½ ounces, 21 inches, caught by John Bringleman, Jacksonville, Fla., Aug. 1965. Food value good.

Metallic-brassy and silvery reflections. Usually found on shallow, sandy shores, in the gulf and ocean swash channels along the beaches. Fairly common in the Pacific, south of San Diego.

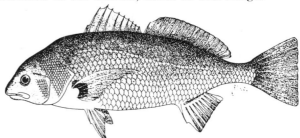

● **SPOTFIN CROAKER**   *Roncador stearnsii*

Also called Spot, Surf Fish, Golden Croaker.

Average weight one pound; largest on record, 5 pounds, 3 ounces, caught by Col. LeRoy Lester, Palm Bay, Fla., Dec. 9, 1964, surf fishing 10 mi. south of Indialantic, Fla. Native to both coasts of U. S.

Grayish-silver with bluish luster above, becoming silvery below. Sometimes distinctly golden or brassy.

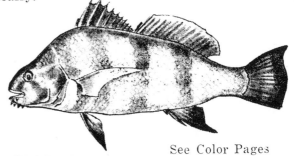

See Color Pages

● **BLACK DRUM**   *Pogonias cromis*

Average weight 9 lbs.; largest reported to Great Outdoors, 115 lbs., caught by Gene Perkins of East St. Louis, Ill., in Tampa Bay near Safety Harbor, Fla., Jan. 8, '67.

Only small fish considered edible. When taken in bays the Drum is dusky with indistinct stripes. Adults in gulf, silvery with dark bands. The Drum has barbels on lower jaw.

American Food Fish

THE TABLES OF AMERICA are supplied with seafood, mostly from the sea species of deep water fish. They are caught by the millions and sold by the tons from nearly every port of America.

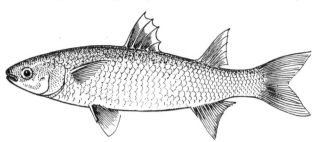

● STRIPED MULLET   *Mugil cephalus*

Also called Jumping Mullet; in Fla., Black Mullet. Another Mullet closely resembling this Mullet is the White Mullet *Mugil curema* which lacks the stripes and is more silvery in color—and does not compare in size.

Average size 2 pounds; largest on record 23 pounds, caught by Alonzo Regar, Tampa, Fla., in the Gulf of Mexico off Clearwater, Fla., 1953. Food value, excellent.

Caught mostly by commercial fishermen. Large numbers are taken annually in nets and sold throughout the markets of the United States. They are vegetarians and live exclusively on grasses. Instead of a stomach as most fish have, the Mullet has a gizzard comparable to that of a chicken.

● ATLANTIC HERRING   *Clupea harengus*

Average size 10 inches; largest on record 18 inches; food value, good.

Bluish, silvery below with bright reflections.

The Herring is considered the most important food fish of the Atlantic. Statisticians of the Atlantic coasts estimate the annual catch to exceed three billion fish. The catching affords occupation to immense fleets of boats.

Fishing for Herring is chiefly by means of brush weirs, gillnets and torching. Of the three, gillnetting is the most popular. Torching for Herring is primitive and effectual only in cool weather.

The method is to fix a light in the bow of a small boat which is moved through the water at a steady pace. The fish will rise to the light and a dipnet wielded from behind the light will scoop up the fish. The light is also used to lure the fish into weirs for that type of fishing.

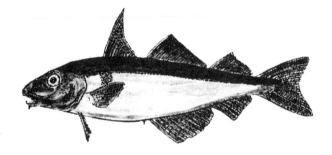

● HADDOCK   *Melanogrammus aeglifinus*

Also called Egrefin, Haddie, Schellfisch.

Average weight 4 pounds; largest on record 25 pounds; food value, good.

Dark or purplish-gray above, becoming paler towards belly then pearly-gray or white. Copperish or pink over sides. Black lateral line running from head to tail. A deep water fish found on both coasts of the North Atlantic. Usually not farther south than Hatteras. This is the "Finnan Haddie" of the commercial world and is of much more interest to commercial fishermen than sportsmen.

Usually found in depths exceeding 60 feet. Taken mostly by hand lines such as Grouper are taken in the Gulf of Mexico. A heavy sinker is needed to keep the bait down and hold it against the bottom currents. They feed on crabs and other crustaceans. Will not take lures.

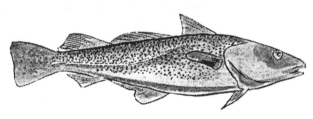

● ATLANTIC COD   *Gadus morhua*

Also called Bank Cod, Black Cod, Shore Cod, Cod, School Cod.

Average 12 lbs.; largest on record, 98 lbs., length 63 inches. reported to Great Outdoors by George Fleming of Ridgefield Pk., N.J. Alphonse Bielevich fishing with two companions in a 25 ft. boat off Island of Shoals, N. H., using a 20-lb. test line, boated this fish after a 30-min. fight. Cods over 200 lbs. have been taken commercially in trawls.

This has been an important and well-known staple food fish from the days of the early colonies. It is not classed as a gamefish though thousands of persons do go after them in party boats off the middle and north Atlantic coast.

They feed on crabs and shrimp or most anything which they come across. They are not an artificial lure fish. although they have been known to strike such baits as River Runt and Vamp.

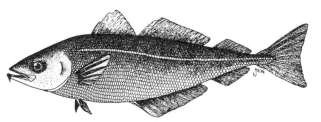

● POLLOCK   *Pollachius virens*

Also called Green Cod, Quoddy Salmon, Sea Salmon, Boston Bluefish.

Average weight 5 pounds; largest on record 42 lbs., even; 4 feet, 4 inches length, 39 inches girth, caught near Scituate, Mass., Aug. 13, 1960, by Francis C. Ward. Food value just fair.

Dark greenish-blue above, shading into lighter greenish sides with a silvery cast, silvery below. White or light-colored lateral line running from head to tail.

While the Pollock has never been regarded as an important gamefish and always has provided bulk in commercial fishing operations at great depth, in recent years fishermen of the Atlantic coast have discovered that they can be taken on artificial lures, by trolling. This is in the spring when they appear in large numbers off the Long Island coast. When in the schools, the fish strike fast and furiously at trolled lures.

They feed principally on smaller fish, but most of the year live near the bottom, feeding on crustaceans.

Best lures are strip bait, squid or feather jig.

● ATLANTIC STURGEON   *Acipenser oxyrhynus*

Average size 3 feet; largest on record, 1,500 pounds. caught in the Snake River near Pavette, Idaho in 1911 by Nephi Purcell. Food value fair. (New record announced in 1966 by Field & Stream).

Covered with bony plates. Mouth under snout is equipped to gather food off the bottom. Two barbels.

This is the famous fish which produces caviar. Known in every state of the eastern seaboard from the Florida rivers to Canada.

The Atlantic Sturgeon is the living reminder of what happens to fish when they are destroyed by man. When the white man came to America the rivers were teeming with Sturgeon. They have been fished out to such extent that today the fish is considered a rarity.

Spend much of their time in salt water, but come into the fresh water streams to spawn. Most noticed in Florida in the West Coast rivers and on the Atlantic from South Carolina to Maine.

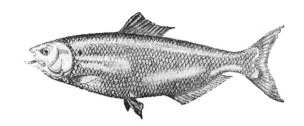

● AMERICAN SHAD   *Alosa sapidissima*

Average weight 3 pounds; largest on record 13 pounds, 8 ounces; food value, excellent.

Bluish above, sides silvery-white; a dark spot behind opercle.

The Shad is one of America's popular food fishes. At one time they were so numerous as to completely fill streams of the Atlantic coast they entered to spawn in the spring. Curiously the males enter the rivers first, then followed by the females. They seldom eat until the eggs are dropped, after that will strike at flies or any type of lures resembling insects.

Some experts claim the American Shad and the Alabama Shad, common to the Gulf of Mexico, are the same species; however, Jordan and Everman state the Alabama Shad (identified in Freshwater Section) are slightly different and give them their own species name; *Alosa alabamae*.

They spend most of their time in the ocean and make their annual runs up and down the coast, appearing in Florida earliest, usually in December. Because these fish faced extinction by over commercial fishing the government has developed new methods of artificial propagation and the fish are now holding their own.

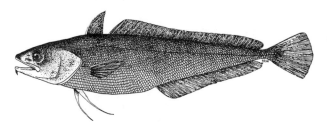

● SOUTHERN HAKE   *Urophycis floridanus*

Also called Ling.

Average size 12 inches; food value, good.

A native of the Gulf of Mexico, but also closely resembling Earl's Ling, Boston Ling and Squirrel Ling, specimens which are very similar.

Feeds on muddy bottoms in the shrimp beds. Active mostly at night.

 # Champion Game Fish

GAMEFISH, PRAISED WITH LOFTY WORDS, are the Tarpon and Bonefish. They have fighting hearts and their game qualities support millions of dollars worth of fishing tackle factories. But as food, only a starving ship-wrecked sailor could **eat one.**

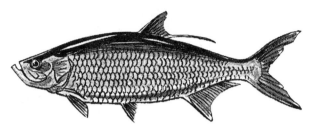

◉ TARPON
Megalops atlanticus

Also called Silverking, Silverfish, Grande Escaille, Sabalo, Savalle, Savavila, Tarpun, Camaripugucus.

Average weight 68 lbs. This game-fish—star of Florida tournaments, reaches a length of 8 ft. and a weight of around 350 lbs.

They have a lung-like air bladder which enables them to take in air from the atmosphere. Extremely prolific; one female may contain more than 12 million eggs. Found from North Carolina (occasionally further north) southward, on both sides of the Atlantic.

Bluish on back, shading to brilliant silver on sides, occasionally with a trace of yellow about fins. Fish taken from clear gulf waters are much brighter than those caught in rivers, some of the latter are classed as "Gold Tarpon" due to tannic acid in the water staining the silver of the scales to a golden color.

At the strike, in deep water, they leap so high as to clear a full sized cabin cruiser. In the course of a battle to subdue a Tarpon the fish will leap from six to twelve times.

This is one of the world's greatest gamefishes, caught on the open waters of gulf and ocean, backwaters and bays and inlets and in the deep waters of harbors in the great ports of the Gulf Coast.

They are caught on a wide variety of baits and by a wide variety of methods. In some areas best method is to troll with a live crab; in other spots casting with a live pinfish is the accepted method. In inland waters a dead fish on a large hook lying on the bottom is all you need to hook the largest of the inland gamefishes.

No matter how they are hooked, the fight is the same. Leaping and cavorting in the water like an enraged demon from the deep.

The Tarpon is not a food fish, sharing the attribute of most gamefishes. The Tarpon is a scavenger as well as a gamefish and the flesh of this beautiful fish can be as foul as the food he often feeds on.

Most exciting of Tarpon fishing is that of the inlets and waterways of the Everglades, where the young Tarpon are found. Here the impish youngsters will hit a fly, a bug, or any well handled lure—and furnish the thrill of a lifetime as you match wits with the fresh and vigorous youngsters, usually in the 10 to 25-pound class.

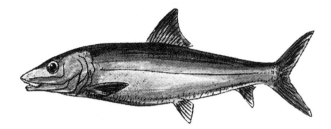

● BONEFISH
Albula vulpes

Also called Banana Fish, Grubber, Macabi.

Average size 5 lbs., largest on record, 19 lbs., 39 inches long; 17 inch girth, caught by Brian W. Batchelor, Zululand, South Africa, May 26, 1962. Not considered edible.

Burnished silver sides which reflect sunlight much as polished silver. Darker olive tinge on back.

This fish is in a distinct class by itself. A world-famous shallow water gamefish which has lured anglers from all over the world to the bottoms where they might be found. Many experts consider them the fastest of all gamefish. This is because they are hunted particularly and the correct weight tackle can be used to fish for them.

They are most prevalent on the flats of the Florida Keys. To catch one it is necessary to stalk it in a small boat, silently. They are always observed before the angler presents a bait.

Casting is practically the only method of fishing for these true gamefish. Live bait is used almost exclusively, although some experts have developed a fly fishing technique. They feed on crabs and shrimp and bait used is conch, crawfish and similar bottom baits.

● LADYFISH
Elops saurus

Also called Ten Pounder, Banana Fish, Flip Flap, Big-eyed Herring, Horse Mackerel, Bonefish, Silverfish, Chiro, Skipjack Macabi.

Average weight 2 pounds; largest on record 12 pounds; food value, poor.

Olive-green on back, shading off to glittering silver sides and white underneath.

This is one of the true gamefish, although it never has received the attention from anglers which is deserved. Without exception it is one of America's greatest gamefish for its size.

Strictly a light tackle fish, the "Lady" will strike vigorously at any artificial lure and jump high in the air the second it feels the prick of the hook.

Sportsman's Favorites

See Color Pages

● **BLUEFISH**　　　*Pomatomus saltatrix*

Also called Blue Snapper, Flatback, Tailor, Greenfish, Skip Mackerel, Snapping Mackerel.

Average weight 2 pounds; largest on record, 24 pounds and 3 ounces, caught near San Miguel, Azores, August 27, 1953 by M. A. da Silva Beloso. Excellent eating.

True to its name the Bluefish is a greenish iridescent blue shading off to silver at the sides. The pectoral fin is gray-black at the base.

The Bluefish is the only one of its kind in the family. Which is probably just as well, for they are the most gluttonous fish in the water, often referred to as a fin-covered chopping machine.

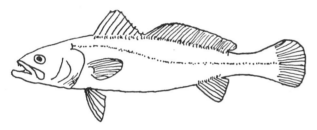

● **WEAKFISH**　　　*Cynoscion regalis*

Also called Squeteague, Summer Trout, Salt water Trout, Silver Trout.

Average size 2 pounds; largest on record 19 pounds and 8 ounces, measuring 3 feet, 1 inch length and with 23¾-inch girth, caught near Trinidad, West Indies, April 13, 1962 by Dennis B. Hall. Food value good.

Dark on back, changing to silvery below. Soft flesh and easily torn mouth. Very similar to Spotted Sea Trout except without the spots.

Although they bear no relation actually to the fresh water Trout, similarity of color patterns has been the cause of naming of this species of fish in common parlance, "Sea Trout".

The name "Weakfish", also is no indication of the strength or fighting ability of this fish. The name applies to the mouth, which is delicate and tender — and a heavy-handed angler can easily tear the hook out when a strike is felt.

The Weakfish in general is found in northern waters and his brother, (or at least first cousin) the Spotted Weakfish, is taken in abundance in southern waters.

They will take most properly handled artificial lures and especially live shrimp, which is the bait most fishermen use.

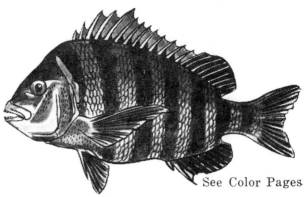

See Color Pages

● **SHEEPSHEAD**　　　*Archosargus probatocephalus*

Also called Convict Fish, Sardo Raiado.

Average size 2 lbs.; largest on record 15 lbs. 4 oz. caught by James J. Percival, Hanahan, S. C., fishing in Trident Tournament, Sept. '69. Reported by R. M. Fabian of Charleston.

A deep compressed body with 12 or 13 black and white alternating vertical stripes along sides from top to bottom.

The Sheepshead is a popular and well known salt water fish, deriving its name from the resemblance of its teeth to that of a sheep. The powerful jaws and strong teeth used to clip the bait in quick bites make it a difficult fish to hook. This is probably one of the best known of the sport fishes caught along coastal fishing grounds.

Most unusual aspect of the sport of fishing for this species is hooking him in the first place. It is said that "you have to jerk before he bites." This is literally true. The expert Sheepshead angler has perfected a system to the point of true excellence in timing. To understand it one must visualize what is going on at the bait end of the line.

The Sheepshead, when he sees a baited hook (usually with small shrimp, small fiddler crab, oyster or best of all sea worm) descend to his area, he swims close by and watches.

After due meditation he moves close and nudges the bait with his nose, backing off a bit at the same time. This is when the amateur angler, feeling the touch, thinks he has a bite and yanks on the line.

The experienced angler holds still and counts. One, two, three—and then jerks ever so lightly. This is about the exact time the Sheepshead moves in again to taste the bait. The jerk here catches him in the lip. His teeth and mouth are solid bone, so if he had taken the hook, it is more than likely a good jerk would pull the hook out, without catching anything.

There is a trick to it, and a good one, but when you have mastered Sheepshead fishing, the action is great and the excitement of an interesting catch unmatched for size. A real Sheepshead fisherman is one that lives his lifetime and seldom mentions any other fish.

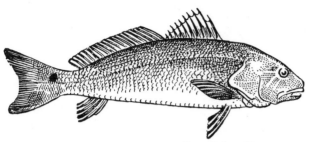

See Color Pages

● **RED DRUM**   *Sciaenops ocellata*

Also called Bar Bass, Reef Bass, Saltwater Bass, Red Bass, Sea Bass, Red Horse, Channel Bass, Redfish.

Average weight 8 pounds; largest on record, 83 pounds, caught by Zack J. Walters, Salisbury, Md., Sept., 1949. Food value excellent to 10 pounds; fair to 20 pounds; poor over that size.

Grayish, iridescent sides which shade to a copperish-red towards the back. As the fish grows larger it becomes red all over. A black spot about the size of half a dollar is always found at base of tail. Sometimes double spot or even triple.

● **DOLPHIN**   *Coryphaena hippurus*

Also called Dorado, Dourade.

Average size 8 pounds; largest on record, 87 pounds, 8 ounces, caught by Robert Kaiser of St. Petersburg, Fla., on a skin-diving expedition at Marathon, Florida Keys, August 15, 1966. Delicious as food.

Male: Iridescent bluish-gold, merging to blue-black on back. Back and sides covered with small purple spots. Fins and tail a golden yellow. Head of male differs from that of female in that it is high in forehead and comes down to lower jaw in almost a straight line. Female: Green-gold instead of bluish-gold, and head curves down to snout in an arc.

Dolphin is said to be the most beautiful of all gamefish and is considered the fastest fish that swims, regardless of size. Its gorgeous coloring is likened to a rainbow, which is most appropriate. They have been seen to out-swim a flyingfish, keeping pace in the water with the fish in the air.

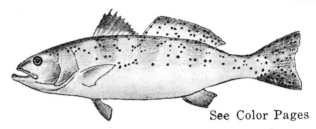

See Color Pages

● **SPOTTED SEATROUT**   *Cynoscion nebulosus*

Also called Spotted Squeteague, Speckled Trout, Weakfish.

Average weight 1 pound and 8 ounces; largest on record 15 pounds and 3 ounces, caught by C. W. Hubbard, Fort Pierce, Fla., in 1949. Excellent food fish.

Dark on back with bright black spots, changing to silvery below. Soft flesh and easily torn mouth which is the reason the fish are called Weakfish.

Mainstay of all southern coastal fishing is the Spotted Seatrout, or more widely known as Speckled Trout. They are good fish for the table, being on the lean side and fillet nicely. The skin is delicate and the scales easily scraped off.

Fishing seasons for these fish are quite pronounced. Best time of the year for larger sizes is from mid-September to the end of December. After the first of January they are hard to find. The large ones usually go into hibernation and the young ones are not interested in the grass flats, so they go up the rivers.

In the spring the middle of March and thru most of June, Trout fishing is again in the works. Fish are then scattered out over the grass flats and respond to casting with artificial lures—and are wonderful sport for a popping cork. Live shrimp is good anytime, anywhere.

After the first of July when the water warms up, it is best to forget the spotted babies. They get sluggish and don't care too much for food—and are often infected with worms, which is not good for food. The flesh is soft and nothing like as palatable as in cool weather.

Not until the first cool breezes of the fall should an angler go in search of Trout again.

While shrimp is undoubtedly the best bait under all conditions, other acceptable baits include small-cut minnows, clams, soft-shelled crabs, squid and eels such as used for fresh water bass are effective.

Artificial lures most used are the white jigs, which are cast out and "jumped" on the bottom to imitate a live shrimp. Many artificial lures are successful and can be had in all tackle shops. There are so many and varied as to cause confusion if listed here.

A popular artificial fishing method, not too widely known consists of the "trailed" lure. That is a standard floating lure which has attached to the tail hooks, a short leader and a small jig. This represents a small fish following a larger bait fish—and apparently fascinates the Trout.

Piscatorial Dynamite

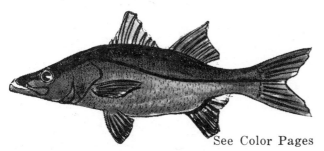

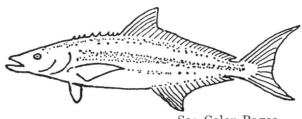

See Color Pages

● SNOOK
Centropomus undecimalis

Also called Robalo, Ravillia, Sergeant, Salt Water Pike, Sergeantfish.

Average size 5 pounds; largest on record 50 lbs., 8 ozs. J. W. Anderson, Panama, January, 1944.

Olivaceous on back shading into greenish-silver on sides above lateral line, silvery below. A pronounced black lateral line or stripe runs from top of gill cover to center of tail.

This is a salt water tackle buster of top rank. Take to artificial bait with a vim which endears them to all sportsmen. They prefer anything that moves on top water.

Most Snook fishermen haunt docks and bridges to get a chance at enticing the big fish which have a habit of lying motionless in the shadows and charging the bait with a resounding crash.

The Snook is the one fish which has created a new type of angling called "puddling" in which a top water bait is moved on the surface of the water in the manner of figure eight until he comes crashing out of the shadows to smash at the lure.

See Color Pages

● COBIA
Rachycentron canadum

Also called Sergeantfish, Oceanic Catfish, Ling, Lemonfish, Flathead, Cubby-yew, Crab-eater, Coalfish, Cavco, Carbio, Cabbeo, Black Salmon, Black Bonito.

Average size 12 pounds; largest on record 149 lbs. 12 oz., length 6 ft. 3 in. caught by Garnett L. Caudell, Texas City, Texas, aboard the M/V FRIENDSHIP off Grand Isle, La., May 15, 1965.

Dark bluish-slate color on top, shading to a lighter blue-black on sides and white below, often has a dark stripe from eye to caudal fin. Has flat head and protruding lower jaw.

A lone-wolf type of fish, usually found around buoys and channel markers and off-shore wrecks. They will lurk around channel edges especially where old rotted pilings offer food for small fishes. They dart out and strike at the bait tossed close to them.

Their natural food is most anything alive they find, from crabs and shrimp to shiners and small flounders.

These fish are found all over the world and in every locality are known by different names. If properly prepared by bleeding while alive, or trimming off dark meat, even the big ones are good eating.

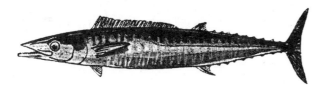

● WAHOO
Acanthocybium solanderi

Also called Ocean Barracuda, Pacific Kingfish, Peto, Guahu, Queenfish, Guarapucu.

Average 15 pounds; largest on record, 149 pounds, measuring 6 feet and 8 inches in length with 37½-girth, caught near Cat Cay, Bahamas, June 15, 1962 by John Pirovano. When prepared by separating the light meat from the dark, it is excellent food.

Upper sides dark greenish or steel-blue shading to paler silver. Fins dark. Gray or yellowish bands run down from the back. These are more distinct in the young.

Termed the fastest fish that swims. The first sizzling run of this powerful speedster defies all star drag reels or human exertion. Why he is called "Wahoo" nobody knows, unless it is because anglers have been known to make this yell when the bruiser strikes.

They do not run in schools as the Cero or King Mackerel, but range all through the deep water. Never are abundant, although in winter and spring many more are caught than other seasons.

● GREAT BARRACUDA
Sphyraena barracuda

Also called Sea Tiger, 'Cuda, Salt Water Pike, Picuda, Muskellunge, Sea Pike.

Average weight 8 pounds; largest on record 103 pounds and 8 ounces, caught by C. E. Benet, West End, Bahamas, 1932. Food value, fair.

Dark gray on back, sometimes appears smokey-black. Pronounced spots on sides which turn silvery below lateral line. Has very long sharp teeth, slightly hooked inward. Built like a torpedo, and very swift to start, but does not run great distances on one impulse.

This is one of the most savage fish of the sea. They often slash at objects in the water more from meanness than hunger. Many fish are cut into by Barracuda while being hauled up from the reef. They strike heavily and fight savagely at first, however, when stopped they quit cold. Usually they lie in wait for their prey and strike like a rattlesnake. Caution. Edibility depends on area where caught. Check with natives, could be poisonous.

Flatfish

THE FLATFISHES form one of the most remarkable groups of fishes in existence. They are apparently only half fish. Spending their entire life on the bottom, only one side is marked. The bottom side is always pure white. The bones are so twisted that both eyes are on one side, the top.

The young, however, are born with the normal arrangement of organs. As they grow older they lean on one side and one eye migrates around to join the other on top, sometimes on the right, sometimes on the left. Strangely there are left-handed Flounders and right-handed Flounders, with no particular reason for this.

The largest grow to immense size and one specimen of Halibut has been found which weighed 500 pounds and was 8 feet long. Usually they weigh up to 5 pounds, with 3 pounds average.

All the Flatfishes are good food fish, most of them excellent eating. They live on whatever food can be captured. Mostly small bottom feeding minnows, or soft crabs. They have teeth which are quite sharp. Because live food attracts them, Flounders can be caught with artificial baits which are made to work on the bottom. Most catches are made with spears, however, and "fire fishing," spearing by lantern light, is the popular type of Flounder fishing.

● **REX SOLE**　　　*Glyptocephalus zachirus*

Also called Long-Finned Sole.

Average size 9 inches; largest on record 18 inches; edible.

Light brown, fins darker shading.

Right-sided Flounder. Tapering shape. Small mouth. Nearly straight lateral line.

An important food fish, taken on hook and line and commercially.

Native to the Pacific, Southern California to the Bering Sea.

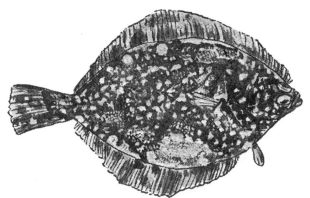

● **ROCK SOLE**　　　*Lepidopsetta bilineata*

Also called Double-Lined Flounder, Broadfin, Flounder. Average weight 1½ pounds; largest 6 pounds. Edible.

Dark brown, marked with lighter shades of brown spots and bars.

Right-sided Flounder, with small mouth. Quite broad and has a high arch in lateral line.

Native to Pacific, all northern waters.

● **PETRALE SOLE**　　　*Eopsetta jordani*

Also called Brill, Jordan's Flounder, English Sole, California Sole, Round-Nosed Sole.

Average weight 2 pounds; largest 8 pounds. Edible.

Olive-brown, sometimes with paler blotches.

Right-sided Flounder. Has small scales. Large mouth, even teeth on both sides.

Popular hook and line fish, also taken commercially in trawls.

Native to the Pacific, Alaska to Mexico.

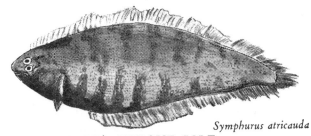

Symphurus atricauda

● **CALIFORNIA TONGUE SOLE**

Average length 6 inches; largest not known; not edible.

Brownish with dark ventral bars extended from the dorsal and anal fin bases toward the center of the body.

A left-handed Flounder. Eyes are small and close set. The mouth is small and rather twisted. Body tapers to a point at the tail. No discernible lateral line.

Taken in drag lines occasionally or hook and line. Plentiful throughout the year.

Native to the Pacific, central California to southern California.

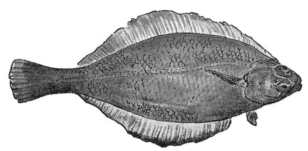

● **SLENDER SOLE** *Lyopsetta exilis*
  Average size 8 inches; largest 12 inches; edible.
Pale brown, with dark points forming edgings
on each scale.
  Right-sided Flounder, has large and loosely
attached scales. Large mouth.
  Native to Pacific, Alaska, Mexico.

● **FANTAIL SOLE** *Xystreurys liolepis*
  Average size 6 inches, largest 15 inches. Edible.
Brown and olive mottled. Gray and reddish
blotches with distinct black spots.
  Abrupt and high arch in lateral line makes
positive identification. May be either left or right
sided.
  Native to the Pacific, mostly in the Gulf of
California.

● **BUTTER SOLE** *Isopsetta isolepis*
  Also called Scaly Fin Sole.
  Average size 8 inches; largest 18 inches; edible.
Brown and gray mottled.
  Right-sided Flounder. There are rough scales
on the eyed side.
  Native to the Pacific, caught on the California
coast from southern California to Alaska.

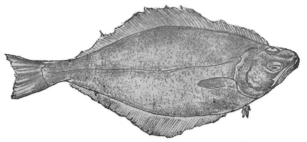

● **ARROWTOOTH FLOUNDER** *Atheresthes stomias*
  Also called Arrowtooth Halibut, Long-Tailed
Flounder. Average length 12 inches; largest 30
inches. Edible. Brown or olive-brown. Black dots
on the blind side. A right-sided Flounder. Has a
large mouth. Taken mostly in trawls, occasionally
on hook and line.
  Native to Pacific, central California.

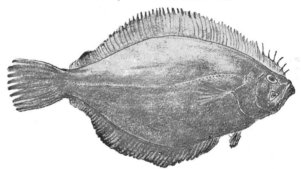

● **SAND SOLE** *Psettichthys melanostictus*
  Also called Fringed Sole, Spotted Flounder.
  Average length 8 inches; largest on record 20
inches (4 to 5 pounds). Edible.
  Brownish, mottled in darker brown, completely
speckled with brown and black. A right-sided
Flounder. Has small eyes with wide space between.
Jaws and teeth equally developed on both sides.
First few fins of dorsal are elongated and not mem-
brane connected for about half their length.
  Native to the Pacific, southern California.

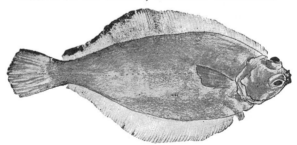

● **DOVER SOLE** *Microstomus pacificus*
  Also called Slippery Sole, Slime Sole.
  Average length 10 inches; largest 24 inches.
Edible, but not comparable to other Flatfishes.
  Various shades of brown, sometimes with
blotches of lighter or darker brown.
  Right-sided Flounder. Identified by the large
amounts of slime secreted. Pacific Ocean.

Flounders

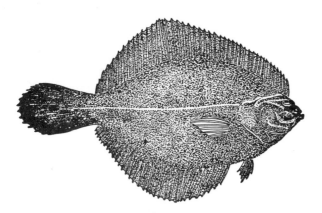

● SMOOTH FLOUNDER   *Liopsetta putnami*

Also called Smoothback Flounder; Eelback; Foolfish; Christmas Flounder; Plaice.

Average size 8 inches; largest on record 12 inches and 1½ pounds weight. Food value, fair.

Grayish to dark muddy or slaty-brown; fins mottled.

A right-handed Flounder which feels smooth to the touch. Sometimes confused with the Dab. Can always be recognized by prominent straight lateral line.

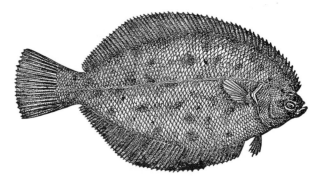

● GEORGE'S BANK FLOUNDER
Pseudopleuronectes dignabilis

Also called Lemon Sole.

Average size 20 inches; largest not known; food value, fair.

Light yellowish-brown color, more or less dark blotched and mottled.

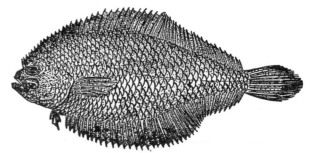

● GULF STREAM FLOUNDER *Citharichths arctifrons*

Average size 3 inches; largest on record 4 inches; food value, nil.

Light brown.

A small left-handed Flounder; very thin with large scales; found mostly in deeper water.

● HOGCHOKER   *Trinectes maculatus*

Average size 3 inches; largest on record 8 inches; food value, poor. A small Flounder easily recognized by the rounded nose. Lives in shallow water, usually preferring brackish content in river mouths. Occasionally ascends to fresh water.

The illustration portrays the Hogchoker as a left-handed Flounder when in fact it is right-handed. To determin if a Flatfish is right or left-handed, lay the fish belly-side down at your feet with the dorsal fin pointed away and the pectoral and anal fins closest to your toes. The head of a right-handed Flounder will be on your right.

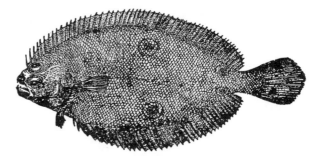

● FOURSPOTTED FLOUNDER
Paralichthys oblongus

Average size 10 inches; largest on record 17 inches, weighing 2 lbs., 15 ozs., caught by Mrs. Henry Nichols, from Teatable Bridge near Tavernier, Fla. Keys, Jan. 10, 1965.

Mottled gray back with four spots, two in the center and two at base of tail.

92

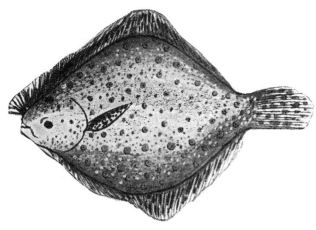

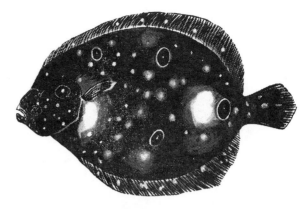

OCELLATED FLOUNDER *Ancylopsetta quadrocellata*

This pretty Flounder is quite common in Fla. However is different from the more northern Fourspot as the spots are not always placed in pairs and they usually have white centers.

● **WINDOWPANE** *Scophthalmus aquosus*

Also called Sand Dab.

This is a small Flounder, so thin it is possible to see light through the body. A perfect job of camouflage to resemble the coarse sand over which fish are found. They are edible but not worth much commercially.

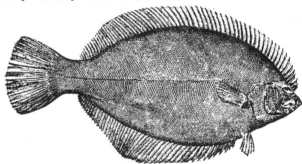

● **WINTER FLOUNDER** *Pseudopleuronectes americanus*

Also called Common Flatfish.

Average size 12 inches; largest on record 30 inches; food value, good.

Brownish-gray with scattered whitish spots. White belly. More uniformly rounded and of oblong shape.

See Color Pages

● **SOUTHERN FLOUNDER** *Paralichthys lethostigma*

Also called Gulf Flounder, Southern Fluke.

This Flounder together with the species known as "Albiguttus" is common in South Atlantic and Gulf waters. Markings are similar to that of the Summer Flounder.

Largest on record 17 lbs. gigged by Frank Usina just north of the Usina Fishing Camp, St. Augustine, Fla., in Dec. '68. Reported by Thomas B. Lewis of that city.

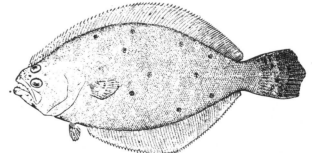

● **SUMMER FLOUNDER** *Paralichthys dentatus*

Also called Fluke. Average 2 lbs.; largest on record 21 lbs., 4 ozs., caught by Daniel Varas Serrano at Maitencillo, Chile, Dec. 8, 1959. Food value, good.

Has a very large mouth with prominent canine teeth. The eyes are usually on left side. Most common on New England coast although is found in southern waters.

93

Flounder and Turbot

● **DIAMOND TURBOT**   *Hypsopsetta guttulata*

Also called Diamond Flounder.

Average size 12 inches; largest 50 inches; edible.

Dark greenish and brown, usually mottled with paler shades.

Right-sided Flounder. Takes its name from diamond-shape of body. Has a small mouth, with teeth on blind side.

A sports fish taken mostly in bays and the mouths of rivers. Quite often found well up in brackish to fresh water.

Native to the waters of California.

● **CURLFIN SOLE**   *Pleuronichthys decurrens*

Also called California Turbot.

Average length 5 inches; largest 12 inches; Edible and desirable.

Dark brown to yellowish-brown, mottled lightly with gray. Fins are dark.

Right-sided Flounder. Has small mouth. A bony prominence is noticeable in front of each eye.

Caught mostly in trawls, occasionally by hook and line.

Native to the Pacific, Mexico to Alaska.

● **HORNYHEAD TURBOT**   *Pleuronichthys verticalis*

Also called Sharpridge Flounder.

Average size 6 inches; largest 10 inches; not edible.

Brown with scattered pale spots on body, irregularly mottled.

Right-sided; small mouth; teeth only on blind side. Several small blunt spines around upper eye; one blunt spine in front of lower eye. Narrow bony ridge between eyes.

Native to the Pacific, mostly in the Gulf of California.

● **STARRY FLOUNDER**   *Platichthys stellatus*

Also called Great Flounder, Rough Jacket, Flounder.

Average weight 4 pounds; largest on record 20 pounds, edible.

Black with dark brown markings. Fins are striped with black, orange and whitish colors.

Either a left or right-sided Flounder. Has rough and scattered plates made of scales. Black bars on the dorsal fins.

This is the sportsman's most desired Flounder, especially in shallow water or inland bays. Has a yen for brackish water and at times moves far up stream.

Native to the Pacific, all waters.

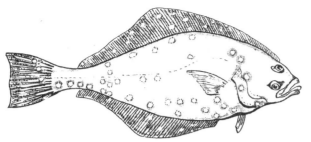

● **ATLANTIC HALIBUT**   *Hippoglossus hippoglossus*
Also called Giant Flounder, Turbot.
Average weight 25 pounds; largest on record 720 pounds. Food value, excellent when less than 100 pounds.
Usually brown or greenish-brown on top and whitish mottled on underside.
This is the supreme member of the commercial fish. A true Flounder, is born in upright position and left eye migrates as fish grows to adult age.

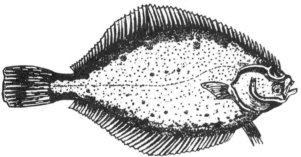

● **YELLOWTAIL FLOUNDER**   *Limanda ferruginea*
Also called Rusty Dab. Average weight 1 pound; largest not known; food value, good.
Greenish-brown. Body covered with rusty dots. Tail and fins edging yellow. Eyes are on the right side and separated by narrow ridge. Has prominent humped nose.   Distributed from New York, south through Gulf of Mexico.

● **PACIFIC HALIBUT**   *Hippoglossus stenolepis*
Also called Right Halibut, Genuine Halibut, Northern Halibut and Alabato.
Average size 20 pounds; largest on record 9 feet long and weighing 500 pounds. Considered a food delicacy. Uniform dark brown with little-defined paler spots.   Native to the Pacific.
Considered a right-sided Flounder, although **there have been instances of left-handed fish.**

● **CALIFORNIA HALIBUT**   *Paralichthys californicus*
Also called Alabato, Monterey Halibut, Southern Halibut, Chicken Halibut, Bastard Halibut.
Average size 16 pounds; largest on record 60 pounds. Excellent for food.
Greenish and grayish-brown, sometimes mottled with darker and lighter spots.
Can be either a left or right-sided Flounder. The eyes are small with flat area between them. Large jaws, strong, sharp teeth. A high arch in the lateral line. Important sports fish on the Pacific Coast.

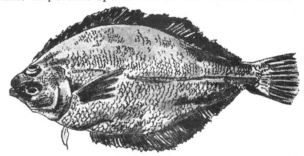

● **PACIFIC SAND DAB**   *Citharichthys sordidus*
Largest 2 pounds; considered a delicacy.
Sometimes tan and often brown shades spotted with black or dull orange.
Has a nearly straight lateral line. The scales are large. The lower eye is longer than the snout.

● **ENGLISH SOLE**   *Parophyrs vetulus*
Also called Common Sole, California Sole.
Average length 10 inches; largest 21 inches; edible.
Brown to pale brownish, dorsal and fins tipped darker. Right-sided Flounder. Has smooth scales; pointed jaws.
Most plentiful of the Soles in the Pacific. Taken **commercially and by sports fishermen.**

Spearfish

SPEARFISHES are the terrors of the ocean. They grow to great size and are the most sought after of all gamefish. In food value they differ considerably. While the Marlins and Sailfish are strong and oily, the Broadbill Swordfish is a delicacy.

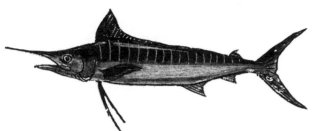

● **WHITE MARLIN**   *Makaira albida*

Also called Billfish, Great Billfish, Skillygoelle, Spikefish, Spearfish.

Average size 60 pounds; largest on record 161 pounds; food value, poor.

Bluish-black with purplish cast which shades into silvery sides. Violet hues predominate the upper portion. Has a smaller and lower dorsal fin than a Sailfish.

● **STRIPED MARLIN**   *Makaira audax*

Average weight 150 pounds; largest on record 692 pounds and 13 feet 5 inches in length, caught near Balboa, Calif., Aug. 18, 1931, by A. Herman. Illegal to use as a food fish, or to buy and sell.

Purplish-blue above, shading into silvery below. Back crossed with 15 vertical light blue stripes.

A highly prized gamefish, roams the Pacific mostly, and caught in largest quantities off Central America and Hawaii.

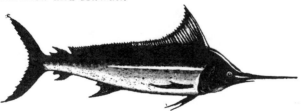

● **BLUE MARLIN**   *Makaira nigricans*

The Blue Marlin are found both in the Atlantic and Pacific. There is some argument as to whether they are identical.

Largest Blue Marlin on record; 845 lbs. caught by Elliot Fishmant aboard Caneel Bay Plantation's fishing boat. Reported to Great Outdoors by David Guinazzo, Bronx, N. Y.; Silver Marlin (so-called in the Hawaiian area), 911 lbs., 13 feet, 5 inches long, 76-inch girth, caught near Kona, Hawaiian Islands, Nov. 16, 1957 by Dale Scott.

● **SAILFISH**   *Istiophorus platypterus*

Also called Pez vela, Spearfish, Sail, Spikefish.

Purple, overlaying a bright blue, with green stripe, shading into greenish-white on sides. Dark spots over entire body, including dorsal fin.

Atlantic, 141 lbs., 1 oz., length 8 feet, 5 inches, caught on the Ivory Coast, Africa, Jan. 26, 1961 by Tony Burnand; Pacific, 221 lbs., length 10 feet, 9 inches, caught near Santa Cruz Islands, Feb. 12, 1947. Food value fair. Only edible if flesh is smoked.

Sailfish roam the Gulf Stream in large numbers. They school in January and sometimes July, but usually are lone rangers of the deep.

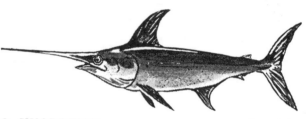

● **SWORDFISH**   *Xiphias gladius*

Also called Alabacora, Espada, Sofia, Vehuella.

Average length 8 feet; largest on record 14 feet, 11½ inches, weighing 1,182 pounds.

Dark purplish-blue on back, shading into a lighter purplish-blue on sides, belly silvery. Fins a very dusky-purple, top sword black. Excellent food value.

The Broadbill Swordfish is considered by big game anglers to be the world's greatest game fish. While related to the Marlin, the Broadbill is the only true Swordfish and its sword differs from that of the Marlin as it is heavier and broader instead of rounded and pointed.

SPEARFISH   *Tetrapturus belone*

Average size 14 lbs.; largest on record 38 lbs.; length 76 in., caught by George Shelley off Ft. Lauderdale during Blue Marlin Tournament. Fish was mounted by Reese.

Gulf and Ocean Fish

● SENORITA   *Oxyjulis californica*

Also called Kelpfish.

Average size 3 inches; largest 7 inches. Not edible. Brown on top, cream color below. Scales have centers of orange-brown. Streaks of bluish on sides of head. Large black spot at base of caudal fin.

Noted for small sharp teeth which project forward. The single dorsal fin running from just behind the head to base of tail has nine weak spines.

A common small fish inshore around kelp beds of the Pacific, usually in the southern latitude of California.

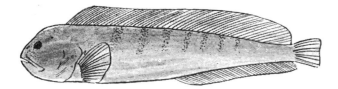

● WOLFFISH   *Anarhicas lupus*

Also called Ocean Catfish.

Average weight 8 lbs. Old records state this fish reaches a weight of 50 lbs. The only recent record is 17 lbs., caught by Philip A. Pirrone, Mattapan, Mass., June 1, 1968. Food value fair.

Dark in color, almost black.

A large and carnivorous fish of the ocean. Has powerful jaws armed with strong canines and large molars. The canine teeth protrude so they are visible even when the mouth is shut, which gives the fish a ferocious aspect.

● SPOTTED WOLFFISH   *Anarhichas minor*

Also called Spotted Catfish.

Average size 3 feet; largest on record 6 feet; food value, fair.

Pale chocolate upper parts, sprinkled with blackish-brown spots of irregular sizes.

Chief difference between this fish and common Wolffish is the arrangement of fins and spots. Although the Latin name indicates the Spotted Wolffish is smaller, it is fully as large as the common variety. Keeps to cold deep waters mostly.

● CHIMAERA   *Chimaera affinis*

Average size 14 inches; largest 3 feet; food value, nil.

A deep water fish, of which little is known. Related to the Sharks although gills resemble the bony fishes.

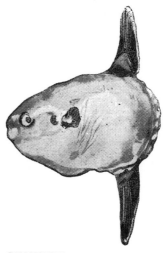

● OCEAN SUNFISH   *Mola mola*

Also called Headfish.

Average weight 500 pounds; largest on record 2,000 pounds; attains length of 8 feet; food value, poor.

A drab-colored, leathery-skinned fish, which appears to be all head.

The Headfish is often found swimming lazily on the surface of gulf or ocean. The skin is over two inches thick and has a small amount of elasticity. Movement and stability are accomplished by waving of the two fins.

They are captured easily when found and are valuable for the oil contained in a large liver.

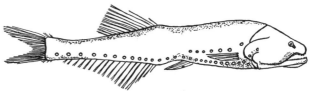

● CYCLOTHONE   *Cyclothone signata*

Average 6 inches; largest 9 inches; no food value.

Pale gray with blackish, dark silvery lining of abdominal cavity. A deep-sea fish with phosphorescent-rimmed organs. The mouth is large, extends back of the eye. The dots along both sides are light buttons.

● ATKA MACKEREL   *Pleurogrammus monopteryguis*

Average weight 2 pounds; largest on record 4 pounds; food value, good.

Brownish on back, to yellow tint below. Has long wide dorsal fin.

A cold water fish, which feeds on small shellfish as a rule and travels in large schools. Mostly inshore during June to late September.

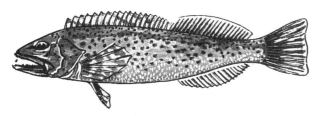

● LINGCOD   *Ophiodon elongatus*

Also called Ling, Cultus Cod.

Average weight 4 pounds; largest on record 40 pounds; food value, good.

Usually a mottled grayish with small brown and yellow spots. Sometimes the flesh is green.

An open sea fish, which is abundant on the Pacific coast and a rarity on Gulf and Atlantic.

They feed on small fish and crustaceans.

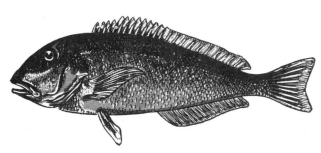

● OCEAN WHITEFISH   *Caulolatilus princeps*

Also called Blanquillo, Whitefish.

Average weight 6 pounds; largest on record 45 pounds; food value, good.

Grayish-blue on top turning to pinkish at lateral line and silverish on belly. Has small mouth and thick lips.

A tropical fish, liking warm water entirely and never found in northern waters. Usually around coast line with good supply of rock. Quite often caught at the ends of rock jetties.

98

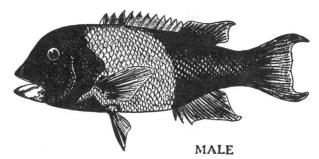

MALE

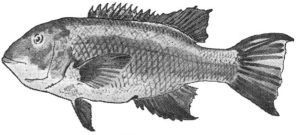

FEMALE

● CALIFORNIA SHEEPSHEAD
Pimelometopon pulchrum

Also called Redfish, Fathead, Humpy.

Average size 3 pounds; largest on record 26 lbs., 29 in. long, caught by Harry J. Devann, Venice, Calif., fishing off Malibu Pier, Malibu, Calif., and reported by pier mgr. Kenneth L. Briggs, Oct. '68. Food value good.

Male is black, fore and aft, with pinkish band around the middle. Female, dull red to rose over all. Young, rose to crimson.

Commercial men use them for lobster bait. They are most always present around the kelp beds of the Pacific.

Native to the California coast, Monterey Bay and the Gulf of California.

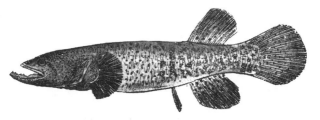

● ALASKAN BLACKFISH   *Dallia pectoralis*

Average size 8 inches; largest on record 14 inches; food value good.

Black-speckled with large fins placed well aft.

This is the famous Arctic Blackfish which forms the main article of food for northern wanderers. Natives as well as the dogs live on this fish for months.

Shown here to differentiate from the many other Blackfish of tropical waters and settle confusion in discussion. It is agreed that of all the fish called "Blackfish" this is the most important.

Soft Fishes

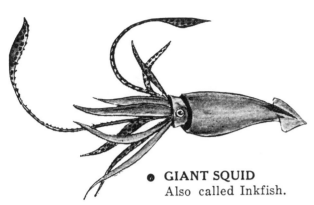

● GIANT SQUID
Also called Inkfish.

Average weight 3 lbs.; largest 200 lbs.; edible.

Dusky in color when grown — the young are transparent in appearence.

A dangerous fish both in and out of water. It can inflict deep wounds with its claw-like feelers and when caught, its ink-like secretion can be painful to the eyes of the unwary.

Native to Gulf of Mexico.

● RINGED OCTOPUS   *Hapalochlaena maculosa*

Average size, 1½ inches across body; largest known, 8 inches across body, reported by Vincent Serventy, Darwin, Australia and Loretta Bolland, Brisbane. Located in a tidal pool on the shore of Northern Australia.

Brightly colored with iridescent blue-purple bands. This species is common in southern Australian waters, especially in rock pools along the shoreline.

Tests have proven that this octopus has a poison more deadly than any living creature. The poison is injected by a bite from the parrot-like jaws. The effect is numbness, nausea, then paralysis. Many persons have died from the bite, which is almost always fatal. No antidote has ever been found.

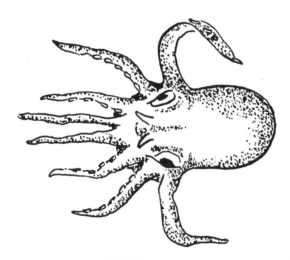

● BAIRD'S OCTOPUS   *Octopus bairdi*
Also called Small Devilfish.

Average size 3 inches; largest 6 inches; nonedible.

A translucent bluish-white spotted with purpish-brown, or orange-brown. It may change color slightly.

The body is short and thick, the head nearly as broad. Around the eyes are many cone-shaped tubercules, and the space between is concave. The upper side of the body is covered with small warts. There are eight arms, each having two rows of suckers on the inner side — they are connected by a web for about 1/3 of their length.

Found in water from 75 to 500 fathoms.

Native from the Bay of Fundy to South Carolina.

● INKFISH
Also called Sea Ostrich.

Average size 8 inches; largest 10 inches; nonedible.

A dull green, its wings scalloped with white.

It resembles a jellyfish, but unlike the latter, has a digestive tract and can see, also it is more solid. When molested, it discharges a purple ink.

Native to Florida coastal waters.

Deep Ocean Fish

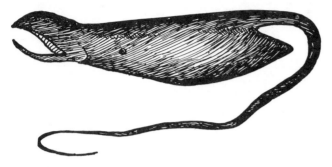

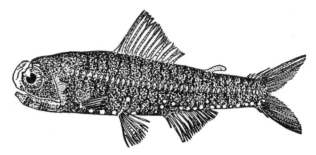

● **GULPER**   *Saccopharynx ampullaceus*

A long-tailed, deep-sea fish which is often pictured and quite common in deep water latitudes. Especially known by its ability to swallow other fish larger than itself.

● **LANTERNFISH**   *Aethoprora effulgens*

Average size about 6 inches.

Black or dark shade with phosphorescent organs of pale blue or green.

Has large eyes situated at the end of nose.

Usually a deep water fish, but rises to surface at night, creating phosphorescent blotches in the water. In some parts of Atlantic are quite common, although rare in the Gulf of Mexico.

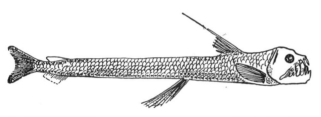

● **VIPERFISH**   *Chauliodus sloanei*

Average size 10 inches; largest on record 14 inches; food value, nil.

Greenish above; sides glossy, belly black.

Recognized by long needle-like teeth.

A deep water fish, thrown up occasionally by disturbances and sometimes found in bellies of deep water fish. Very little known of life cycle.

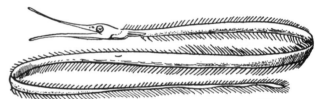

● **SNIPE EEL**   *Nemichthys scolopaceus*

Average size 2 feet; largest on record 36 inches; food value, nil.

Pale to dark brown above. Belly black.

Although this is commonly called a "deep-sea" fish, it is actually of the mid-depths. Probably 100 fathoms. There is record of one being caught as it clung to the tail of a Red Snapper.

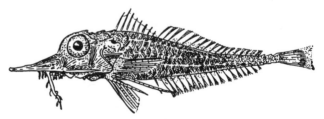

● **COELACANTH**   *Latimeria chalumnae*

Scientists consider this the "missing link" in the evolution of land animals from the age when the earth was populated only by fishes—it had been believed to be extinct for 60 million years when the first living specimen was found in 1938 off the coast of South Africa. It was 5 ft. long, weight 127 lbs. A second was caught 15 years later off Madagascar, and others have been identified since then.

The fish has elongated fins resembling arms and legs.

● **ARMORED SEAROBIN**   *Peristedion miniatum*

Average size 6 inches; largest, 10 inches; no food value.

Light cream or straw color above, belly white. Has appendage under lower jaw like a piece of seaweed.

Usually found in deep water. Very little known about the species.

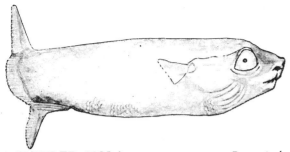

● **SLENDER MOLA** *Ranzania laevis*

Also called Molidone, Vardo.

Average size unknown; largest on record is 30 inches, taken by Ary Ebroin, in the waters adjacent to Guadeloupe, French West Indies.

Resembles somewhat the Moonfish family. Compressed, fairly elongate b o d y terminated abruptly, close behind the dorsal and anal fins in a manner that suggests it has been cut off. Very small mouth. Smooth velvety skin. Gillrakers free, pointed. No caudal fin.

This is an extremely rare fish. Only a few ever found. The family habits of this species are virtually unknown.

● **TOTUAVA** *Cynoscion macdonaldi*

Also called Totuba; Tutava; Mochoro; Pez Grande; Cabrilla; Ora.

Average size 18 pounds; largest on record 200 pounds even; caught by Mrs. Gertrude Watts, of Hubert, N. C. fishing near San Felipo, Mexico, May 30, 1960. Hooked 3 miles off shore in 5 feet of water. Edible.

It is our opinion and generally accepted that male and female of this fish are known as Totuava and Mochoro. The female is the largest. Both prefer live shrimp for food, but the record fish was taken with a 2-pound Corvina.

Strongly resembles a California White Sea Bass. Has a yellow mouth, like a Weakfish. Tail has a central peak. Might be said to resemble a Salmon in shape. Sold commercially in the markets of Mexico, although not many fishermen have seen them outside of Mexico.

These fish appear along the Mexican coast in the vicinity of Puerto Libertad in October and stay several months. Believed to go to the upper end of the Gulf of California to spawn. There is very little knowledge about the life of this fish.

Feed in shallow water on crustaceans. Smaller fish taken inshore; larger ones out on deep banks. They take bait, shrimp mostly, trolled slowly, deep.

Native to Gulf of California.

● **LOUVAR** *Luvars imperialis*

Also called Red-fin Tuna.

Largest on record 278 pounds, taken in the vicinity of main dock at LaPaz, Mexico. The fish was harpooned by Capt. Allan Douglas Jr., of LaPaz, May 16, 1965. Food value excellent.

Have a head like a Dolphin and general shape of a Tuna. The bluish skin is covered with minute mushroom-like pink scales which give it a reddish cast. In general the body has a rounded, well-filled appearance of an Albacore or Bonito.

This is quite a rare fish and so far as records go, only 30 have ever been caught anywhere in the world.

● **OIL FISH** *Ruvettus pretiosus*

Also called Tapioca Fish or Escolar. Not considered good food as the flesh is rich and oily and reputed to have a purgative effect.

Average size 10 pounds, largest on record 87 pounds, caught by Pete Patronas of Dauphin Island, Ala., in January, 1968. He found the fish floundering in a tidal pool and caught it with his hands.

Dark gray to black, belly lighter, body fusiform, no keel on tail stem; skin studded with bony plates; 13 dorsal spines.

These are solitary and rare gamefish, traveling the Atlantic coast from the Caribbean to the Grand Banks off the coast of Newfoundland. More plentiful in northern latitudes, very rare in the Caribbean.

The specimen above was captured and photographed by G.O.A. member Ary Ebroin of Basse-Terre, Guadeloupe, French West Indies.

101

Rare Fish of the World

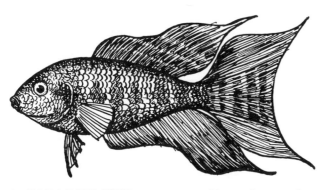

● **PARADISE FISH**   *Macropodus opercularis*

A fish of Southeastern Asia remarkable for the extension of its fins. Much admired for its beautiful coloration.

● **NARWHALE**   *Monodon monoceros*

A species of whale, the male of which has a long twisted spike protruding from the upper jaw.

Average size 13 to 16 feet.

The Narwhale, rarely seen by anyone except Eskimos, lives above the Arctic Circle and attains a length of 20 feet when full grown. The male has an 8 to 10-foot spiral tusk that for several centuries has helped contribute to the legend of the unicorn.

● **PIRANHA**   *Serrasalmo rhombeus*

Average size 12 in. Native to the Amazon. Have short, strong, sharp teeth capable of cutting a hook in half as easily as tin shears. Travel in large packs attacking any living thing, including humans. Victims soon reduced to bare skeleton.

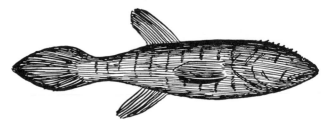

● **NORTHERN CAVEFISH**   *Amblyopsis spelaea*

Also called Blindfish.

A type of small fishes with functionless eyes found in subterranean streams. Best examples in Mammoth Cave, Kentucky.

● **BOARFISH**   *Capros aper*

An unusual small fish of the Mediterranean marked by a projecting snout. Works its way northward to south coast of England, where it's abundant in summer. Odd shape makes it a curiosity in aquariums.

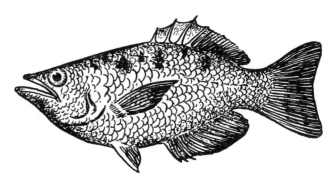

● **ARCHERFISH**   *Toxotex jaculator*

A fish of the East Indian Ocean which has the ability to squirt a stream of water into overhanging trees and knock down insects.

102

Dolphins And Porpoises

Most interesting animals of the ocean are the Porpoises, or Dolphins. Of a dozen families there are many variations, none of which are much different from the other except for size of snout and coloring of skin.

Dolphin gets the nickname Porpoise because of his habit of porpoising in the water while playing about ships or small boats under way. As a group they are quite fond of the human race and his equipment. Throughout the world they are regarded as a friend. Many legends have been told of the Dolphin saving sailors. This was begun by the Greek fable of Arion of Lesbos, lyric poet and player of the cithara—who was saved by a Dolphin. He was returning to Corinth from Sicily carrying money and trophies he had amassed with his talent, when sailors, jealous of his wealth, plotted to kill him. He heard of the plot. By playing his cithara, he attracted Dolphins to the ship and jumping into the sea he was borne to safety on the back of one of them.

The Dolphin or Porpoise is quite intelligent and can be taught any number of tricks. He is in great demand at aquariums and water circuses where he jumps for food or pulls boats with riders. There is apparently no limit to the number of tricks they can be taught. As a whole, the flesh is not considered edible and they have no commercial value, except for their hide. This is not pursued because of the great expense in capturing them.

Some are herbivorous and are considered edible by natives of the Kamerun River. All species are considered good luck omens.

● **COMMON DOLPHIN**   *Delphinus delphis*
Average size 7 feet; largest 9 feet.
Black or dark brown on back and white on belly. Slender and streamlined.

Ranges throughout the world. May be seen in warm and cold waters in all seasons. There are many stories of them saving drowning sailors.

Feed on fishes, mostly Herring, Pilchards, Mullet or such. Extremely fast swimmers, considered the fastest of all Porpoises. Not known, but estimated, their speed may be 60 miles an hour. They have been seen to play and cavort while keeping pace with a ship traveling 30 knots, finding it not difficult to keep up.

At one time the flesh of Dolphins was eaten, but not considered edible nowadays.

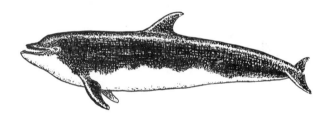

● **BOTTLENOSE DOLPHIN**   *Tursiops truncatus*
Also called Common Porpoise.
Average size 9 feet; largest 12 feet.
Black on top ranging to dark brown on sides and white belly. Under surface from vent to flukes is pigmented. Upper lip edges are white and whole lower jaw is white.

The largest of the Dolphins, or Porpoises. Ranges in all oceans of the world and particularly numerous in the Gulf of Mexico.

Food is entirely of fishes and even small Sharks have been found in the stomachs of these mammals. Renowned for their jumping ability.

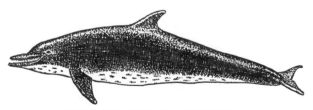

● **LONG-BEAKED RIVER DOLPHIN**
Sotalia guianensis gadamu
Average size 5 feet; largest 8 feet.
A type of bottle-nose Dolphin identified by the long and distinct beak, recurved flippers, broad at the base. There are a dozen or more of the *Sotalia* genus of River Dolphins. All are found in the regions of South American rivers as well as rivers of Asia. Not known on the American continent or north of the Equator.

● **SMOOTH-TOOTHED DOLPHIN**
Prodelphinus euphrosyn
Average size 8 feet; largest not known.
Distinguished by teeth which are smooth, and short jaws. Very much like a Common Dolphin. Back is black, belly white. Extremities of both jaws are black. A black band connects eye and anal fin.

Ranges the Atlantic and found on all coasts of this ocean. Feeds on fish.

103

Small Whales

● **ROUGH-TOOTHED DOLPHIN** *Steno bredanensis*

Average length 8 feet; largest not known.

Distinguished by long beak. Teeth are rough or furrowed. Body is slender. The upper surface slate colored, or purplish black. Has irregular star-shaped blotches. Under surface slightly rose-color.

Very little is known of this Dolphin. One specimen was found stranded off the coast of France. Believed to inhabit the Atlantic and Indian Oceans.

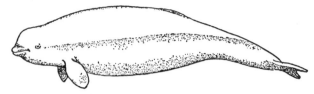

● **WHITE WHALE** *Delphinapterus leucas*

Also called Beluga.

Average size 14 feet; largest known 18 feet; used as food.

Whiteness distinguishes from all other Whales. Has no spots or markings of any other kind.

A Polar species, usually limited to the Arctic latitudes. Found in Atlantic off Gulf of St. Lawrence, also in Pacific off Alaska. Sometimes known to dart into shallows after Flounder and bottom fish.

The skin makes valuable leather.

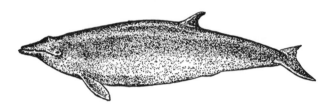

● **NORTH SEA BEAKED WHALE**
  Mesoplodon bidens

Also called Sowerby's Whale.

Average size 10 feet; largest 16 feet; no food value.

Bluish-black, sometimes grey or white on undersurface.

One of a family of the beaked Whales. Sowerby's Whale is considered the most common of the genus. A North Atlantic species.

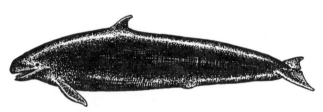

● **FALSE KILLER WHALE** *Pseudorca crassidens*

Average size 12 feet; largest 18 feet, 6 inches. No food value.

Body is entirely black.

World-wide in range with the possible exception of the Polar seas. Sometimes found in shallow waters. Numerous instances of the stranding of these Whales has been recorded.

Feed mostly on Cuttlefish, but also eat Cod or other fish of such nature. Sometimes hunted for blubber, but not hunted in commercial quantities. Have a plentiful supply of sharp teeth but is not aggressive as the true Killer Whale.

● **PIGMY SPERM WHALE** *Kogia breviceps*

Also called Lesser Cachalot.

Average size 5 feet; largest 9 feet weighing 573 pounds, caught by Antonio Belismelis of Santa Ana, El Salvador, January, 1959. No commercial value.

Body color is black and light grey to pinkish and at times red underneath.

Wide distribution, although a rare species. The specimens taken have been found stranded while in throes of childbirth.

Practically nothing is known of the swimming or breeding habits.

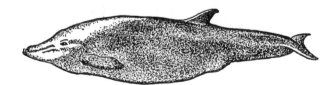

● **GOOSE-BEAKED WHALE** *Uiphius cavirostris*

Also known as Cuvier's Beaked Whale.

Average size 21 feet; largest 26 feet; has no commercial importance.

Bluish-black on top, white beneath. Has two large teeth in lower jaw.

Widely distributed in Atlantic and Pacific. A rare species however and practically nothing is known of its habits.

Valuable Whales

● **SPERM WHALE** *Physeter catodon*

Also called Cachalot.

Average size 40 feet; largest recorded 84 feet. Important for oil, blubber, spermaceti and ambergris, all valuable products.

Very dark on top, shading to silvery-grey underneath. Does not have a dorsal fin, but a hump where it should be. Identification by box-like head.

A toothed whale, feeding on giant Cuttlefish. Often they have scars from battles with these immense creatures.

Widely distributed through all oceans but prefer the warmer regions. So widely hunted they are now near extinction.

● **SEI WHALE** *Balaenoptera borealis*

Also called Rudolphi's Rorqual.

Average size 40 feet; largest 60 feet; valuable for food, blubber and whalebone.

Bluish-black. A white area stretching from the chin to the region of the flippers identifies the species.

Resembles the Blue Whale in some ways, but more graceful. Usually appears along the Norwegian coast with the Sardines.

World-wide in range. Noted for speed.

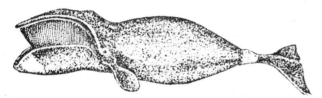

● **BOWHEAD WHALE** *Balaena mysticetus*

Also called Greenland Right Whale.

Average size 40 feet; largest 60 feet. Predominately black with white area under lower jaw.

Three qualities made this Whale a favorite target of the old-time whaling industry—slower motion, greater buoyancy and exceeding richness of oil. They were pursued so extensively as to render them almost extinct—rarest whale of the ocean.

● **BLUE WHALE** *Balaenoptera musculus*

Also called Sibbald's Rorqual.

Average size, 60 feet; largest over 100 feet; largest producer of oil and blubber; largest of all living animals; might weigh over 120 tons.

Distribution is world-wide. Has been the object of intense pursuit by whalers. Feeds on minute organisms known as "krill." Like most animals of tremendous size is actually timid, never aggressive. The sound of a man's voice over the water is enough to cause a Blue Whale to bolt. Cannot be overtaken.

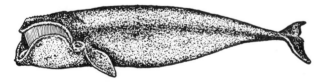

● **BLACK RIGHT WHALE** *Balaena glacialis*

Average size 40 feet; largest 60 feet; valuable for oil, blubber and whalebone.

Usually black all over; sometimes with white patches irregularly distributed on under surfaces.

Are known to collect barnacles and parasites to greater extent than other Right Whales. They are pursued so extensively the species is almost extinct.

Found in most all oceans from the Arctic to the tip of South America, there are several variations of this Whale. The southern species as well as the northern.

● **FINNER WHALE** *Balaenoptera physalus*

Also called Common Rorqual or Razorback.

Average size 68 feet; largest on record 82 feet; important for oil, blubber and whalebone.

Light grey in color and pure white below. Inner sides of flippers and flukes are white.

This is the greyhound of Whales. Fastest in the water. Feeds on smaller animals, usually krill or shrimp. Distribution world-wide. Mostly Atlantic.

Rare Whales

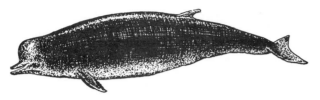

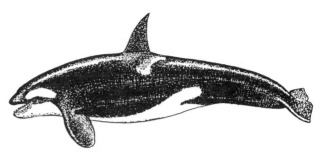

● **NORTH ATLANTIC BOTTLE-NOSE WHALE**
Hyperoodon ampullatus

Average size 26 feet; largest 35 feet; valuable.
General body color is dark grey to black. Flippers are dark, both upper and lower surface.
Travel in small schools in Arctic. They often become stranded when a mate is wounded and goes into shallow water. Hunted extensively for oil in the head cavity.

● **KILLER WHALE**   *Orcinus orca*

Average size 15 feet; largest 30 feet. No food value.
Black on back, belly white. Chin is white, flippers are black on both upper and lower surfaces. White patch above eye. Large teeth. A ferocious mammal and known to attack live Whales as well as those being towed to whaling ships after being killed. They kill Seals and Porpoises for food.
Found mostly in Arctic and Anarctic Oceans. Usually hunt in packs, comparable to a pack of wolves. Have a habit of rising under ice floes to knock animals into the water to devour them.

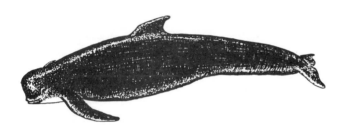

● **PILOT WHALE**   *Globicephala melaena*

Also known as Blackfish, Pothead. Valuable for oil. Average size 15 feet; largest 26 feet.
Range in many oceans of the world, spending the summers in northern latitudes. Move south in November to bear their young. Sometimes found stranded on Florida coasts. Known to follow a leader blindly on to the beach. Valuable for oil in heads and blubber.

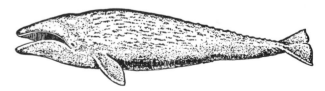

● **HUMPBACK WHALE**   *Megaptera novaeangliae*

Average length 30 feet; largest 50 feet; valuable for oil and blubber.
Hunted by whalers because of ease in handling compared to larger Whales. Has a spectacular leap from the water. Migrate from Antartic to Africa.

● **LITTLE PIKED WHALE** *Balaenoptera acutorostrata*

Also called Lesser Rorqual. Average size 24 feet; largest known 33 feet; food value excellent.
Blue-grey on back, pure white underneath. Has white patch on outer surface of flipper.
One of the smaller whales. Feeds mostly on fish and prefers the ice-floe Arctic area. Noted for leaps and gamboling about vessels under way, in the manner of a Porpoise.
Range is world-wide, abundant off Norway.

● **CALIFORNIA GREY WHALE**
Eschrichtius gibbosus

Average size 20 feet; largest on record 45 feet.
Grey in color with elongate body, less head than other Whales. A lover of shallow water. Often referred to as a "shore swimmer" a habit which is fatal to many that strand in the surf.

Fresh Water Bass

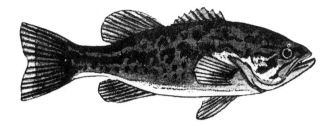

LARGE MOUTH

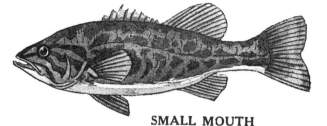

SMALL MOUTH

● **LARGEMOUTH BASS**   *Micropterus salmoides*

Also called Bronzebacker, Trout, Government Fish, Chub, Green Bass, Linesides, Mossback, Yellow Bass and Big-mouth.

Average weight, 4 pounds; largest on record 22 pounds and 4 ounces, caught in Montgomery Lake, Ga., June 2, 1932 by George W. Perry.

The color of a Largemouth Bass varies widely according to the waters they swim in. When in clear water they are greenish, shading to white belly. In moss-bottom lakes they are black with yellowish belly. Regardless of the color they always have a dark stripe along the sides from gill to tail.

Called an "unpredictable but lovable scoundrel" by the famous authority, Bob Waterman, this fits the case quite well. They have courage, stamina and versatility, stubbornness and plenty of fight. They are considered the top American fresh water gamefish. They often will smash at anything that's offered to them, then there are times when they sulk and will not touch any bait.

They eat most anything that might come their way. Minnows, insects, frogs, small animals, or what they take a fancy to.

Caught on practically every kind of artificial lure, from pork rind to large wooden plugs. They rise to flies, spinners, bucktails and most any combination. It's all according to the water and the type of lure a fisherman finds best suited.

● **SMALLMOUTH BASS**   *Micropterus dolomieui*

Also called Black Bass, Redeye, Bronze Backer, Chub, Green Trout, Jumper, Linesides, Oswego Bass, Swago Bass, Welshman, White Bass, White Trout, Yellow Bass, Yellow Perch.

Average weight 2 pounds; largest on record, 9 pounds, 13½ ounces, taken at Birch Lake in the Province of Ontario, Sept. 26, 1954. The fish was hooked and landed by Engnar Anderson of North Tonawanda, New York. This for Canada. In the United States the largest on record is 10 pounds and one ounce, taken in Alabama in 1950. A Florida record, not recognized nationally, because Florida is not a Smallmouth fishing state, is 14 pounds and one ounce, caught by Charles M. Hooks, Green Cove Springs, Fla., in 1949. Food value excellent.

Has a bronze-golden green color lighter than Largemouth Bass as a rule. The darker bronze markings tend toward vertical patches. It is difficult to distinguish the Smallmouth from the Largemouth Bass but by counting the scales the identity can be proven. Smallmouth Bass have 72 rows of scales between gill and tail, the Largemouth never more than 70 and mostly 65. The Smallmouth Bass of course has a smaller mouth as shown in accompanying illustration.

Fishing experts call the Smallmouth Bass the Sunfish aristocrat. Many will claim there is no fish equal in fresh water for energy and the unscrupulousness of a fish roughneck.

In Florida the Black Bass grow to largest size in the world. Stories continually pop up about bass which weigh 30 pounds. It is known that Great Grouper, a salt water twin, have been put into lakes to create such a story. Records of many years standing compiled by commercial fishermen in Lake Okeechobee and by the Florida Fish Commission prove that a bass exceeding 24 pounds has never been found.

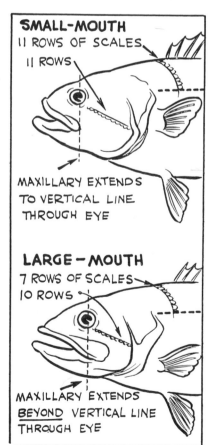

SMALL-MOUTH
11 ROWS OF SCALES
11 ROWS

MAXILLARY EXTENDS TO VERTICAL LINE THROUGH EYE

LARGE – MOUTH
7 ROWS OF SCALES
10 ROWS

MAXILLARY EXTENDS BEYOND VERTICAL LINE THROUGH EYE

 # Fresh Water Bass

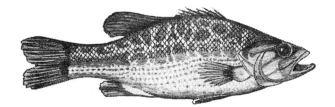

● **SPOTTED BASS**   *Micropterus punctulatus*

Also called Kentucky Bass.

Average size 10 inches; largest on record 8 lb., 12 oz. caught by Harvey L. Simms, in Brushy Creek, Ala., July 22, '68. Food value excellent.

The coloration of the Spotted Bass is so near that of the Largemouth Bass, they are easily confused. They are a distinct and separate species, however.

Most outstanding characteristic is the evenly arranged black spots in alternate rows below the dark lateral line. These rows of spots vary in intensity, appearing quite sharp in the region of the caudal fin and becoming less distinct farther forward. Very sharp on fish taken from clear, cold water, but appear faded on Bass taken from muddy water. It must be remembered the dark coloration of the Largemouth lies below the lateral line in irregular blotches, presenting a haphazard arrangement.

Another characteristic which should be of help in identifying the Spotted Bass is a pronounced dark rough spot on the tongue. The spot is usually not more than an eighth of an inch long in a 10-inch specimen. Also, dorsal fins of the Largemouth are separated; on Spotted Bass, connected.

Ohio is the northern limit of range which reaches southeast to Virginia, Georgia, and southwest Florida; south and west to Texas and west through Kansas and Oklahoma. In Missouri the Spotted Bass is present in rivers of the southwest plains.

The Spotted Bass is commonly found in quiet, silty pools of fairly deep water in the northern streams. In the south it is generally found in the cooler, clear streams with gravel and sand bottoms. It is not normally present in the rocky, boulder-strewn streams with fast currents, which is the home of the Smallmouth Bass, nor in quiet bayous and overflow ponds of Florida inhabited by the Largemouth.

In many respects the Spotted Bass seems to be intermediate between the Largemouth and the Smallmouth. Baits and lures taken by either Smallmouth or Largemouth will work for the Spotted Bass.

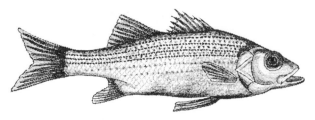

● **WHITE BASS**   *Roccus chrysops*

Also called Striped Bass, Silver Bass.

Average weight 1 to 2 pounds. Largest on record in 1964 is a three-way tie. All three holders from Arkansas and the published world record is four pounds and two ounces. Record holders are J. R. Hulseman, Hot Springs, Ark.; J. R. Chamberlain, Hot Springs, Ark.; Bill Stackhouse, North Little Rock, Ark. Recorded by James T. Petigrew, Tupelo, Miss., and first published by Henry Reynolds in The Commercial Appeal of Memphis, Tenn. Good food.

The White Bass is silvery with its underparts tinged with yellow. The sides are marked with longitudinal stripes, The lower of which is usually intermittent. The mouth is medium-sized and horizontal; the head is scaly and somewhat conical. The body is flattened and the back is high. If Black Bass and White can be compared, there is hardly any possibility for confusion.

The dorsal fin of the Black Basses is a single fin made up of two sections which always are connected by a membrane. In the White Bass these two fins are separated distinctly. Furthermore, the White Bass has four or more longitudinal stripes, the lower of which is usually interrupted. Most of the stripes are located on the upper half of the body.

The range of the White Bass extends from New Brunswick and Minnesota southward through the St. Lawrence River, the Great Lakes region and the Ohio and Mississippi River valley to the Gulf of Mexico. The greatest concentration is found in Ohio water of Lake Erie.

The general habitat of the White Bass is deep, still water over sand and gravel bottoms. It most often frequents medium or large lakes and large, deep rivers. It rarely is found in small streams or ponds.

Although these fish prefer deep, open water, they usually spawn in shallow, flowing water. In the spring, usually during March and April, the adults migrate upstream to their spawning grounds. If they are lake dwellers, they seek out stream inlets. On the spawning grounds the eggs are deposited among rocks or weedy areas in the riffles.

Its gregarious habits and the voracity with which it feeds often result in good catches when the fish are running. In smaller lakes and streams White Bass may be found almost anywhere where food is abundant. Points at the edge of a channel or in the narrows of the stream are preferred angling spots.

Pikes and Pickerel

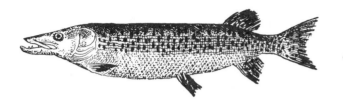

● MUSKELLUNGE
Esox masquinongy

Also called Barred Muckqua, Muskalonge, Chataualonge, Blue Pike, Chatauqua Pike, Great Pike, Leopard Muskie, Longe, Lunge, Muskie, Spotted Muskie and Tiger Muskie.

Average weight 18 pounds; largest on record 69 pounds, 11 ounces; food value good.

A cross breed known as Tiger Muskellunge has both spots and bars.

This is the largest and most ferocious of the Pike family and is called by many, the king of fresh water fish. There is none to equal it for size and the savage battle which results when they are hooked.

Like the salt water Barracuda they are lone wolves of the lakes and rivers, prey on all species as well as their offspring. Usual method of feeding is to lie in hiding and pounce on unwary fish which pass. They are caught casting and trolling.

● NORTHERN PIKE
Esox lucius

Sometimes erroneously called Chain Pickerel in northern Midwest.

While some experts say that two varieties are common in America, this is not so. There's no difference whatever on both sides of the Atlantic, according to Expert Jason Lucas.

Average size 8 pounds, largest on record 34 pounds, 1 ounce, caught by Arthur R. Wittmayer, Pick City, N. D., fishing in Garrison Reservoir, Jan. 10, 1967. The Pike is a real fighter and good eating, a rare combination.

The Pike is usually a brownish-green on back, shading to greenish-yellow on sides and belly with olive green blotches, arranged in lines or chains.

They are voracious feeders and most frequently found in deeper streams and lakes, though sometimes in sluggish or shallow streams. The Pike is very cosmopolitan, ranges from Canada to New York to the upper Mississippi Valley, also found in Asia and Europe.

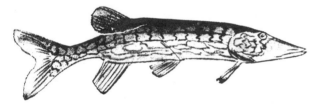

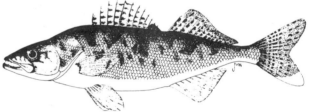

● EASTERN PICKEREL
Esox reticulatus

Also called Banded Pickerel, Jackfish, Duck-billed Pickerel, Black Pike, Green Pike. Average weight 2 pounds. Jason Lucas, fishing editor of Sports Afield says there is no record over 10 pounds and the largest apparently are found in Florida. Authentic records solicited. Food value fair.

Usually a brownish-green on back shading to greenish-yellow on sides and belly. Marked with blotches of olive-green and lines or chain-like markings of the same color, only lighter.

This is the smallest member of the Pike family which includes the Great Northern Pike and Muskellunge, yet it is the largest member of the Pickerels. They are voracious feeders and prey on smaller fish and minnows. Likes to conceal itself behind logs or weeds and dash out to seize whatever comes past.

They strike trolled baits and are active for bait casters. Their natural foods are worms, frogs, minnows and small fish.

Primarily a lake fish, but found occasionally in slow moving rivers Florida to Canada.

● WALLEYE
Stizostedon vitreum

Also called Glasseye, Marble-eye, Jackfish, Jack Salmon, Sauger, Susquehanna Salmon, Walleye Perch; White Yellow Pickerel, Yellow Pike, Perch, Dore.

Average weight 5 pounds; largest on record 25 pounds even; measured 41 inches in length; 29 inches girth, caught by Mabry Harper, Hartsville, Tenn. in Old Hickory Lake. Food value excellent.

Generally dark olive in color, mottled with yellow; indistinct black blotch on dorsal fin.

Considered a solid denizen of the rivers, the Walleye has a tremendous following among sportsmen. Misjudged as a Pike by a great number of fish fanciers because of shape and teeth, the Walleye is a Perch. This is positively shown by two dorsal fins like a Perch, while the Pikes have but one rear fin.

They are a fine gamefish due to willingness to strike at any kind of lure. Moving lures are preferred. Prolific spawners, the Walleye is equipped to hold its own against the inroads of nature.

109

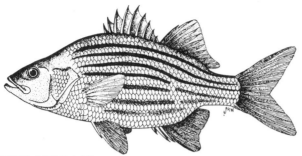

YELLOW BASS
Roccus mississippiensis

Also called Brassy Bass, Striped Bass.

Average weight three-quarters of a pound; largest record solicited; food value, excellent.

Colored a brassy yellow with seven distinct black longitudinal stripes. These stripes are broken or offset about midway of body. In appearance this fish is very similar to the White Bass, but with a more yellowish cast.

This fish is a true member of the Sea Bass family and closely related to the White Perch and White Bass. They might be called a fresh water edition of the Striped Bass. Primarily a southern fish, the species has been found as far north as Wisconsin and Illinois.

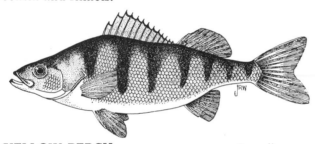

YELLOW PERCH
Perca flavescens

Also called American Perch, Convict, Jack Perch, Raccoon Perch, Red Perch, Yellow Ned, Ringed Perch, River Perch.

Average weight three-quarters pound; largest on record not established; food value excellent.

Bluish-gray on back, merging into golden yellow on sides, which extend to belly. Has six to eight broad dark colored bars which extend from back to below lateral line. Vertical and anal fins are reddish orange.

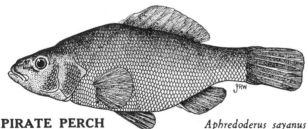

PIRATE PERCH
Aphredoderus sayanus

Average size one pound; largest not known; food value fair.

Dark olive, sometimes lavender tinged. Usually found in sluggish waters. a small voracious fish.

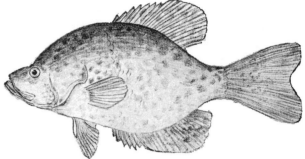

● SPECKLED PERCH
Pomoxis nigromaculatus

A greenish, large-mouthed fish distinguished by the fact that the anal fin is nearly the same size as the dorsal. Female is a silvery-olive color while male is a darker, more olive-green. Both have speckles or black spots.

Adult attains weight of 3 to 4 pounds but averages less. Found throughout Florida in large lakes and rivers. Food value: Excellent.

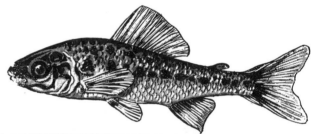

● TROUT-PERCH
Percopsis omiscomaycus

Also called Sand Roller.

Has a peculiar translucency. Recognized by two spines in the short, median dorsal fin and one spine in the anal. Scales have saw-toothed edges. Record solicited.

This is a popular panfish especially for junior fishermen. Although never in large quantities, there are times in Lake Michigan when great numbers are caught from the piers. They are found from the west coast to the east coast and down the Atlantic coast.

Take a bait readily. Feed on small crayfish and insects.

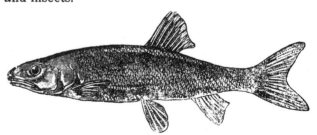

● SACRAMENTO SQUAWFISH *Ptychocheilus grandis*

Also called Sacramento Pike.

Average size 12 inches; largest on record 48 inches; food value fair.

Muddy green with silver on sides. Fins yellowish-red becoming brighter in spawning season.

Sunfish Family

THE SUNFISH FAMILY is a large and diversified group of fish. Besides the specimens treated in these pages there are others less known but quite often located in the rivers and lakes. Exclusively North American, abundant from Florida to Canada. They are active carnivorous fishes, often brilliantly colored. It has been established that many species of Sunfish interbreed naturally, so that the species blend into one another in such a manner as to make it difficult to determine where one species ends and another starts. They are all alike in habit.

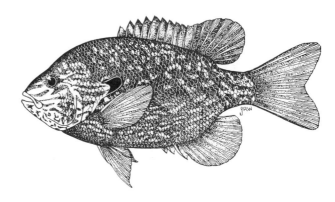

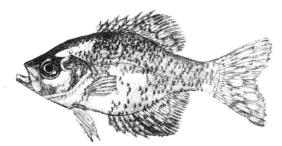

● **WHITE CRAPPIE**   *Pomoxis annularis*
● **BLACK CRAPPIE**   *P. nigromaculatus*

Also called Old Spots; Calico Bass.

Average size 12 ounces; largest on record 5 pounds and 3 ounces, caught by Fred Bright, Memphis, Tenn., in Enid Reservoir, Miss.

One of the Sunfishes with a much shorter dorsal fin. Deep-bodied, flattened profile. Sprinkled with black spots on a silver background. There is a wide variety of pattern in these spots. Some are loosely or carelessly spaced; some in vertical bars and some as aimless as a calico quilt.

Two distinct varieties are the White Crappie and the Black Crappie. The Black Crappie has seven or eight dorsal spines and the White Crappie usually has six.

They take most any kind of bait, but tiny minnows appear to be the best. Fly and bait casting equipment take quite a few fish. The best spot to find these fish is around a submerged brush pile.

● **LONGEAR SUNFISH**   *Lepomis megalotis*

Also called Bigear, Black-tailed Sunfish, Tobaccobox, Red-bellied Bream. Maximum weight about a pound, record solicited. One of the handsomest of Sunfish family. Gill cover flap unusually long.

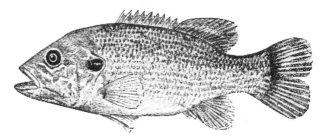

GREEN SUNFISH   *Lepomis cyanellus*

Also called Blue-spotted Sunfish, Blackeye Sunfish, Little Redeye, Creek Sunfish, Blue Bass.

Recognized by the fact the black gill cover is only on the bony part, not on the membrane back of it. Found in small streams from the Great Lakes to Mexico. Good panfish for small boys.

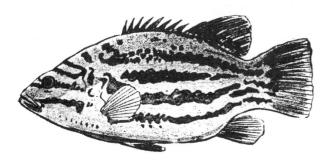

● **MUD SUNFISH**   *Acantharchus pomotis*

Average size 6 inches. Edible.

Dark greenish with indistinct dark bands on body and cheek. Caught in lowland streams from New York to Carolinas.

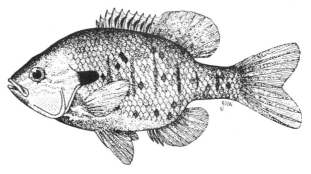

● **REDBREAST SUNFISH**   *Lepomis auritus*

Also called Yellowbelly, Red Sunfish, Robin Perch. Average size 8 to 10 inches. Breast of male generally yellow or orange-red, body olivaceous. Found all over Eastern U.S. and Texas coast.

Sunfish Family

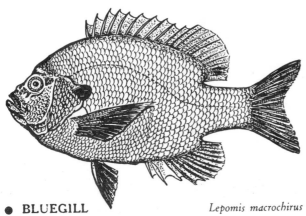

● BLUEGILL
Lepomis macrochirus

Also called Black-eared Bream, Blue Bream, Blue-mouthed Sunfish, Blue Sunfish, Bream, Brim, Copperhead Bream, Coppernosed Sunfish, Pollades, Sun Perch. Average weight 10 ounces; largest on record 3 lbs. 8 oz., girth 15½ in., length 14 in. Taken from 10-acre pond near Junction, Texas, by Dick White, Texas State biologist, March 15, '68.

The color of this fish varies greatly with water conditions. Usually they are dark greenish-olive on back with a purple lustre and chain-like transverse greenish bars. Belly sometimes a reddish-copper color. Fins greenish and cheeks an iridescent blue. Very noticeable is a marking on top of the head resembling a bruise or injury. This mark is the reason for the term "copperhead".

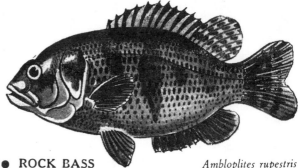

● ROCK BASS
Ambloplites rupestris

Also called Bream, Frog-mouthed Perch, Goggle-eye, Lake Bass, Redeye, Redeye Bream, Redeye Sunfish, Sunfish, Sunfish Bass, Sun Perch, Warmouth, and White Bass.

Average weight half a pound; largest on record 1 pound and 4 ounces, caught by S. Lane Craig, of Roanoke, Va., fishing in Carvin's Cove Reservoir, during August, 1965. Food value excellent.

Olive-green on back becoming lighter and tinged with yellow on sides with darker mottling. Yellowish-white on the belly, red eye.

The Rock Bass is considered the missing link of panfish between the Sunfish and the Bass. They are taken trolling mostly by still fishing or fly casting. They will hit a small lure but most of all they like flies. A smart fisherman looking for a mess of Rock Bass will cast around lily pads.

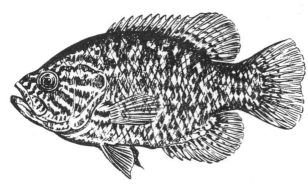

● WARMOUTH
Chaenobryttus gulosus

Also called Big-mouth Sunfish, Black Sunfish, Black Warmouth, Bream, Buffalo Bass, Chub, Mud Sunfish, Perch, Perchmouth Bream, Red-eye, Rock Bass, Sac-a-ait, Sun Trout, Warmouth Bass, Wide-mouthed Sunfish, Yawmouth Perch.

Average weight 8 ounces; largest on record 16 ounces, caught by Jay Kaffia of Cherokee Village in Myatt Creek, off Spring River, near Tupelo, Miss. Sept. 9, 1965. Food value fair.

Dark olive-green, mottled with darker colorings and sometimes flecked with yellow or green. Shades into a lighter yellowish color on belly. Similar to—and often confused with the Rock Bass. At times reddish markings are present.

● PUMPKINSEED
Lepomis gibbosus

Also called Shellcracker, Red-ear, Indian Fish, Quiver, Stump Perch, Ruff, Roach, Redbreast, Creek Sunfish, Blue Bass, Stumpknocker.

Average weight 8 ounces; largest on record 4 pounds, 8 ounces, caught in Lake Panasoffkee, Fla., in 1956. Angler unidentified. Considerable variation depending on distribution. Usually greenish-olive above, shaded with purplish-blue, sides spotted with orange; belly orange; cheeks orange, with long wavy blue streaks. Distinguished by the brilliant reddish-orange spot on the edge of gill flap.

The Pumpkinseed is one of a family of 40 different species, all nearly alike. Like the Bluegill, which they very clearly resemble, this fish is a popular panfish for all ages. They are Sunfish one and all and go for worms whenever presented on a hook.

Gars and Bill Fish

● ALLIGATOR GAR *Lepisosteus spatula*

Also called Great Gar, Manjuari, Billfish, Jackfish, Garjack.

Average weight 18 pounds; largest on record 180 pounds, caught by Ray Kirk, Akron, Ohio. Recorded June 24, 1959. Not considered edible.

Greenish-brown on back, ranging to light brown and yellow below.

This strange fish is one of the largest of the Gars—and one of the largest of freshwater fishes. As one of the immense fishes of North America, there have been many tales built up around this fish, including the belief they are man-eating.

Stories of Garfish weighing up to 300 pounds and 20 feet in length are often told in the Ozarks, although this is not borne out by authenticated fact.

The Garfish is a holdover from the Carboniferous age, many millions of years ago. They have existed mainly because of a head covered with bones and a body with scales which cannot be dented by an axe.

● SHORTNOSE GAR *Lepisosteus platostomus*

Average size 14 inches; largest on record 18 lbs. 3½ oz. (50½ in. long), caught off pier on north end of Anna Maria Island, by Jack Jones of Bradenton, Fla. in Oct. of '68.

A small edition of the Longnose Gar, except this fellow does not have the bright spots. Has some spots on the tail but body is solid greenish to light color on belly.

The Shortnose Gar can be found in Florida rivers, where they travel in schools, leaping much like the famed Tarpon. Except for the short snout they enjoy the same unenviable reputation as their big brother.

● LONGNOSE GAR *Lepisosteus osseus*

Also called Garfish, Billfish, Longnose.

Average size 2 feet; largest on record 6 feet; top weight not determined. Food value, absolutely none.

Elongate body, greenish black on top and yellowish towards belly. Covered with an armor plate of heavy scales which defy any instrument except a heavy axe. Have a series of black spots along lateral line.

● SHOVELNOSE STURGEON *Scaphirhynchus platorynchus*

Also called Sturgeon, Shovelnose Switchback, Whiskers, Hackleback.

Average size 36 inches long; largest reported to Dictionary of Fishes weighed 200 pounds, caught in Missouri River in 1911. White Sturgeon, *Acipenser transmontanus*, has been reported at 360 pounds, caught by Willard Cravens, Snake River, Idaho, April 24, 1956.

Recognized by rows of armorplate bones which partly cover the body. The mouth is bordered by four fleshy barbels, located beneath the long and pointed snout.

There are several varieties. Mississippi Sturgeon are different from Atlantic and Pacific seaboard Sturgeon, which have conical snouts. The most common Sturgeon "Shovelnose" is found from Canada to New Mexico. The White Sturgeon is a rare species, similar to the Shovelnose. Lake Sturgeon can be distinguished by a pair of openings in the head called spiracles. This species has a short pointed snout.

These fish are very long lived, growing ever larger for 90 years or more. They lay a preponderance of eggs in 60-degree water, usually one female surrounded by four or five males. They spawn in spring and take to deep holes in winter.

● PADDLEFISH *Polyodon spathula*

Also called Spoonbill.

Average weight 12 pounds; largest on record 73 pounds, measured 64 inches in length and 56 inches girth. Caught by Marvin E. Stratton, Springfield, Neb., July 5, 1967 fishing near Oahe Dam. Food value poor.

Grayish-brown throughout with very little marking. Leathery appearance of skin. Most conspicuous feature is the long paddle or snout.

While they mature to great size, they feed entirely on minute organisms, which are taken from the water by an elaborate and efficient straining mechanism, borne on the gills. The feeding of these fish is so difficult they are seldom found in captivity.

These fish are caught largely in nets and traps, and on rare occasions sports fishermen have taken Paddlefish on a hook baited with minnows or worms. Such catches are thought to be accidental.

No one has yet discovered exactly where and how the Paddlefish spawns, but the evidence available indicates that spawning occurs in the spring over hard sandy bottoms. The young start life without the paddle.

 # The Salmon Family

PACIFIC COAST SALMON include five species of which the Chinook is the largest. They eat flies and aquatic insects, crustaceans, worms. When in salt water they will take herring, anchovies, sardines, candlefish and other small fish. They also like shrimp and other small shellfish.

Spoons, spinners and plugs are the best artificial bait for Salmon and are usually caught when they leave the open sea to start spawning migration into fresh water, taken at the mouth of rivers and also the brackish waters above the mouth. They do not feed and rarely strike when fresh water is reached.

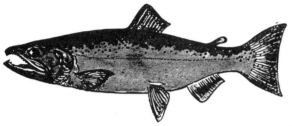

● **CHINOOK SALMON**   *Oncorhynchus tshawytscha*

Also called Black Mouth Salmon, Quinnat Salmon, Columbia River Salmon, King Salmon, Spring Salmon, Tyee Salmon.

Average size 20 pounds; largest 88 pounds.

Dusky above, silvery below; black spots on back, dorsal fin and tail.

Found on both coasts of Pacific—one of the most commercially valuable fishes in the world. Both male and female die after one spawning.

SILVER OR COHO SALMON   *Oncorhynchus kisutch*

Also called Hoopid Salmon, Medium Red Salmon, Kisutch, Quisutch.

They average 5 to 10 pounds in weight.

Bluish-green back, silvery sides, spots obscure and fewer than on Chinook. Caught from San Francisco northward, both coasts of Pacific.

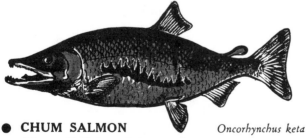

● **CHUM SALMON**   *Oncorhynchus keta*

Also called Dog Salmon, Calico Salmon. Averages 5 to 8 lbs. Coloring like Chinook but no spots.

Ranges from San Francisco to Alaska, both coasts of Pacific. Not as good a food fish as other varieties, but Japanese dry-salt it and call it sake.

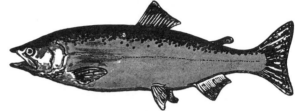

● **PINK SALMON**   *Oncorhynchus gorbuscha*

Also called Humpback Salmon, Haddo and Holia.

Smallest of Pacific Salmon, they take artificial lures and will break water when hooked. Average 4 to 8 pounds.

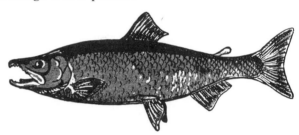

● **SOCKEYE SALMON**   *Oncorhynchus nerka*

Also called Blueback Salmon, Fraser River Salmon, Krasnaya Ryba, Redfish, Sawkeye. Average 5 to 8 lbs. Found on both coasts of Pacific. In certain lakes of northwestern U.S. a dwarf form occurs—it seems to be the same species which has become landlocked.

Salmo salar

ATLANTIC SALMON is universally acclaimed the most famous of fresh water game fishes. Since time immemorial, this fish has been known for food value and game qualities. The name is derived from the Latin *Salio,* meaning "to leap".

Like the Pacific Salmon, they migrate to salt water to spend most of their lives and then return to fresh water to spawn. Unlike the Pacific Salmon, they do not die after spawning, but return to the sea.

On light tackle the Salmon is unbeatable as a game fish. They feed mostly on insect life and when in tidewater feed on shrimp or crustaceans. Mostly fishermen prefer the fly rod for Salmon because of willingness to hit surface bugs.

Whitefish, Grayling, Bowfin

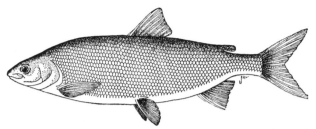

● **MOUNTAIN WHITEFISH**   *Prosopium williamsonii*

Also called Chub, Cisco, Grayling, Mountain Herring, Squawfish, Sucker, Whitey, Williamson's Whitefish.

Average weight 1 pound; largest on record 5 pounds; food value, good.

Light bluish-silver above, silvery sides and whitish below.

These fish are not considered as gamey as Trout, however are the most sporty members of the Whitefish family and readily take an artificial lure.

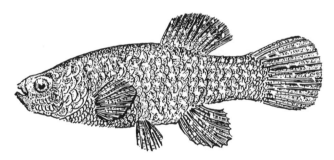

● **MUMMICHOG**   *Fundulus heteroclitus*

Also called Killifish, Chub, Mudfish, Mud Dabbler, Cobbler.

Average weight 2 pounds; largest on record not known; food value none.

A dull green above, pale to yellowish-orange below—males blossoming with georgous colors during breeding season. Occurs in brackish waters from Maine to the Rio Grande.

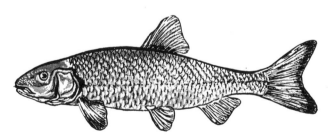

● **FALLFISH**   *Semotilus corporalis*

Also called Chub, Silver Chub, Chivin, White Chub, Windfish, Corporal.

Average size 10 inches; largest on record 22 inches; food value good.

Steel blue on back, sides and belly silver. Eastern Canada south to Virginia.

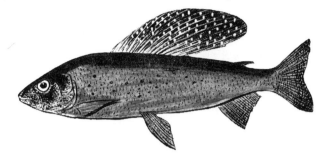

● **ARCTIC GRAYLING**   *Thymallus articus*

Also called Montana Grayling.

Average weight 1 pound; largest on record 5 pounds; food value, excellent.

Montana to Alaska and northward in cold, clear streams. Great game, excellent food, beautifully colored.

Purplish-blue on back, shading into a lighter purple on sides and below. Small black spots on forward part of body. Dorsal fin colored dusky green with brilliant orange and rose markings.

Another species, the Michigan Grayling, with the brilliant hues of a peacock's tail, has become virtually extinct due to destructive methods of lumbering operations. In Montana the Grayling seemed doomed to the same fate, but through improved hatchery and stocking techniques has now staged a comeback.

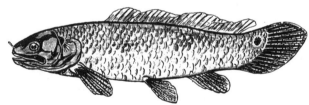

● **BOWFIN**   *Amia calva*

Also called Freshwater Dogfish, Choupique, Grindle, Scaled Ling, Cottonfish, Speckled Cat, Mudfish, Grinnel, Lawyer.

Average weight 1 pound; largest on record 20 lbs. caught by Joe Morris, Lake City, Fla., on 12-lb. test line fishing in Lake Ogden, 8 mi. west of Lake City, June 10, '68; food value poor.

Mottled olive. The breeding male has a black spot rimmed with orange at upper base of tail fin.

A numerous fish throughout the Mississippi basin and the south Gulf. Inhabit sluggish water and prefers weeds or mud in lakes, rivers and swamps. A typical mudfish.

Shad

ONE OF THE BEST KNOWN of the American fresh water fish is the Shad.

The Trout and Salmon are easily identified, but the Shad look so much alike, usually only an expert can tell them apart; yet they are quite different. Some are good to eat; some are valued gamefish and some are worthless.

All have one outstanding characteristic, they are anadromous—but regardless of whether they inhabit salt or fresh water they still pursue the same eating habits—and take the same kind of bait. This is the fish which orginates that delicacy —shad roe.

GIZZARD SHAD   *Dorosoma cepedianum*

Average size 9 inches. Attain a length of 15 inches. No record available on largest size. Not edible.

This Shad, much disliked by fishermen as a whole is recognized by its blunt face and thick body.

Inhabits fresh water lakes and the rivers thruout Florida. When small, they serve as food for game fishes, but they often overpopulate certain lakes making control work necessary.

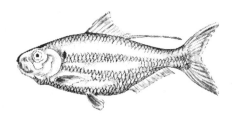

● THREADFIN SHAD   *Dorosoma petenense*

Also called Threadfin Herring.

Found in the large lakes and streams adjacent to the Gulf of Mexico.

Average size 6 inches; largest on record 1 lb. 8 oz., 14 inches long, taken by Roger A. Hovatter from the Hillsboro River, Tampa, Fla., on Apr. 12, 1968. Not edible.

Recognized by the long streamer ray at the end of the dorsal fin, extending to the level of the posterior margin of the anal fin.

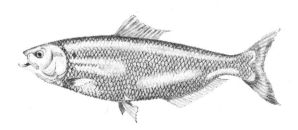

● AMERICAN SHAD   *Alosa sapidissima*

An important commercial fish—good to eat.

Because they are anadromus (spawning in fresh water), over-fishing and pollution have taken their toll; but many are still caught on flyrods in the rivers after egg laying. More are taken in gill nets.

Range, along the Atlantic coast and in the large rivers of the Florida eastern seaboard.

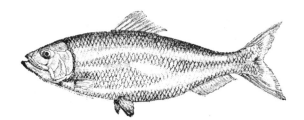

● ALABAMA SHAD   *Alosa alabamae*

Average size about 12 inches. Have been mentioned to 24 inches. No record weight has been reported. Edible.

Distinguishing characteristic is a pointed face.

These Shad migrate to fresh water in the spring and the young return to the sea in the fall. They do not return again to fresh water until mature enough to spawn.

Native to the large rivers emptying into the Gulf of Mexico on the western side of Florida and to Alabama.

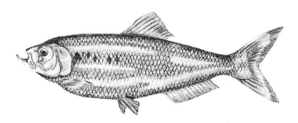

● HICKORY SHAD   *Alosa mediocris*

Average size 1 pound; largest about 3 pounds. Record size is solicited. Edible.

Spend most of their lives in the Atlantic Ocean and then come into east coast rivers, which empty into the Atlantic, to lay their eggs.

This Shad can be recognized by the long lower jaw, comparable to a small Tarpon.

Fresh Water Trout

AMERICAN TROUT, members of the Salmon family, inhabit the rivers and lakes of the United States from Canada to the Gulf of Mexico and the Atlantic to the Pacific. They are the backbone of the fly fishing industry and the most written of fish in the world.

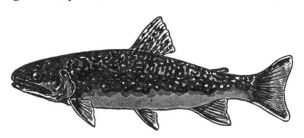

● BROOK TROUT
Salvelinus fontinalis

Also called Eastern Brook Trout, Coaster, Squaretail, Mountain Trout.

Average size 12 ounces; largest on record weighing 14 pounds and 8 ounces; 31½ inches long and 11½ inches girth, caught by Dr. W. J. Cook, from the Nipigon River, Ontario, Can., July, 1916. Food value excellent.

If the Black Bass is the king of plug casters, then the Brook Trout is tops for fly fishermen—and sought after more than any other fish in the streams of America. They feed on flies, worms, insects, small fish and minnows.

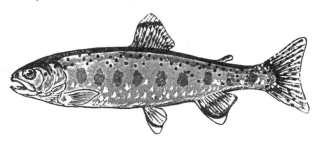

● GOLDEN TROUT
Salmo aguabonita

Also called Bonita Roosevelti, Roosevelt Trout, Volcano Creek Trout.

Average size, three-quarters pound; largest on record is 11 pounds and 8 ounces, caught by Ernest Theoharis, Nashua, N. H., from Lake Sunapee, N. H. in 1957. Food value, excellent.

Olivaceous on back, shading into golden yellow which extends below lateral line to lower sides. A broad rose lateral band, marked by 10 or so dark blotches extends along sides and a reddish strip along the belly. Black spots on dorsal and caudal fins and the peduncle.

Lou Caine says the Golden Trout deserves a niche in the hall of fame, if for no other reason than that of its exotic and gorgeous coloring, which makes it the most beautiful of all trout. Also it is first in fighting qualities, due to its unusual breadth of fins. Can do credit to a much larger fish.

Usually found in small streams and fished for with the lightest of tackle. They like such flies as Royal Coachman, Silver Doctor, Professor and the Black Gnat.

● BROWN TROUT
Salmo trutta

Also called Brownie, German Trout, European Brown, Loch Leven Trout, German Brown.

Average size 22 ounces; largest on record 25 pounds even, caught by Tommy Gully in the White River, below the dam near Bull Shoals, Ark. Recorded by James T. Pettigrew, Tupelo, Ark.

Food value good.

Dark brown on upper part of body blending into lighter brown. Marked heavily on sides and back with red and black spots. The Brown Trout was introduced into the waters of America in 1883.

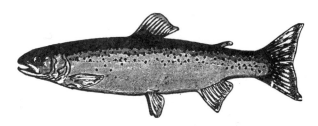

● KAMLOOPS TROUT
Salmo gairdneri

Also called Kamloops Rainbow.

Average size 2 pounds, not uncommon at 30-40 lbs.

Actually a Rainbow Trout found only in British Columbia. They grow unusually large and strong due to a diet of a species of small fat salmon.

● ARCTIC CHAR
Salvelinus alpinus

Average size 10 pounds; largest on record, 27 pounds, four ounces, caught by Guy Murphy of Great Bear Lodge, Northwest Territory, Canada, fishing in the Tree River in 1963.

Males usually seen ascending to spawn have fiery red bellies, olivaceous backs, hooked lower jaw and typically speckled trout spots; red surrounded by blue rings. The females are not as pronounced in color pattern.

An extremely gamey fish, excellent in food value; found only in Arctic waters.

Fresh Water Trout

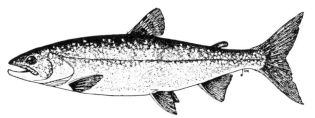

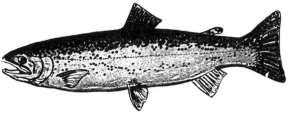

● **LAKE TROUT**   *Salvelinus namaycush*

Also called Gray Trout, Forktail Trout, Great Lakes Trout, Mackinaw Trout, Laker, Togue.

Average size 10 pounds in deep water; largest on record, 63 pounds and 2 ounces, caught in Lake Superior, by Hubert Hammers. Recorded May 25, 1952. Food value excellent.

Usually dark gray but sometimes a paler gray. Profusely covered with pale spots which are often tinged with pink.

This is the largest of fresh water game fish, but despite its size is not considered to rank high in game qualities. This probably is because of the fishing methods employed for deep water fishing.

During summer months, the lake trout is found in very deep water averaging 100 feet. Popular method of fishing is trolling with large spoons or plugs like the Muskie Vamp or Zig-wag. It is necessary to use a monel metal or copper wire line to get the lure down to the depths with a heavy sinker adding several pounds to the weight. It requires a heavy reel and rod to handle such cumbersome equipment.

● **RAINBOW TROUT**   *Salmo gairdneri*

Also called Steelhead, California Trout, Mc-Cloud River Trout, Salmon Trout, Pacific Trout.

Average size 2 pounds; largest on record 37 pounds; 40½ inches in length, caught by Wes Hamlet from Lake Pend, Oreille, Idaho. Recorded Nov. 25, 1947.

Vary greatly in coloration depending on water and part of country they are found. Generally bluish or olive green above with silvery sides, profusely spotted with small black spots. Wide lateral band along sides of purplish-red which is brighter on males.

Like the Salmon, the Rainbow passes freely from ocean to the fresh water to spawn and most naturalists now agree that a Steelhead is merely a Rainbow Trout which has gone to sea and returned. The fish designated as Rainbows have larger scales and are generally smaller and brighter colored than Steelheads. The name Rainbow is in reference to the broad, reddish bands on their sides.

Considered to be the gamiest of the spotted Trouts because of the characteristic of breaking water and jumping when hooked.

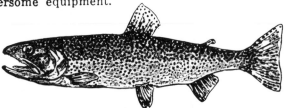

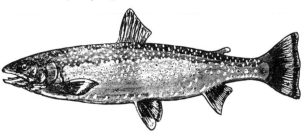

● **CUTTHROAT TROUT**   *Salmo clarkii*

Also called Black-spotted Trout, Rocky Mountain Brook, Columbia River Trout.

Average size 2 pounds; largest on record 41 pounds and 39 inches in length. Caught by John Skimmerhorn from Pyramid Lake, Nev., in Dec. 1925. Food value excellent.

Varies with water conditions. General characteristics are pronounced red streaks on both sides of lower jaws. Body olivaceous silver, heavily spotted with a rosy tint along the lateral line.

The Cutthroat is said to be the parent from which many others of the famous trouts are descended. Relatives are many. They inhabit fresh water streams and lakes and some do migrate to salt water, where they reach a larger size. As a rule not considered as game as a Rainbow, but will put up a good fight when hooked.

Taken fly-fishing, bait casting, trolling or still-fishing. They like cool, fast waters. They feed on flies, insects, shrimp, crayfish, worms, minnows and small fish.

● **DOLLY VARDEN TROUT**   *Salvelinus malma*

Also called Bull Trout, Malmo Trout, Re-Spotted Trout, Western Char, Salmon Trout, Oregon Trout.

Average size 3 pounds; largest on record 34 pounds by Elmer Dreisbach, Bayview, Idaho, March 14, 1952. Food value excellent.

General color olivaceous, small red and orange spots on back which become larger as they extend to sides. Pale stripe on lower fins. When found in salt water the darker colors assume a silvery cast.

The Dolly Varden Trout is a close relative to the Eastern Trout and the Eastern Trout is a true Char. They prey upon Brook Trout, or Rainbow Trout, yet when caught in clear cool, fast water, put up an excellent fight. Not too much of a favorite with expert anglers, however.

They are found around rocks, logs and obstructions in streams. Eddies, riffles, deep pools and overhanging banks are favorite spots.

Catfish Family

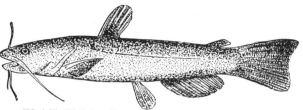

● **FLAT BULLHEAD** *Ictalurus platycephalus*

Also called Brown Cat.

Average size, 2 pounds; largest on record, length 43 inch, girth 27 inch, weight 82 pounds, caught by Glenn T. Simpson, Indianapolis, Ind. Taken from the White River about 4 miles below the Williams Dam, August 14, 1966. Food value good.

Olive brown, varying into yellowish or greenish. Has a dark horizontal bar at base of dorsal. Slender and nearly round. This is the herbivorous member of the Catfish family. Has a diet almost exclusively of water plants. They do not take a hook except rarely. A fine eating fish. Carolinas to Florida.

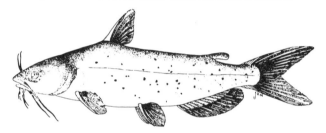

● **CHANNEL CAT** *Ictalurus punctatus*

Also called Silver Cat, White Cat, Fiddler, Speckled Catfish.

Average size, 4 pounds; largest on record 24 pounds, 12 ounces, caught by Al Linares, Escondido, Calif., fishing in Lake Wohlford, May 15, 1967. The fish measured 37 inches length and 21 inches girth. Food value good.

Color slate gray with bluish tint to silvery on belly. Black speckled.

This is a freshwater Catfish which has migrated into the gulf waters and turned white. They are known all the way from Canada to the Gulf.

It is one of the Catfish family which is good food. They are not scavengers as other breeds of Cats, but feed on shellfish, mussels and other small bait fish.

● **ELECTRIC CATFISH** *Melapterurus electricus*

Also called Shocker.

Average size 2 pounds; largest on record 6 pounds; food value not known.

Dark brownish with scattered black spots. White band at tail and anal fin. Has very small adipose fin and no dorsal. Barbels on both upper and lower lips.

When handled this fish is capable of delivering a severe electric shock.

This is a native of Africa and is not common in the United States. They live well, however, in American rivers and are believed to have been introduced by immigration from Africa.

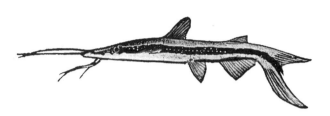

● **FLAT-NOSE CATFISH** *Sorubim lima*

Also called Dwarf Catfish.

Average size 6 inches; largest on record 18 inches; food value poor. Light silver with black stripe running from fork of tail to nose.

A curious fish recently imported from the Amazon by fish fanciers. Their long barbels and flat head are equipped to search the surface waters for minute particles of algae or top water minnows.

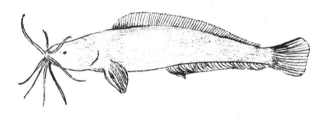

● **WALKING CATFISH** *Clarias batrachus*

An unwelcome new Fla. resident unwisely imported by tropical fish dealers. A few escaped—they breed prolifically and have now become a menace to Florida's ecology, devouring and crowding out native fish. They will eat anything, including water plants.

First imports were albino; offspring reverting to catfish colors of gray, brown or black. A lung-like organ adapted to air or water allows it to cross the land to other ponds, lakes and canals to satisfy its gluttonous appetites.

Cold weather may deter further migration north. No control has been discovered by baffled Fla. biologists. Largest Fla. specimen 18 in., it's known to grow to 22 in. in India.

Catfish and Bullheads

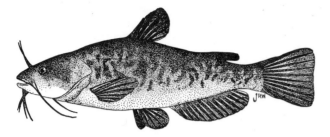

● **FLATHEAD CATFISH** *Pylodictis olivaris*

Also called Mud Cat, Goujon, Yellow Cat, Pied Cat, Granny Cat, Brown Bullhead, Bashaw, Russian Cat.

Average size 5 pounds; largest on record not known; food value good.

Color yellowish mottled with brown and greenish; paler below.

This is a large and coarse fish, second only to the Blue Cat in commercial importance. Found throughout the southern United States in the lowlands. Most abundant in the bayous and overflow from large streams. While the flesh is equal to that of the Blue Cat, many persons do not care for it because it is a large and repulsive looking fish and not any too clean in its habits.

Not very particular in choice of food, the Mud Cat will eat a smaller fish or its own progeny with as much relish as a crayfish.

● **BROWN BULLHEAD** *Ictalurus nebulosus*

Also called Black Catfish, Bullpout, Horned Pout, Minister, Sacramento Cat, Squaretail Catfish.

Average size 1 pound; largest on record 22 lbs. 15 oz. reported in New Jersey, July 11, '68, verified by A. Bruce Pyle, State Fisheries Biologist. Food value excellent.

Dark yellowish-brown, sometimes clouded with darker brown, lighter colored on belly.

The bullhead is certainly no beauty winner among fishes and it is not sporty on rod and reel, nor is it choosey about where it eats, yet this fish ranks high in the opinion of millions of fishermen.

Practically every boy and girl who has fished in a river or stream can remember catching Bullheads. They would run the Sunfish family a close race for first honors.

● **BLACK BULLHEAD** *Ictalurus melas*

Also called Northern Bullhead.

Average size 6 inches; largest on record 16 inches; food value good.

Greenish-brown to black, shading to green or gold, the under part of body has a leaden cast. is never white. Light bar across the base of tail.

A small Catfish which inhabits the ponds, creeks and rivers, having a fondness for the sluggish water. Feeds on insects and crayfish. Will take a hook baited with worm, grasshopper or such.

● **YELLOW BULLHEAD** *Ictalurus natalis*

Average size 12 inches; largest on record 18 inches; food value fair.

Yellowish mottled with a darker brown. Belly is bright yellow. Has a short heavy body and wide mouth.

A species of Catfish found mostly in large canals and drainage ditches of the north. Feeds on insects or whatever might be handy. Not considered much of a fish for sport.

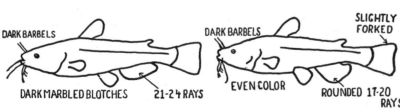

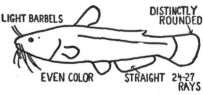

120

 # Catfish and Lungfish

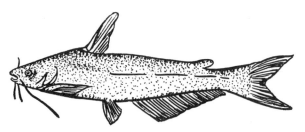

● **BLUE CAT**   *Ictalurus furcatus*

Also called Common Catfish, River Cat, Freshwater Catfish, Mississippi Cat, Florida Cat.

Average size 3 pounds. The largest on record has been said to be 150 pounds, although this weight has not been authenticated. It is known that large specimens of this fish have been taken. For the records this book presents a catch of 30 pounds by W. O. Woolsey of St. Petersburg Beach, Fla., from Withlacoochee River, Fla., in March 1966.

Dull blue or slate colored shading to whitish below. Barbels usually color of body, rarely black.

This is the most important member of the Catfish family. A commercial food fish throughout the southern part of the United States.

REDTAIL CATFISH   *Phractocepholus hemilioptuas*

Also called Gravel Cat.

Average size 3 pounds; largest on record 40 pounds; food value good.

Has a hard bony head like a Sturgeon. White stripes runs from nose to tail which is pinkish red. Top bluish gray. Head mottled brown and black spots. Dorsal fin tipped with pink.

One of the largest South American Catfishes.

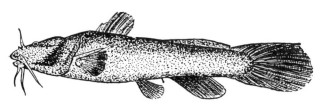

● **STONECAT**   *Noturus flavus*

Also called Little Yellow Cat, Mad-tom.

Average size 6 inches; largest on record 12 inches; food value, poor.

Uniformly yellowish brown, sometimes blackish above fins edged with yellow.

This little Catfish has a wicked poison stinger at the base of the pectoral spine—and a well developed poison sac. They are capable of inflicting a painful sting.

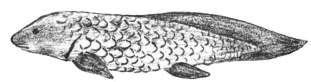

● **AUSTRALIAN LUNGFISH**   *Epiceratodus forsteri*

Also called Mudfish.

Average size 18 in.; largest 100 lbs., 6 ft. long, reported by E. A. Hauser, Chief Inspector of Fisheries of Australia.

Greenish-gray with mottled appearance.

A strange fish with a functional lung as well as gills and 4 leg-like fins resembling 4 legs of an animal. Edible in smaller sizes and have been credited with saving travelers by providing food in dry seasons.

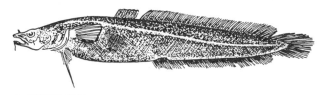

● **BURBOT**   *Lota lota*

Also called Ling, Lake Lawyer, Mud Blower, Fresh Water Cusk, Gudgeon, Eelpout.

Dark olive marbled with black. Sometimes has reddish spots and blotches. Dirty gray on belly.

Average weight 5 pounds; largest on record thought to be 20 pounds; food value fair.

This is called the fresh water member of the Cod family and is widely distributed throughout the waters of the United States. It has some of the characteristics of a Cod and a Catfish.

● **EELPOUT**   *Zoarces anguillaris*

Also called Yowler.

Average size 18 inches; largest on record believed to be three feet; record solicited; food value fair.

Bluish-black with fair sized ventral fins as contrasted to the common Eel. The anal fin is continuous with the tail fin.

Fairly common along the Atlantic coast, especially around the river mouths of Delaware, rarely found in tropical waters. It is used very little for food, although the flesh is said to be sweet.

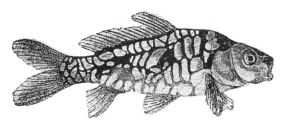

● **LEATHERSIDE CHUB**   *Snyderichthys copei*

Also called Mirror Carp; Leather Carp.

Average size 12 inches; largest on record, 39 pounds, caught by Harry Martin in 1905, fishing near Lewistown, Pa. Not considered edible.

Skin covered with a type of "soft upholstery." Differs from the common Carp in that they are not scaled. This fish, or variety of fishes, is comparatively rare today. It appears that they are steadily disappearing from the waters of American rivers.

In Missouri they were once netted as a commercial fish and found a ready market. Rivers where they are plentiful were almost devoid of Bass. Today the Bass have come back and the Leather Carp are disappearing.

● **CARP**   *Cyprinus carpio*

Also called German Carp, European Carp.

Average weight 5 pounds; largest on record, 40 pounds and 40 inches long, caught by Paul R. Sherman, Portland, Oregon. A 70-pound specimen is said to have been recorded in Europe. Food poor.

Have a varied color of brassy silver or yellowish, greenish or black. Can be recognized easily by barbels.

Here's how you recognize a Carp. Take a chunky scale-fish with a turned-down mouth like the nozzle on a gas hose; see if he has two pairs of antennae-like barbels on his mouth. If he has, it's a Carp.

A nuisance fish and not very well thought of. They like muddy bottoms and stagnant water. Have no teeth in their mouths but do in the throat.

Originally a European fish but introduced to America where it has spread widely.

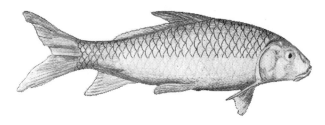

● **RIVER CARPSUCKER**   *Carpiodes carpio*

Also called Silver Carp, American Carp, White Buffalo.

A small silvery fish—may reach a pound or two in size. Identified by nipple-like structure on lower lip. Food value poor.

There appear to be a number of subspecies in different areas. Found in rivers and lakes from the Great Lakes to Texas.

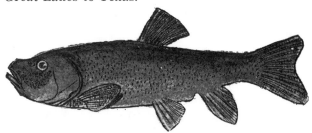

● **TSWAM**   *Chasmistes copei*

Also called Klamath Sucker.

Average size 12 inches; largest on record 20 inches; food value fair.

Upper parts dark, under parts whitish. Pectoral fin dark on inner surface.

Inhabits the Klamath Lakes.

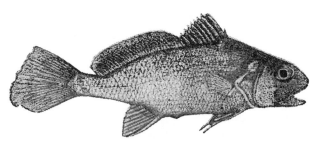

● **FRESH WATER DRUM**   *Aplodinotus grunniens*

Also called Gaspergou, Crocus, Thunder-pumper, Sheepshead, Perch.

Average weight 4 pounds; largest on record 41 pounds, caught by Herman Fehring, Fort Sill, Oklahoma, August 5, 1967, from Lake Lawtonka. Larger fish have been reported but not authenticated. Food value poor.

Grayish, silvery, dusky above, sometimes very dark, resemble a salt water Drum to a great extent.

This fish has no relatives. The genus has but a single species. Found in southern lakes and sluggish streams from Mexico to the Florida Keys. It is also abundant in the Great Lakes.

Suckers

THE SUCKER FAMILY is a large and varied one, rivaling the Catfish in numbers. They are found throughout the American continent, in waterways of every state. Not ranked highly as food fishes because they are mostly well filled with small bones. Some of these fish reach a large size although none of them has a high rank as game fish. They do like worms and will take a hook thus baited.

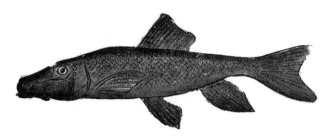

● **FLANNELMOUTH SUCKER**   *Catostomus latipinnis*

Average size 12 inches; largest on record 3 inches; food value fair.

Dark olive, shading abruptly to paler below. Sides and fins have an orange tint.

Mostly a western fresh water fish, very rare in the eastern United States or south.

● **MOUNTAIN SUCKER**   *Pantosteus platyrhynchus*

Average size 5 inches; largest on record 12 inches; food value, poor.

Recognized by a cartilaginous sheath on each jaw.

Mostly found in brooks and ponds in the more rocky or arid regions of western U.S.

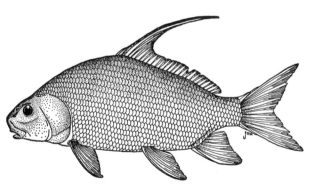

QUILLBACK   *Carpiodes cyprinus*

Average size 12 inches.

Silvery to dusky color; dorsal fin half as long as body; lower lip does not have nipple-like structure of other Carpsuckers. Food value poor.

From Canada and Great Lakes region to Kansas and Fla. Panhandle.

● **SMALLMOUTH BUFFALOFISH**   *Ictiobus bubalus*

Also called White Buffalo.

Average size 5 pounds; largest on record 41 lbs., caught by Larry Mize, Bedford, Ind., in the White River, July 20, 1967. Food value fairly good.

Pale color, almost silvery; fins dusky.

This large fish, is the best known and largest of the Buffalofish which inhabit the larger rivers of the South. They are much like the Carp in habits and are the largest of the sucker-type fishes.

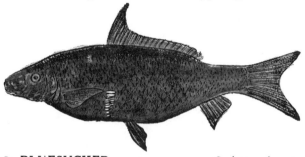

● **BLUESUCKER**   *Cycleptus elongatus*

Also called Gourdseed Sucker, Missouri Sucker, Sweet Sucker, Blackhorse.

Average size 12 inches; largest on record 40 inches. Caught by W. C. Tabor in the Arkansas River, Feb, 18, 1953. Food value good.

Very dark color, almost black.

One of the highest in esteem as a food fish. Most common in Mississippi Valley. Usually caught with set lines.

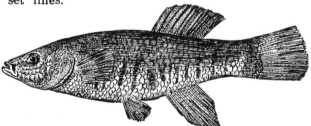

● **STRIPED MUMMICHOG**   *Fundulus majalis*

Also called Mummichog; Mummy; Killifish.

Average size 5 inches; largest on record 8 inches; food value nil.

Dark olive green above with silvery sides; greenish-yellow belly; male has dark bars on sides.

Brackish water, Cape Cod to Florida.

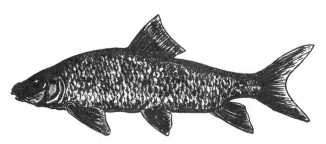

● **SILVER REDHORSE**   *Moxostoma anisurum*

Also called Redfish, Large-scale Sucker.

Average weight 1 pound; largest on record believed to be 12 pounds.

There are about 20 different species in the Redhorse group. All are silvery to reddish-brown. Only about 5 species grow large enough to make them worthwhile as food.

A wanderer in the streams of the eastern half of the U.S.; feed along the mud of the bottom, sometimes picking up a piece of bait cut from a minnow or a worm.

Hardly a good fish for food or game qualities.

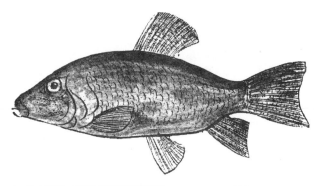

● **LAKE CHUBSUCKER**   *Erimyzon sucetta*

Average size 8 to 10 inches.

Uniformly dark color—young have a broad black lateral line.

Range from eastern Minnesota to New England and south to Texas and Florida. Food value poor.

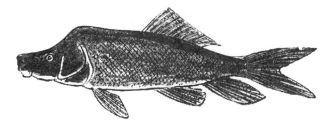

● **HUMPBACK SUCKER**   *Xyrauchen texanus*

Also called Razorback Sucker.

Average weight 4 pounds; largest on record 12 pounds. Color is plain olivaceous.

Native of Colorado Basin and rare elsewhere. In this area is quite abundant.

124

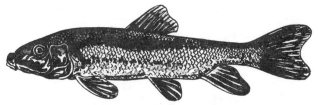

● **WHITE SUCKER**   *Catostomus commersoni*

Also called June Sucker, Blackhorse, Mullet.

Average size 12 inches, weight 14 ounces; largest on record 40 inches, caught by W. C. Tabor in the Arkansas River, Feb. 28.

Usually olive color with a black longitudinal band in males. Below body is cream colored.

A fish inhabiting streams and lakes, mostly with clear water. They are widely scattered until spawning season, then gather in schools. Eat aquatic plants mostly with insects and small crayfish and worms. Not much of a sport fish and very seldom taken on a hook. Edible, though bony.

● **HOGSUCKER**   *Hypentelium nigricans*

Also called Hog Molly, Hammerhead, Hog Darter.

Average size, 4 inches; largest believed to be 12 inches. Information on weight and length solicited. Edible.

Identified by a large head and four broad oblique bars or saddles on the body. The eye is behind the middle of the snout. The whole body appears to be conical and is covered with large scales. The lower fins are a dull red.

Only found in clear streams, prefers a stream with plenty of riffles. Likes shallow water near the mouth of a stream.

Found from central Minnesota eastward to New York and south to Alabama.

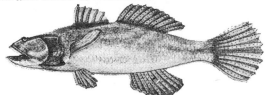

● **SPINYCHEEK SLEEPER**   *Eleotris pisonis*

Also called Sleeper.

Average size 8 ounces; largest known caught by John Sanders, Miami, in Snapper Creek near the Tamiami Trail in 1958. Weighed 4 pounds and 8 ounces; 18 inches in length. No food value.

Color brownish—pelvic fins not united. Found from Gulf of Mexico to Brazil in ditches, canals and streams where it has a habit of lying quietly among the weeds—thus it's name "Sleeper".

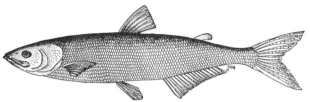

● **EULACHON**   *Thaleichthys Pacificus*

Also called Candlefish.

Average size 8 inches; largest 15 inches; food value good.

Dark above; silvery-white below. California coast northward.

An excellent panfish, said to surpass all fish in delicacy of flavor and the flesh texture is superior to Trout. The oil is sometimes extracted and used as Cod Liver Oil. It is solid and lard-like at ordinary temperatures.

When dried these fish have been used as candles by inserting a wick in one end and burning it. The records do not state which end.

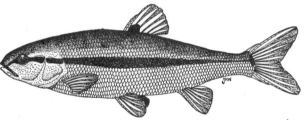

● **CREEK CHUB**   *Semotilus atromaculatus*

Also called Horned Dace.

Average size 4 inches; largest on record 12 inches; food value, poor.

Dusky bluish above, belly whitish, conspicuous black spot on dorsal fin.

This is the commonest fish on a small boy's fishing string. Also considered the bait supreme for Walleyed Pike or Pickerel. It is everywhere abundant, particularly in small creeks, where it is often the most voracious inhabitant.

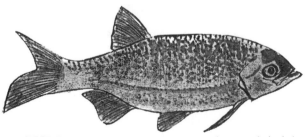

● **RUDD**   *Scardinius erthröpthalmas*

Also called Pearl Roach.

Average size 3 inches; largest 7 inches; food value poor.

Silvery color with fins of bright red.

A close cousin to the Golden Shiner, and often called by that name, the Pearl Roach can be distinguished by the red fins. They are native of Europe, but often found in American ponds, especially in the East. A good bait fish.

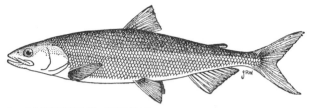

● **AMERICAN SMELT**   *Osmerus mordax*

Average size 6 ounces; largest not known for certain, records solicited. Food value good.

Greenish above, silvery sided with tiny dots.

A small food fish which migrates into rivers and brackish bay waters, mostly of the northern coasts. They run in great schools in spring and bring out crowds of fishermen who favor them as panfish. Usually they feed on insects and very small shellfish.

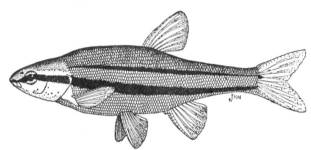

● **SOUTHERN REDBELLY DACE**

     Chrosomus erythrogaster

Average size 4 inches; largest on record not known; food value poor.

Brightly colored, black on top with general splashes of scarlet and gold.

This minnow of the fresh waters is considered the most beautiful of American fishes. In the spring at breeding time, the colors come out in rainbow fashion. It is a lively fish and does well in aquariums, for which most specimens are captured.

Found in running water of clear streams.

● **SAUGER**   *Stizostedion canadense*

Also called Sand Pike.

Average weight 16 ounces; largest on record 5 pounds and 8 ounces, caught by S. W. Robinson, Pocohontas, Tenn., April 2, 1966, in the Tennessee River near the dam at Pickwick. Reported by James T. Pettigrew, Tupelo, Miss.

Olive-gray with brassy sides and dark mottling. Has a large black spot at base of pectoral fins.

A river fish not very plentiful these days. Once was a favorite in the Indiana rivers. Resembles the Walleye in manner of feeding and finding game. Known mostly in the Mississippi basin.

Minnows

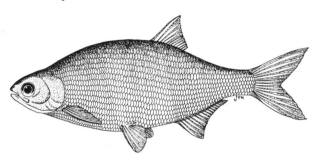

- **MOONEYE**   *Hiodon tergisus*

- **GOLDEYE**   *Hiodon alosoides*

Also called Toothed-herring.

Average size 5 inches; largest not known, probably 12 inches; excellent when smoked. Not used as food in Midwest.

Large silvery scales, flattened crappie-like mouth filled with teeth, large eyes.

There are two distinct types of fish, which look almost exactly alike except that one has translucent eyes and the other golden eyes.

They range from Hudson Bay in Canada to Alabama. Mooneyes are most abundant in the Mississippi River system and Goldeyes abundant in the Missouri River.

They will smash into a plug or fly and occasionally take a small spinner or minnow. Not too many are caught on hook and line.

- **STONEROLLER**   *Campostoma anomalum*

Also called Slick Dick, Horny Head, Rot Gut and Brown Chub.

Average size 2 inches; largest not known. Edible.

The Stoneroller is much the same in habit as the Creek Chub, but is much more hardy as a bait minnow. In coloration they resemble the Common Shiner, although their interior is quite different.

These minnows have a long intestine, which is wound tightly around an air bladder. They feed entirely on tiny plants which grow on rocks and other projections in the stream bottom.

The Stoneroller can withstand high temperature and thrive in mildly polluted waters which would not sustain other fish. It is an important bait minnow and is raised commercially.

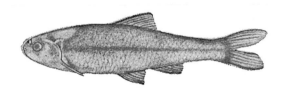

- **FATHEAD MINNOW**   *Pimephales promelas*

Also called Blackhead Minnow.

Average size 2 inches; largest not reported. Information solicited.

Recognized by the black head and number of rough tubercles on snout and chin which appear during spawning season.

This is the prime commercial bait minnow. They can be raised easily. A female lays up to 12,000 eggs and they hatch in about a week. A healthy female may nest several times in a summer.

With proper feed and fertilizer, the minnows will attain two inches length in three months. Some operators say they can raise 1,000 pounds per acre. As the demand is greater for three-inch bait, quality is sometimes more lucrative than quantity.

- **COMMON SHINER**   *Notropis cornutus*

Also called Missouri Minnow.

Average size 2 inches; largest not known.

These minnows are widely used as bait and shipped great distances. They are extremely hardy. Although most plentiful in Missouri, they can be found throughout the United States east of the Rocky Mountains.

 # Darters, Shiners, Chubs

THE DARTERS are diminutive Perches found in clear streams throughout the length of the United States. Graceful in form, they are beautifully colored, some say the most beautiful of all fresh water fish.

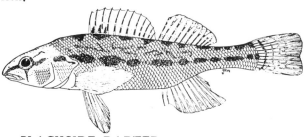

● **BLACKSIDE DARTER**   *Percina maculata*
Average size 3 inches; largest on record 8 inches. Dark on back with series of blotches of black on sides. Belly yellowish. Good aquarium fish.

● **FOURSPINE STICKLEBACK**   *Apeltes quadracus*
Average size 1½ inches; largest on record 2½ inches; food value, nil. Skin like Jacks, with four spines on the back and a stout spine in front of each ventral fin, can be set at right angles.

Live mostly in brackish water where they are noted for their nest building habits. The nest is constructed by the male and held together with threads spun like that of a spider. They protect this nest against all invaders and although small, can put up a formidable defense.

They are very pugnacious and often attack other fish and their nests where they do considerable damage.

Besides the Stickleback described there is a Twospine, Threespine, Ninespine and Brook Stickleback, all in the same *Gasterosteidae* family. Only the Brook Stickleback is restricted to fresh water, the others are anadromous.

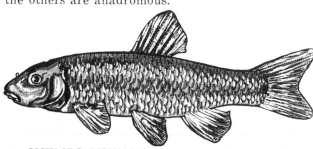

● **CUTLIPS MINNOW**   *Exoglossum maxillingua*
Also called Butter Chub, Negro Chub.
Average size 4 inches long; largest 8 inches; no food value. A three-lobed lower lip, composed of a tongue-shaped bone in center, flanked by fleshy lobe on either side. No barbel.

A minnow of the streams, preferring those with a strong current. They cling to the bottom and feed on small mollusks.

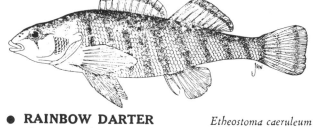

● **RAINBOW DARTER**   *Etheostoma caeruleum*
Average size 3 inches, largest 7 inches; food value, small.

Variegated colors of alternating reds, yellows and blacks.

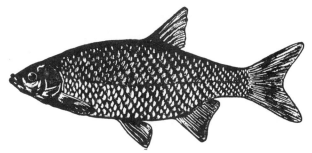

● **GOLDEN SHINER**   *Notemigonus crysoleucas*
Also caller American Roach, Roach Shiner, Dace, Bitterhead, Chub, Gudgeon, Windish, Southern Roach, Bream.

Average size 4 inches; largest on record 12 inches and weighing about 24 ounces.

Greenish on back, pale yellowish-silver on sides, fins sometimes yellowish-red.

This is the largest of the "minnows" found in the deep south and Florida lakes. It is highly valued as a bait fish for Bass. Reproduces abundantly The bright color varies from silver to gold according to the type of water. They like quiet shallow water. Are easily caught with doughball baits.

HORNEYHEAD CHUB   *Hybopsis biguttata*

Average size 6 inches; largest on record taken by W. D. Huckate, Jr., Rochelle, Va., from the Rapidan River. This fish weighed 1 pound, 4 ounces and measured 15 inches. Food value fair.

Dark on back and silvery belly. Have distinctive spot on tail.

A small game fish for youngsters, widely distributed throughout the rivers of America. Although small, it is very gamey and quite popular for juvenile fishermen.

● CICHLID
Cichlasoma severum

Also called Grande Perch.

Average size 12 ounces; largest on record five pounds; food value good.

Mottled brownish-blue with yellowish blending to white on belly variegated black spots which appear to be in rows of even numbers.

The Cichlids are a large family embracing over one hundred species. Only a few of the species are found in American rivers and lakes and these in the southern part. Basically this family is a South American fish.

● NILE BREAM
Tilapia nilotica

Also called Tilapia.

Average size one pound; largest on record 2 pounds and 4 ounces, taken by Ed Shepard of Dover, Fla. In Pleasant Grove Lake near Plant City, Fla., May 10, 1963.

Color bronze-green above, shading to brassy-red on sides, to light gray on belly. Shaped like Bream.

This fish, a member of the Cichlid family, was introduced into Florida lakes in 1962. This now appears to have been a major mistake. It was hoped the fish would get rid of excess algae and provide a new sport for fishermen; however, as a vegetarian it refuses most bait and its exploding population is rapidly devouring valuable plants which provided breeding grounds for gamefish.

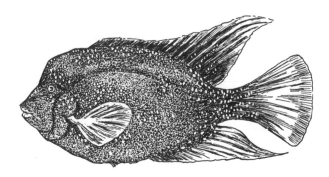

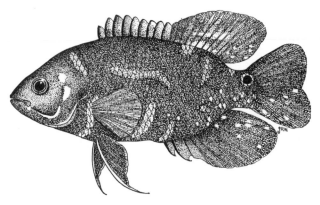

RIO GRANDE PERCH
Cichlasoma cyanoguttatum

No records available for average or record size. Fishermen are urged to report largest size. Fair food value.

Greenish-grey in color with dark blotches along the lateral line. Well covered with blue dots. During spawning season, forepart of body turns white. Has long, pointed dorsal fin.

Shaped like a Sunfish, with breeding habits resembling a Black Bass, yet they are neither. Belonging to the family *Cichlidae*, a very familiar tropical fish family. Although their natural habitat is in waters of the equator, they are found in Texas, in the United States.

They were planted in waters about San Marcos, Texas by the U. S. Fish Hatchery, there they thrived and multiplied so fast they drove out the Bass in some waters. When they are taken away from the vicinity of a warm spring these fish do not survive.

PERUVIAN PEACOCK BASS
Cichla ocellaris

Average size 12 ozs; largest size about 3 pounds. Information solicited.

The Florida Fresh Water Game Commission, in partnership with other biologists of southern latitudes are planting the famous Peruvian Peacock Bass in American waters. This fish is considered to be the fightingest gamefish to be found in this hemisphere.

In the first test, 500 baby Bass did not make it, but in the second try several hundred survived. The plan is to introduce them into every freshwater fishing area bordering the Gulf of Mexico.

These fish, seldom seen by the average angler can be recognized by their glistening tail marked with twin black bars and a flaming red ocellus or false eye. The body of the fish is colored gold.

Index -- Fresh and Salt Water Fish

Boldface Page Numbers indicate accepted common names. Other
names are regional or dockside *nom de plumes*.

Index -- Fresh and Salt Water Fish

Boldface Page Numbers indicate accepted common names. Other
names are regional or dockside *nom de plumes*.

Index -- Fresh and Salt Water Fish

Boldface Page Numbers indicate accepted common names. Other
names are regional or dockside *nom de plumes*.

Index -- Fresh and Salt Water Fish

Boldface Page Numbers indicate accepted common names. Other
names are regional or dockside *nom de plumes.*

Index -- Fresh and Salt Water Fish

Boldface Page Numbers indicate accepted common names. Other names are regional or dockside *nom de plumes*.

Index -- Fresh and Salt Water Fish

Boldface Page Numbers indicate accepted common names. Other names are regional or dockside *nom de plumes*.

PARTS OF A FISH

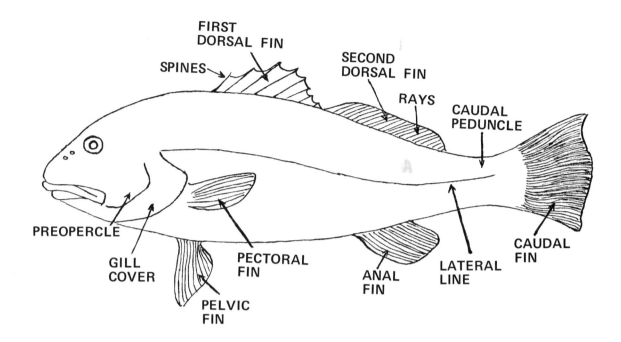

References:

The Fishes of North and Middle America	by Jordan & Everman
Game Fish of the World	by Vesey-Fitzgerald and Francesca LaMonte
Field Book of Marine Fishes	by Charles M. Breder, Jr.
The Sea Fishes	by J. L. B. Smith
American Fisheries Society—Special Publication No. 2	
Guide to the John G. Shedd Aquarium	by Walter H. Chute
American Food and Game Fishes	by Jordan & Everman
The World of Fishes	by William K. Gregory and Francesca LaMonte
The Fishes of North Carolina	by Hugh M. Smith
Fishes of the Gulf of Maine	by Henry B. Bigelow and William W. Welsh
The Fisherman's Encyclopedia	by Ira N. Gabrielson and Francesca LaMonte
Caribbean Reef Fishes	by John E. Randall
Fishes of the Bahamas	by Bohlke and Chaplin
Shark	by Thomas Helm
Salt-Water Fishing	by Robert A. Dahne
Common Marine Fishes of California	by Phil M. Roedel
Marine Game Fishes	by Francesca LaMonte
Sportsman's Guide to Game Fish	by Byron Dalarymple
Pacific Game Fishing	by S. Kip Farrington, Jr.
The Freshwater Fishes	by Samuel Eddy
The Ways of Fishes	by Leonard P. Schultz
A Book of Fishes	by S. Kip Farrington, Jr. and Lynn Bogue Hunt
Giant Fishes, Whales and Dolphins	by J. R. Norman and F. C. Fraser
Sharks and Survival	by Perry W. Gilbert and members of the Shark Research Panel
New Genera and Species of Fishes from Tortugas, Florida	by William H. Longley and Samuel F. Hildebrand